Quality Leadership Skills
Standards of Leadership Behavior

Richard W. Leatherman

HRD Press, Inc. • Amherst • Massachusetts

Published by: HRD Press, Inc.
                  22 Amherst Road
                  Amherst, Massachusetts 01002
                  1-800-822-2801 (U.S. and Canada)
                  413-253-3488
                  413-253-3490 (fax)
                  www.hrdpress.com

ISBN 978-1-59996-131-6

Production services by Jean Miller
Editorial services by Suzanne Bay
Cover design by Eileen Klockars

To my son, Matt Leatherman

May he have many "turtle days" with his sons,
Tanner and Trevor

Table of Contents

Preface

Human resource departments have traditionally provided leadership training only for supervisors and managers, focusing on participative leadership. More often than not, those same supervisors and managers finished their training and entered a world of work that did not encourage or even allow participation. Good leadership practices were ignored, and vast segments of this country's industries have become noncompetitive in the world market as a result.

There have been significant shifts in organizational focus over the past decade. Work teams that were usually led by traditional managers are now more likely to be cross-functional or organized by marketing, service, research, and operations areas. And many are self-directed.

Today's organizations are trying to achieve quality, effectiveness, and productivity by downsizing, reducing the middle management population ("flattening"), delegating responsibility downward, and giving the responsibility for quality to front-line employees.

Unfortunately, some that turned to downsizing, right-sizing, reengineering, or divesting report mixed results, mostly bad. According to Cameron and Quinn (1999), most focus on cutting expenses and personnel and changing processes and do not try to improve leadership skills. This leads to worker cynicism, frustration, loss of trust, and deterioration in morale.

In a growing number of organizations across the country, the CEO says,

"Executive Vice President Jones, we are going to win that quality award for excellence!"

The executive VP replies, "Right, boss."

Vice president Jones then calls the senior VP of Human Resources and says, "The chief wants us to win that award for excellence. What do we have to do to make it happen?"

The senior VP replies, "I don't know, boss. But I'll find out."

The senior VP calls in his VP of Training and Development and states, "The chief wants us to win that prize for excellence! What do we need to do?"

The training department VP responds, "Let our supervisors and managers do what they have been trained to do—create an environment that supports change. And while you're at it," he continues, "give the non-exempts training in how to take on the new responsibility that change creates."

"But what about the budget?" cries the senior VP of HR. "Where are we going to get the money to continue our regular supervisory and management training—and train all the employees at the same time?"

"Use one of the oldest teaching tools in the trade," replies the training manager. "Buy them a book!"

"You're nuts!" snorts the senior VP. "You mean you expect me to tell my boss to buy books for our supervisors and managers?"

"Yes," replies the training manager. "I do."

Quality Leadership Skills addresses today's need for quality performance. It is a practical how-to-do-it manual for new and future leaders that explains the basic leadership tasks in a simple, step-by-step manner. It can also be used by individuals who have been trained and retrained—and trained again—in leadership principles and want to pick up new techniques.

And it's easy to use. Would you like to know how to *really* empower your employees so that they will take greater charge over their own careers? To teach your employees how to take more responsibility for their performance appraisals? To learn how to effectively delegate work to employees? The old saying *You can't delegate responsibility—only authority* is 99% myth.

In the chapters that follow, you will find clear directions on how to develop your employees. And the exciting thing about it is that you and your employees will produce more, better, and faster—and enjoy doing it, too!

Introduction

A machine is easy to run. Hit this button, and it starts. Push that one, and it stops. And a machine usually produces more, better, and faster than a manual worker could ever hope to do. We have automated most of our highly skilled jobs in a continuous effort to make everything bigger, better, and faster.

But there is one high-skill area that can never be automated: human interactions that take place between a leader and the members of his or her team.

It often takes more skill than most of us possess to deal with the great variety of employee needs and problems we encounter. Remember your feelings of discomfort when you had to handle a major discipline problem? You're not alone. Most of us have had those same feelings in dealing with employee situations.

I believe that it's good that we experience these uncomfortable feelings, because they serve as motivation—motivation to learn more about how to lead employees.

A number of years ago, I felt like a very lucky supervisor. I had four very competent employees. It was fortunate for them that they were outstanding, because I was the original "gutless" supervisor. I found it very easy to praise my employees on their good work, but extremely difficult to tell them how they could improve.

So I didn't. I didn't give them feedback on improvement, because it made me feel uncomfortable. They were deprived of important opportunities to develop and grow because I didn't give them accurate information.

Then one day my manager asked me if one of these employees was ready for a promotion. "Not yet," I replied. "There are a couple of areas she needs to work on. Let's give her another year."

The next morning, the employee stood in my office doorway and said, "Can I see you for a minute, Dick?"

"Sure," I replied.

She stepped inside and shut my door. "Dick," she asked, "did you turn me down for a promotion?"

"Well… yes," I replied.

"Why?" she asked.

"Because I felt you weren't ready."

"Why not?" she responded.

"Well, there are two particular areas I feel you need to work on." I began to lamely spell out the problems.

"But you never told me this," she replied. And she was right.

Two months later, she quit our organization. At that point in my career, I had a great need to know how to truly lead my employees. Much of what I have learned since then has come the hard way, by making mistakes and learning from them.

I also watch other leaders closely, good ones and poor ones, and I regularly attend leadership programs and read books on leadership. I've also learned a lot from 30 years of teaching leadership skills.

This book is my learning process, put into writing for those leaders who want common-sense ideas on how to handle the often-bewildering array of employee problems they face as they carry out their organizational responsibilities. It is full of practical advice, not theories, and outlines clear standards of performance. The chapters show you how to handle the many day-to-day interactions that are key to empowering your employees and helping them be more productive and fulfilled.

Part 1

Introduction to Leadership

1

Leadership in the 21st Century

"If you did not hold a position of authority, if your name was not on the door, would anyone follow you for what you believe in, who you are as a person, and where you want to go?

– Bruce E. Thom

Incredible changes are being made in today's organizations. Most are in transition—downsizing, rightsizing, merging, acquiring, and moving products and services offshore. They change to enhance their value to stockholders. They change in order to survive in today's competitive world markets. And they change their internal structure to reduce department boundaries in order to enhance creativity and communication. These organizational changes also force change in the workforce.

First, employees do not look at their life's work the way they always did. The good employees, the ones the organization wants to keep, no longer see anything wrong with leaving the company to take a better job somewhere else. Few employees, if any, look forward to the gold watch and retirement party. And it's not because today's employees are any less loyal than the employees of yesterday—they are still loyal. That is, until the organization gives them reason to leave.

Think about it. How many employees remember the Great Depression and what it was like to be grateful to have a job—any job? The generation of workers that followed, whose only links to that life-changing time were the stories they heard from their parents, are themselves now retired. Men and women in their twenties and thirties have little or no fear of not being able to find work. They believe that good jobs are readily available, and they're mostly right: organizations always have a need for good people. So, when good employees feel dissatisfied with their jobs or the way that they are being treated, they quit and look for work someplace else. And they find it.

One of the major sources of dissatisfaction for employees is having to work for people whom they consider to be incompetent. Years ago, workers were more willing to put up with an incompetent boss. Today, they are more apt to leave.

Employees are also more willing to leave because it is now socially acceptable. There is little or no stigma attached to an individual who leaves one company to work for another. With the destruction of the psychological employee/organization contract, an employee's loyalty today is more often to his or her profession, not to the organization. Therefore, in order to keep high-quality employees, organizations have to provide high-quality leadership.

The second major change in today's workforce is that there are now wider spans of control. More and more people work for fewer and fewer bosses. The more people a leader has, the more he or she needs to lead—that is, delegate, create, and motivate teams that can take responsibility

3

for their own work. Organizations need people to lead the many teams that have been created as a result of organizational change, but not always supervisors or managers: They might simply need individuals who can step forward and take over the role of team leadership.

The third major change has to do with the fact that traditional boundaries inside organizations are disappearing. Many departments no longer focus only on their own narrow view of the organization's mission. Employees must be able to work across functions and departments. This requires leadership: It requires leaders who are able to create a vision for their employees—a vision of what they are about and where they are going. And it requires employees who realize that they must cooperate with others in the organization in order to complete the mission.

There is one more new workplace reality. Employees used to be promoted to positions of leadership because they were competent at doing the department's tasks. Not anymore: With the rapid changes in technology that lead to changes in the way people work, many employees now know more about the tasks to be done than their leaders. In such circumstances, the supervisor's or manager's authority comes not from his or her detailed and competent knowledge of the job responsibilities, but in his or her ability to lead a talented and diverse team of employees.

An organization's strengths come from many individuals, not just one person. Our workforces are no longer made up of predominately male Caucasians: all ethnic backgrounds, races, faiths, and genders are represented. To manage today's diverse workforce, we need more than management—we need leadership.

Unfortunately, employers don't do a good job preparing their employees to take on the role of leadership. They just promote them and somehow expect them to know what to do. They teach them to complete paperwork and they teach them how to manage, but they don't teach them how to lead. It used to be that the manager had the time to mentor the new supervisor in the subtle skills of leadership. Today, it is difficult for most managers to find the quality time required to help a new supervisor make the transition from employee to leader. Furthermore, many managers are not themselves good leaders—how are they going to teach the new supervisor to lead? Some managers know how to lead, but don't know how to teach others what they know.

Many employees are reluctant to take on the title and role of a supervisor. They feel, with some justification, that it is just not worth the hassle of dealing with problem employees, a never-ending flow of paperwork, increased hours on the job, a diverse workforce, sexual harassment problems, and their own lack of knowledge in how to lead.

J. P. Kotter, noted leadership author and professor of organizational behavior at Harvard, wrote in the *Harvard Business Review*, "Leadership is about coping with change. Doing what was done yesterday, or doing it 5% better, is no longer a formula for success. Major changes are more and more necessary to survive and compete effectively in this new environment. More change always demands more leadership." (Kotter, 1995).

So, how do we teach this thing called "Leadership"?

Kotter offered us one way of looking at leadership: by comparing it to management. He said that management is made up of the activities of planning and budgeting, organizing and staffing, and controlling and problem solving. He states that leadership, however, is about setting a direction and a vision, aligning people to the organization's vision, and then motivating and inspiring employees to achieve their vision.

Management:	**Leadership:**
• Planning and budgeting	• Setting a Direction and a Vision
• Organizing and Staffing	• Aligning People
• Controlling and Problem Solving	• Motivating and Inspiring

Unfortunately, workers who have had a traditional four-year liberal arts education receive little or no training in leadership. Graduates with bachelor's degrees in business administration receive the majority of their training in accounting, economics, statistics, and finance. Good management stuff, but not leadership. Even graduates in a typical MBA program receive little in the way of leadership education and training. Employers are thus left to "grow" their own leaders.

Kotter made another interesting observation: "Most U.S. corporations today are over-managed and under led. They need to develop their capacity to exercise leadership. Successful corporations don't wait for leaders to come along. They actively seek out people with leadership potential and expose them to career experiences designed to develop that potential. Indeed, with careful selection, nurturing, and encouragement, dozens of people can play important leadership roles in business organizations."

John W. Gardner, advisor to six U.S. presidents, wrote this in 1990: "Many dismiss the subject [of leadership] with the confident assertion that 'leaders are born, not made.' Nonsense! Most of what leaders have that enables them to lead is learned. Leadership is not a mysterious activity. It is possible to describe the tasks that leaders perform."

And if we can describe it, we can learn it! We can study famous leaders. We can examine the latest research that has practical, on-the-job application for leaders. We can learn how the environment that surrounds the organization affects leadership. We can study ethics. And we can learn the skills of leadership.

2

Values: The Foundation

Leadership is not a person or a position. It is a complex moral relationship between people, based on trust, obligation, commitment, emotion, and a shared vision of the good.

— Joanne Ciulla

So, what do values have to do with leadership? Everything. Our underlying values guide our actions. We can learn the key behavioral steps required for any given leader/employee situation, but if our values aren't aligned with the needed behaviors, we are not likely to consistently say or do what needs to be said or done. For example, I know that "management by walking around" is important. Taking the time to stop working on a particular task, leave my office, and schmooze with my staff is worthwhile. I knew it when I was an employer, but I didn't consistently do it because I tend to be task-driven and practically unconscious to the outside world. I knew *how* to do it, and I even knew I was "supposed" to do it, but only rarely did I just walk around and talk to people and make casual conversation, such as *"How's everything going?" "What's happening in your life?" "How's your family?" "What concerns do you have about your job?"* If I had walked up to a member of my staff and started asking what I felt were "chit-chat" kinds of questions, he or she would have wondered if I had been taken over by aliens. (Not that they wouldn't have liked me to do it.)

If I had consistently taken time out of my day to interact with my staff, it would have had a positive effect on the workforce. It is a bit embarrassing to write this, but creating strong interpersonal relationships was just not at the top of my list of things to do. Talking one-on-one with others was not something I learned to do as a child, and I was not comfortable doing it. I love teaching groups or making presentations (primarily one-way communication), but taking the time from my busy schedule of doing the things I like to do (like writing this book) to reach out to others didn't "feel" right for me. It was just not a deep-seated value, even though it ought to have been.

We aren't born with values. We acquire them, mostly in early childhood. We learn how to behave, and how not to behave. We learn what's right and not right. We learn values from our parents, teachers, good bosses and bad bosses, and other significant people in our lives. These values are mostly buried in our subconscious. We rarely if ever take the time to say to ourselves, "What are my basic values about leadership?" As I think about my own leadership values, I realize how difficult it is to articulate them. I know that I value integrity, the Golden Rule, respect for all individuals who work for and with me, and helping others who need assistance. I also value hard work, tolerance for others' mistakes, and life-long learning. Is "hard work" a leadership value? I think so. It has always affected the way that I relate to individuals. I tend to invest more of my time in mentoring people who work hard. I also cut them some slack when

7

they make mistakes. I would be more likely to reward a hard worker with salary increases and promotions. This strong value of mine, however, also got in my way: I tended not to be as understanding of individuals who were productive yet put their childcare or family life ahead of their job, taking time off from work or not being available to volunteer for special and important work projects on the weekend. "Wow," you might think, "this guy Leatherman is not much of a leader!" You might be right; in some ways, I was not. What this personal example illustrates is that our values about leadership, especially those that are core to our being, can also be detrimental to good leadership—especially when taken to excess. And there is no question that I took the value of "hard work" to an extreme.

Any of our values can get us in trouble when taken to extreme. For example, many leaders place a high importance on integrity, yet seem to get pleasure out of verbally destroying an employee with "truth," justifying their behavior by saying, "I was only being honest."

It is important to clearly know our values so that we understand why we do the things we do as leaders. This allows us to guard against excess when we project our values onto others, and helps guide our future actions. If you know that you strongly value hard work and want others to do so, you can monitor your own behavior when dealing with subordinates who don't value what you value.

Our core values seldom change over time. What we choose to do (the actions we take as we lead) can change, and do change. But the personal core values rarely change. These values can help us examine how we should treat people we work with and bring to light how we really treat them and why. Then we can look at the gap and figure out what to do about it.

When I was the academic director of the human resource management program at the University of Richmond, I realized that our adult students rarely if ever met the office staff. They likely met a staff member when they first enrolled. Then, over the years, they attended classes in the evening and met a variety of professors. However, the staff worked during the day, and the students attended class in the evening. I thought it was important for the students to feel more connected to the university, so I reluctantly forced myself to do "walk-abouts," where I visited every class each semester. I would tell the students about new initiatives at the university, empathize with their hardships in attending evening school, and answer their questions. Many years later, I still have students come up to me at the mall or supermarket and say, "Dr. Dick, you don't remember me, but I remember the times you visited our classroom. I really appreciated what you did." I worked hard to overcome my own reluctance to engage others in conversation and did what a leader should do.

I strongly encourage you to take a few minutes and consider what is important to you as a leader. Can you list your top five leadership values?

1. _____

2. _____

3. _____

4. _____

5. _____

Now think about the leadership values of the organization for which you work. If your values and your organization's values are similar, then the culture of your organization supports the way that you lead your employees. If not, then you have a problem. (See the next chapter for more discussion on workplace culture.)

Suppose that one of your values is "truth-telling," and you have an employee who is technically very competent and almost irreplaceable. This employee is also very ambitious, and strongly desires a promotion into a leadership position. Unfortunately, he wants a promotion for the wrong reasons: he wants the prestige, money, and recognition that would come with a promotion—he does not have good long-term reasons for wanting to be a leader. You also believe that this employee does not have the personality necessary to lead others. He is abrupt, authoritative, and autocratic when dealing with others, and is basically a loner who prefers to work by himself.

In preparing for your annual performance appraisal interview with this employee, let's say that you discuss the situation with your boss. He tells you that in order to keep this employee in his important job, you must let him think that he has a future chance at being a supervisor. At this point, your key value of honesty is in direct conflict with your boss's wishes. Most of us would try to convince our boss that he or she needs to see the long-term problems that would be created if we don't tell the employee the truth. But if the boss can't be convinced, we have a problem. When faced with an ethical dilemma such as this, a true leader must make the decision that is right for them. If the leader values honesty, the right decision is to tell the truth—no matter the personal consequences.

Working in an environment that is opposed to your core values is a disaster in the making. Not only will *you* be unhappy with the organization where you work, but the *organization* will be unhappy with *you*. If you can't change the environment, you might need to find a new place to work that matches your values.

The decision to move to another job because of major differences between personal values and the organization's values is somewhat easier for your people if they have fewer outside responsibilities (they're not paying for their children's college tuition—yet) and their level in the organization is not as high as it will be later. They have less to lose by leaving one job for another. But as they get older, it becomes more risky to leave one job in order to find another. There are greater consequences to quitting a job because of one's principles. Therefore, it is very, very important that you think through your personal values early in your career, and make sure that they match those of the organization.

In the following chapters, you will see models of leadership behavior for a number of different leadership tasks. But remember that these are models that fit *my* beliefs and values; you may need to adapt or modify a particular model to be better aligned with *your* core beliefs and values. If, however, there is something about the model that bothers you, don't discard the whole model—figure out what part of it bothers you and why that particular step in the model doesn't work for you, and then think of what you would do or say in place of that step. You might discover that the underlying reason for completing a particular step in a model is so important, you will choose to do it in spite of your discomfort.

It's time to spell out my beliefs about leadership that underlie the behaviors I discuss in the book. I believe that:

1. Leaders and employees can and must learn new and better ways of working together.

2. Leaders must show respect for all employees.

3. Leaders must trust their employees to do the right thing, unless proven otherwise.

4. Leaders must trust their employees with information about the organization's mission, vision, and strategic and tactical plans.

5. Leaders have to talk *with* employees, not *at* them.

6. Authority and responsibility can both be delegated and shared with employees, individually or in teams.

7. With the complexity of today's jobs, it is likely that employees know more about their jobs than their leaders, and some of their ideas will be better.

8. Creativity is widely dispersed in the organization—it is not just the province of leaders.

9. Employees must be involved in problem solving, decision making, and planning.

10. Quality discussions with employees take time—time to prepare, and time to conduct. Effective leaders are willing to take the necessary time.

11. Leaders have an unlimited opportunity to provide positive feedback to employees.

12. Employees should be allowed to take appropriate risks, make mistakes, and learn from them.

13. It is almost always better to tell the truth.

3

Influencing Culture

It can be argued that the only thing of real importance that leaders do is to create and manage culture; that the unique talent of leaders is their ability to understand and work with culture, and that it is an ultimate act of leadership to destroy culture when it is viewed as dysfunctional.

— Edgar Schein

You likely already know much about culture. You grew up in one. You know that the culture of the southern part of the United States is different in many ways from the north, and that the culture of New York City is very different than the culture of Staunton, Virginia (population 15,000). You probably know that the culture of Switzerland is significantly different from that of Peru. You have also probably experienced the cultural differences within and between various professions (e.g., medical profession vs. engineering). I can tell you from personal experience that the academic culture is a world unto its own.

I have had significant experiences in five very different "cultures": the military; a small, family-owned electronics business; the 3M Company, a very large organization; my own business; and academia. Each of these cultures required many adjustments on my part. In two of these, I was able to make significant changes in the culture: in my own business, where I was able to instill my own values and beliefs; and surprisingly, in academia, where I was given the responsibility of creating a new department.

If you take the institutions and organizations I listed in the preceding paragraphs and made statements about each of them in terms of their values, beliefs, and assumptions, you begin to describe each organization's culture. You are no doubt familiar with many of your own organization's values. Its mission statement, if there is one, will tell you something. Which assumptions, often unspoken, underlie your organization? Maybe it is focused on the customer and there is an unspoken assumption that "the customer is always right." This leads to very specific behaviors. If the founder of a company had a thing years ago about answering all telephones promptly and stormed out of his office if he heard a phone ring more than four times, this might be why the organization does not make callers push 16 numbers in order to talk to a human being! (I'm embarrassed to say that the founder was me.)

Organizations and departments and sections all have cultures that are different from one another. The extent to which a leader can influence a company's culture is dependent on the maturity of the organization (that is, the degree that the culture is already embedded) and one's hierarchical position in it. In this chapter, I will offer thoughts for those of you who work in mature organizations (perhaps holding leadership roles such as supervisor or manager), as well as for those of you who are founders or key managers in small companies.

A vast number of organizations in this country are small businesses. Much of what is discussed in dealing with culture in a large organization is the same as or is similar to that of smaller organizations.

Influencing Culture within an Organization

Many of the readers of this book manage and lead within cultures that already exist—not as CEOs, but more likely as division supervisors or department managers. This section is about you and how you lead your division or department within an established organization. Founders of small businesses and key leaders will also find helpful information in this part of the book.

First, it is only fair to tell you about my bias. I strongly believe in President Harry Truman's philosophy "The buck stops here." The renowned consultant and author Peter Drucker believes that effective managers don't worry or complain about what they cannot do. They figure out what can be done. Yes, top management establishes important, organization-wide values that probably drive your organization's culture, but I have seen examples of extraordinary work ethic in sections and departments of dysfunctional organizations. Of course, the reverse is also true: there are outstanding, vibrant organizations with great cultures that had one or more sections or departments that were dysfunctional. Here, however, I will focus on you and what *you* can do to influence the culture of your area of responsibility.

What is your organization's culture? It is important to understand the cultural environment that surrounds your area of responsibility, because it influences what you and your associates value and believe, and the assumptions you make about the way things are done. Hopefully, the organization's culture matches the culture of your area of responsibility. (Unfortunately, it may not.) In this case, it is important to know how the organization supports your values and in what ways it does not (through its culture).

I try to provide clear, step-by-step, prescriptive leadership behaviors, but when it comes to the culture of an organization, the first step in understanding is not about taking action—it is about how to think about the culture. For insight into the culture of your organization, answer the questions in this section. At first glance, these seem to be simple, easy questions to answer. They are not. Take some time and write the answers to the following questions on a separate sheet. It's important.

1. **What are the parables, myths, or legends of your organization?** At the 3M Company, everyone knew the story of the Post-it note: A bad batch of adhesive was found to have unusual properties: the adhesive would stick to paper, but could be easily released. The engineer who examined this phenomenon decided to use the adhesive on small pieces of paper that could be used to mark his choir's selections of hymns to be sung in church on Sunday. The 3M Company allowed discoverers of a new product idea to lead a new business to promote their product, and this is how a large new division was created to manufacture Post-it notes, headed by the same individual who had originally discovered a new way to use a bad adhesive.

    Briefly note on separate paper the events or people in your organization that have become legendary.

2. **What do your organization's legends mean?** (How do they play out in everyday life?) The Post-it story from the 3M Company has, over the years, evolved into a company-wide belief that anyone can come up with a clever idea and become an executive of the organization. This single event created and supported a culture of innovation, fostered a sense of pride in the organization, and enhanced the morale of all of 3M's employees.

How have the things you listed in #1 above changed or affected present life in your organization?

3. **What does your organization value?** Does it, for example, value innovation; healthy profit margins; decentralization of business units; a strong marketing orientation; acceptance of world-wide, international cultures; honesty; square dealing with customers; promotion from within; or education and training of all employees?

4. **How do you know what the company values?** I had an interesting personal experience with one of 3M's key values, "square dealing with customers." I worked in the Electro Products division. We produced an innovative product for the utility market called a "high-voltage terminator" that was cheaper to purchase and operate, saved labor, and cost far less for materials than existing methods. It was used to terminate the ends of high-voltage cable, which is usually installed at the top of electrical poles. It was a highly successful product and large numbers were sold to utilities across the country. A year after its introduction to the marketplace, some of the terminators failed. The division marshaled its sales people and sent them out in the field to determine the scope of the problem. They discovered a number of additional units that needed to be replaced. The area salespeople were told to hire a local industrial electrical contractor, coordinate with the local utility, take a bucket truck and experienced electricians out to the field, and replace every one of the units that had ever been sold. I don't know what the final cost was, but I'll bet it was in the millions of dollars. Nobody made them do this and there were no threats of litigation. 3M did it because it was the right thing to do—it was "square dealing." This decision reinforced the values embedded in the culture at 3M. To this day, the story is passed down to new salespeople.

A word of caution here: What we *think* is going on in an organization may not be at all what is actually happening. When I was the founder and owner of my own small business, I valued participative leadership and believed that I practiced participative leadership as an ingrained part of the company culture. (After all, I taught the stuff.) One day, I gave each of my associates a survey form to complete anonymously. I asked each of them to rate me on each of the survey items and to frankly state how they perceived me as their leader. I discovered two things: (1) My staff also valued participative leadership. (2) My staff did *not* perceive me as being at all participative! I set up a meeting where I consciously created an atmosphere of trust, and I asked questions to obtain more understanding about my behavior. The staff was able to give me clear examples of the many times I was not a participative leader. My cherished assumptions about my leadership were shattered, and it almost moved me to tears.

Which events or actions have you personally observed or heard that support the values of your organization?

5. **What are the physical, outward signs of what your organization values?** If a corporation has centralized training departments for each of the major divisions where education and training is ongoing, one rightly concludes that it puts a high price on training. If there are newspapers from Germany, England, Russia, France, and Italy in the waiting room of one of the executives, it suggests that the company really does value other cultures and international relations. Support for innovation is demonstrated when individuals in the research and development departments are allowed to spend a certain amount of time working on their personal pet projects in the hope that they will come up with a new invention for the company.

What tangible evidence do you have that indicates your organization's outward support for its values and beliefs?

6. **What values are implicit?** Implicit values, beliefs, and assumptions are those that everybody knows are true but that are not actually written down. At many companies, the staff is expected to wear business attire (suits and ties for the men), but this is often not spelled out as a requirement. Everyone understands that this is what the company expects, however.

   Consider your organization. What are the implicit values and beliefs or assumptions that make up your organization's culture?

7. **What specific values are included in the organization's mission statement?** The mission statement "To solve unsolved problems innovatively" tells us that the values of *innovation* and *customer problem solving* are clear.

   What are the values in *your* organization's mission statement?

8. **What is the organization willing to spend money on?** 3M spent a huge amount of money on education and training. Almost all divisions had their own fully-staffed training department and their own budgets that coordinated sales and marketing training, management development, and employment training.

   What is your organization willing to spend money on?

9. **How is the organization's physical layout consistent with its values?** An example: If a corporation's training departments are housed in separate facilities, each well-equipped with the latest in technological audio/visual equipment, plush carpet, and comfortable chairs for the participants, everyone can see that training and development are important values and are part of its culture.

Now that you have thought about how these questions relate to your own organization, you are ready to move to the next step: thinking about how *you* influence the culture of your section, department, or small company.

Influencing the culture of your section or department. How do you influence the culture of your area of control? Again, by asking questions. For example, what are your assumptions about the way things are "supposed" to work? What do you pay attention to? What don't you pay attention to? What do you believe and value? Do you pay attention to the things that you believe and value? For example, do performance appraisals measure and rate the values you hold important? You may value participation when conducting performance appraisals and want your associate to have input into his or her own appraisal, but if you have to have a written appraisal signed by your boss before you can conduct the appraisal meeting, then you can be assured that your associate will not see the appraisal as being participative.

Do you model what you want your associates to believe and value? This is more difficult than you might imagine. For example, suppose I value open communication, yet I insist that there is only *one* way we should do things—my way. I won't get much feedback on ideas—especially those that the staff thinks are nutty. If what I say does not match what I do, my associates will take their cues from what I do, not from what I say. If you value open communication, do you take the time to walk around and make yourself available to all your associates? Or do you wall up in your office and require associates to come to you? If you have an office and your door is open, do you stop what you're doing and make yourself available when they stick their head in the door?

Are your associates rewarded with pay and/or promotion when they take on your values and thus help you create your desired culture? Do you hire and retain associates who believe in and value what you value? Are you more apt to assign plum jobs to individuals who hold and espouse the same beliefs and values that you feel are important? Do your systems and processes support what you believe and value? (For example, if you value informality in your weekly meetings, have you ever taken your associates outside of your organization's walls for a couple of hours to help create the informality you desire?) Schein (2004) states, "What leaders consistently pay attention to, reward, control, and react to emotionally communicates more clearly what their own priorities, goals, and assumptions are." Is what you believe and value also valued by the people who report to you? What do you do to consistently reinforce what you believe in and value?

Beliefs and Values

Now, take a few minutes and think about your own values. Pencil in notes to yourself, if you wish.

Check what you personally agree with or believe in.

- ☐ I believe in being honest with others.
- ☐ Participative leadership is critically important.
- ☐ I believe people should get an honest day's pay for an honest day's work.
- ☐ Hard work should be expected of everyone.
- ☐ Quality is important.

Check what you personally agree with.

- ☐ Employees should do what is expected.
- ☐ Employees should care about each other.
- ☐ Work and fun are not mutually exclusive.
- ☐ The customer's or client's needs must come first.
- ☐ The customer or client is always right.

Check what you personally agree with.

- ☐ Training and development of all employees is important.
- ☐ People are an organization's most important asset.
- ☐ Teams are more effective than individual workers.
- ☐ Employees should never be laid off.
- ☐ Employees should not be primarily motivated by money.

Check what you personally agree with.

- ☐ Recognition is the primary motivator for doing good work.
- ☐ Creativity should be valued in the organization.
- ☐ The organization should be environmentally friendly.
- ☐ Take risks. It is always more risky to say yes to a new idea than to say no—but say yes.

☐ Social events off the job with all employees are important.

☐ All leaders should have an "open-door" policy with their direct reports.

☐ Whistleblowers are not troublemakers. Honor them.

What are your key values and beliefs?

In your section or department, what do you *really* pay attention to?

What *don't* you pay attention to?

In what ways do you demonstrate or reflect what you believe in and value?

How do you model what you want your associates to believe in and value?

How do you reward your associates (e.g., pay, promotion, etc.) when they embrace your values?

Consider the last five people you have hired. How close was the match between what you value and believe and *their* values and beliefs?

Are you more apt to assign plum jobs, almost without thinking, to individuals who espouse the same beliefs and values that you feel are important?

How well do your systems and processes reflect what you believe in and value? Which processes get in the way of your desired culture? Which processes support the culture you wish?

What kind of culture do you want? The next step in your analysis is to define your desired culture. To do this, you need to answer the following difficult questions:

Do you want to maintain an earlier culture that is threatened? Or do you want to make stronger an existing culture? Do you want to integrate a new culture?

What specific ways would you like to see your section or department's culture enhanced?

Why do you want this?

How well does the organizational culture support your area's culture? (Skip this question if you work in a small organization.)

How do the specific departments that work closely with you match the culture of your area's culture? (Skip this question if you work in a small organization.)

How is what you want different from what you have?

What can you do to close the perceived "culture gap" in your area of control?

How can you evaluate the effects of your efforts to maintain and build on the changes you introduced into your company's culture?

Your values, beliefs, and assumptions drive what you do. And what you do determines the culture in your area of control. Recognize that some values and beliefs are contradictory. For example, if you value and believe that participation is necessary for the survival of your organization and you also value and believe that the organization should respond quickly to market conditions, then there is likely going to be trouble. Your drive for quick and decisive action may be in conflict with the often time-consuming need for participation.

Finally, if you want to engage in an interesting project that is almost guaranteed to bring about surprises (not always pleasant) and positive change, get together with the people in your area of control and distribute the preceding questions to each person. When everyone has had time to respond, facilitate a discussion. You'll be amazed at what you will learn!

4
Motivating Employees

Extrinsic motivation deals with the satisfaction or the reward gained for having done something. . . Intrinsic motivation deals with the satisfaction gained from the activity itself, such as the pleasure of walking not for where it takes you, but just for the action itself; the pleasure of doing a job not for what it pays, but because of its interest. These satisfactions are the opposite of boredom.

- Norman R. F. Maier

There are many reasons why employees want to excel, which is why it is difficult to establish hard and fast motivational "rules." But because people are similar in so many ways, we can make some general statements about how to motivate others.

For example, if your boss informs you that she is going to give you a big raise because of your outstanding contributions over the past year, you will probably feel—at least for the moment—highly motivated to work harder.

However, suppose you are already making big bucks in your job, but you feel unappreciated because your boss never takes the time to tell you how much she appreciates your work. Odds are that a sincere compliment might mean just as much—maybe even more—than a somewhat bigger paycheck.

Some people feel uncomfortable when they receive a compliment. For these employees, a more challenging job (or even a different job) might be a better motivator. Employees are motivated by *their* needs—not yours.

So how do you motivate your employees? By knowing something about the dynamics of motivation and by using this knowledge appropriately. Let's look, then, at some general theories concerning motivation.

Theories about Motivation

Of the many persons who have contributed to our knowledge about motivation, Douglas McGregor, Abraham Maslow, and Frederick Herzberg have been particularly helpful. These three individuals began the search for answers to the "How in the heck do I motivate my employees?" question. Parts of their theories don't hold up in light of modern-day research, but they still offer us the best way of looking at the issue of motivation.

Douglas McGregor studied the relationship between a *leader's attitude* toward his or her employees and the resultant employee behavior. Abraham Maslow investigated *employee needs*. And Frederick Herzberg looked at how the *employee's job* affects his or her motivation. All three of these factors—the leader's attitude, the employee's needs, and the job itself—greatly affect employee motivation. We'll look at what each of these important theorists said about motivation in this chapter.

The Leader's Attitude

McGregor believed that there are two types of leaders: The leader who believes an employee works hard only if he or she is forced to and will goof off if given a chance, and the leader who believes that employees work productively because they enjoy their work. He labeled these leaders X and Y.

McGregor emphasized that a leader's attitude toward employees affects the way he or she manages. If the leader believes that his or her people work only because they are made to work, he or she will probably be a very controlling boss. He or she is more likely to establish strict job standards, set up job controls, observe and monitor his or her people carefully, and let them know that they are being watched.

On the other hand, if the leader believes his or her employees can be trusted to do their jobs, he or she will tend to be less controlling and won't see the need to control employees because they will control themselves. Now, whether or not one's employees need to be controlled is not the point—it's whether or not the leader *believes* they do. What we believe to be true tends to result in our employees becoming what we expect. It's a little like raising children: If we expect children to be dishonest and therefore treat them as if they are dishonest, they are likely to become dishonest.

The same thing is true with adult workers: If we believe that employees have to be watched, monitored, controlled, and forced to work, they will behave in ways that call for such treatment. But if we *expect* people to do their work, then they usually will. A lot of what happens in terms of an individual employee's morale is simply due to our attitude about him or her.

Let's look at an example. Suppose one day an employee takes too much time for his morning break. A type X leader will say to this employee, "You're late. Don't you know that breaks are only ten minutes? Get back to work—and in the future, I'll be watching you!" Here, the leader believes that he or she has to keep a close eye on this employee in order to prevent future problems, because the employee is not to be trusted to behave appropriately on the job. As a result, the employee, not feeling trusted, is more likely to behave in untrustworthy ways in the future.

A less-controlling leader might say to this employee, "I'm surprised that you are late from break. What happened?" Here, the implication is that there may be a legitimate reason why the employee was late returning from break, and that the employee is self-motivated to return to his job on time. The leader has clearly communicated his or her standards ("I'm surprised that you are late from break") and has demonstrated his or her concern for the employee's situation ("What happened?").

In order to see how Theories X and Y can be applied to the work world, read Part 1 of the following case. When you have finished, answer the questions at the end of the case before turning to Part 2.

The Case of the Disappearing Profits: Part 1

The Natural Taste Company's sales and distribution facility is located in Pamplin City, Virginia. It's early Monday morning, and George Dishberger, NTC's vice president of sales and distribution, is waiting for Joyce Havinstock, NTC's senior vice president of marketing, to arrive from New York.

George is not a happy man. Things have not been going well for the organization during the past year. Sales are down, and costs are up. George is afraid that Joyce is coming to fire him, demote him, or "straighten him out" in some unpleasant way or another.

The intercom buzzes. With a deep sigh, George picks up his phone.

"Ms. Havinstock is here," his receptionist reports.

"Send her in," George replies. He sighs again, straightens his tie, and stands to greet Joyce as she breezes into the office.

"Good morning, Joyce," he says, with a strained smile.

"I wish it were a good morning," she replies. "Unfortunately, you have serious problems and I'm here to see that they get fixed. Your sales are miserable and your costs are even worse. Frankly, George, your job is on the line. Now, why don't you fill me in on what's going on?"

"Well, Joyce," he says, "You're right about sales being down a bit, but our competition is a lot tougher than it used to be. And costs are up a little because our labor costs are higher."

"That is just an excuse for incompetent management," Joyce grimly replies. "Sales are down a lot more than a 'bit' and your costs have risen more than 11% during the past two years!"

"Look, Joyce, you really need to look at what we are facing here. Most of our telemarketers are just college kids. We hire them, they work for a year or two, and when they graduate, they quit. You know that high turnover is normal for our type of business."

"Yes, George," she says, "you've always had high turnover, but your operating costs used to be much lower."

"But we used to be the only major employer within 20 miles of Pamplin City! Now there are three other organizations that compete with us in the same labor market."

"So what's your excuse for the decrease in sales?" she replies.

"It's the competition, Joyce. Look, walk out with me to the sales area and see for yourself what they face every day."

"Okay, George. Let's take a look at how your people are doing."

As they walk back to the telemarketing area, George fervently hopes that his people are at their best. For the most part, he knows they are good employees, but this is the first job for most of them. They don't all have good work habits. If they have to stay up studying for a tough exam, they might be a little late coming in the next morning. *Let them all be here,* he thought. He walked in. *Oh no! There are three empty stations. Maybe she won't notice. And where is Betty, the supervisor?*

(continued)

The Case of the Disappearing Profits: Part 1 (continued)

"Joyce, let me introduce you to one of our more experienced telemarketers, Dan Williams. Dan, this is Joyce Havinstock, our senior VP of marketing in New York."

"Nice to meet you, Dan."

"Likewise, Ms. Havinstock."

"Well, Dan, how do you like working for NTC?" she asks.

"It's great," he replies. "They really treat you well. When I have too much class work—you know, a tough report that's due—they give me extra time off to take care of it. And when it's exam time, nobody fusses if we come in late after studying all night. This is a nice place to work. It's like working for my own family."

"I see," Joyce said. "And how do you like the work you do?"

"Well, uh…" he stammers, "I guess it is okay."

"What do you mean, 'okay'?" she asks.

"It's just that who can get excited about making phone calls all day to people who feel like you are intruding on their time? It makes it hard to keep up your enthusiasm day after day."

"I see," Joyce said.

"Say, Dan, where is Betty?" George asks.

"I don't know, boss," he replied. "I think she went to call Randy at home to find out when he is coming in. She should be back in a few minutes."

"Okay," George replies. "Tell her I stopped by."

"You bet, boss. Nice to have met you, Ms. Havinstock."

As they walk away from the section, Joyce says, "I saw several stations empty. Where is everybody?"

"I don't know," George replies. "There's Betty. She'll know."

"Betty, I'd like you to meet Joyce Havinstock. She is our senior VP of marketing. Joyce, this is Betty Thurston, the supervisor of the telemarketing department."

"Hi, Betty."

"Pleased to meet you, Ms. Havinstock."

"Betty," George says, "we noticed a few people missing. What seems to be the problem?"

"Oh, no problem, boss. I think there was a fraternity party over at the college last night and some of our people were probably up pretty late. They'll be along."

"Good, good."

(continued)

Quality Leadership Skills

The Case of the Disappearing Profits: Part 1 (concluded)

"Tell me, Betty. Don't you have set schedules for your people?" Ms. Havinstock asks.

"Not exactly," Betty replies. "Oh, we do have a schedule, but we let the telemarketers keep their own hours because of their studies. We had a strict schedule at one time, but it was too hard to keep good students, especially in their junior and senior years."

"Oh, excuse me, Mr. Dishberger, but could I see you when you are free?" Paul Otts asks.

"Paul, this is Joyce Havinstock, NTC's vice president of marketing. Joyce, this is Paul Otts. He takes care of our computers for us."

"Hi, Ms. Havinstock. It's nice to meet you."

"Yes," Joyce replies, with a grim look.

"It was nice to meet you also," Betty says as she turns to leave. "But I need to get back to the section. See you later, boss."

"Now, what seems to be the problem, Paul?" George asks.

"Mr. Dishberger, there is a serious problem with the computer network, but I don't know what's wrong with it. Frankly, I think there is something wrong with the basic system. Could you call in a technical representative from the computer company and see if they can find out what's wrong? We need to fix it as soon as possible because section B's out of business. They have to write up all of their calls in longhand."

"Sure, Paul. Leave a note on my desk and I'll get somebody out here right away."

"Thanks, Mr. Dishberger. Let me know what you find out. Nice to meet you, Ms. Havinstock."

Joyce doesn't reply, but as Paul leaves, she turns to George and asks, "Why do you have a computer technician who obviously doesn't know his job?"

"Well, Joyce, he is the son of our old shipping and receiving manager, who died last year. So, when Paul needed a job, we felt it was important to find him a place. Actually, it turned out pretty good. He's got a lot to learn, but he's coming along fine."

"Well," Joyce says, "I'm beginning to see why your profits are down and your costs are up. You keep people who can't do their jobs out of respect for the deceased. You let a bunch of college kids run amok and do whatever they want, when they want. You're not running a business, you're running a resort! You need to fire your computer technician and get somebody who knows what they are doing. You need to set up standards and controls to make sure your people come to work on time. And you need a new management team that can keep a close eye on your people. But most important, you need to get tough. And you need to do it all yesterday!"

"Wait a minute," George said. "How long do you think it will take for all my people to leave and join the competition? You just can't treat people like they did 100 years ago!"

"No, you wait a minute," Joyce says. "These people don't work because they like doing what they are doing. They work so they can afford to party at their fraternities. Do you actually think that people work because they're in love with their jobs?"

George hesitates a moment, and says, "No, I guess not."

After reading the scenario, how would you classify the leadership style of Joyce Havinstock: Theory X, or Theory Y?

What did Joyce say or do that made you classify her as you did?

How would you classify the leadership style of George Dishberger: Theory X, or Theory Y?

Did you find it easy to classify Joyce as an archetypal Theory X manager? Was it more difficult to classify George? If you reluctantly decided that George is a Theory Y manager, you are not alone, as others who have read this case also rated him a Theory Y manager.

Consider these points:

1. One of George's employees said, "This is a nice place to work. It's like working for my own family."

2. George agreed to call in an outside computer expert, rather than encourage the employee to make the call. This reinforced the employee's dependency on George. George chose not to use this situation as an opportunity to empower his employee.

3. But the strongest indictment of all occurred when Joyce asked, "Do you actually think that people work because they're in love with their jobs?" Do you remember how George answered that question? He said, *"No, I guess not."* What do you think that George's answer would have been if he had, in fact, been a Theory Y manager? He would have said "YES!"

As you have probably guessed, George exhibits just another form of Theory X leadership. In his own way, he is just as paternalistic as Joyce.

At this point, you can see that McGregor's work was not as simplistic as you might have imagined. In fact, it is even more complex. Read Part 2 and again answer the questions at the end.

The Case of the Disappearing Profits: Part 2

It is one week before the Monday that Joyce Havinstock is scheduled to visit George Dishberger. As George drives to work, a black cloud forms above his car. Suddenly, a bolt of lightning flashes down and strikes his car, instantly changing George into a *true* Theory Y manager. At that moment, he has new insight into his job and a whole new way of looking at his people.

When he arrives at work, his receptionist hands him a phone message from Joyce Havinstock. She is calling to remind him that she plans to visit next week, and expects to meet with him to discuss sales, costs, and profits.

George walks into his office, sighs, and pulls out a legal pad. He begins to make some notes on what must be done before Joyce arrives. He knows his job is on the line.

If you were George Dishberger, what would you do to prepare for Joyce's imminent visit? Remember that poor George has only five working days to get ready for Joyce!

Now, read the following list of actions and see if any of them match yours:

1. Set production targets for the employees.
2. Establish and publish attendance requirements.
3. Review selection procedures to ensure that only people who want to work are hired.
4. Schedule the computer person to take a course in computer maintenance.
5. Call a meeting to inform the employees of all the changes.
6. Tell the employees that Joyce is coming and that they should look sharp when she is around.

Carefully examine this list. Would you say that the style of leadership is participative (Theory Y), or more directive (Theory X)? In other words, which way does the communication flow in each of the above examples—up the organization, or down from the boss?

Right. Down. Most of George's listed actions flow from him down to his people. If George had really been changed into a Theory Y leader, he might have listed the following kinds of actions:

1. Ask all supervisors and managers to meet with their employees to set production targets.
2. Meet with the key employees to determine the problems Joyce might see. Together identify the causes of those problems, and obtain the group's input on possible solutions.
3. Ask the supervisor of the telemarketing department to meet with her employees and identify ways to make their jobs more challenging.
4. Meet with the supervisor of the telemarketing department and several of her key employees to discuss ways to address the attendance problem.
5. Ask the computer person what he needs in order to do his job.

It is easy to agree with McGregor's theories, but as we have seen, when the stakes are high and the pressure is on, many people revert to Theory X behavior because 1) participation takes time, and 2) it is difficult to delegate during a crisis.

But our attitudes and beliefs about how our employees feel about work is only part of the motivational puzzle. Another piece of the puzzle involves our employees' needs and how they are motivated to fulfill those needs.

Maslow's Hierarchy of Needs and Employee Needs

Abraham Maslow studied highly motivated people to determine why they are successful. He discovered that individuals have a series of needs, and that they can be arranged in a hierarchy of ascending order. His premise was that people are motivated by their most-immediate needs. The illustration that follows shows our most-basic needs at the bottom, moving up.

Maslow's Hierarchy of Needs

Let's look at these needs in more detail.

Physiological needs are our most basic requirements. They include the need for food, water, sleep, warmth, and sex. Maslow suggested that employees are motivated to meet these primary needs before they are motivated by the needs at the next level. For example, if you are walking across a desert and haven't had water in two days, you are going to be most strongly motivated to satisfy your thirst. Until you obtain water, you are not going to be interested in other needs. On the job, physiological needs can be satisfied by paying employees fair salaries that enable them to pay their water bills, purchase food, and keep their houses warm.

Safety needs include both the need to be free from imminent danger and the need for security. On the job, safety needs include working in an environment that is not hazardous, having safe equipment, and not worrying about losing your job. If you are genuinely worried about losing your job, you are not likely going to be motivated by higher-level needs. Conversely, if you are dying from a lack of water (a physiological need), you are probably not going to be very concerned about losing your job.

Belonging needs include the need to feel a part of a group, to receive affection from others, and to be in a loving relationship. Do you remember what it was like when you first went to work for your organization? Remember the feelings of uneasiness when you arrived? No one knew you, and you didn't feel included as a part of the work group. The lack of belonging produces strong needs that most people are motivated to fulfill. Maslow believes that all individuals will try to satisfy the need to belong—but only when their physiological needs and safety needs have already been satisfied.

Esteem needs are at the top of Maslow's hierarchy. He states that all people have a need for the esteem of others, as well as a need for self-esteem. On the job, this need is usually met by different forms of recognition. Examples are giving an employee a sincere compliment for a task well done, awarding him or her the "Employee of the Month" parking space, asking an employee's advice, or assigning him or her to a special task group.

Esteem given by others, especially when received in an individual's formative years, usually results in good self-esteem. If an employee did not receive positive feedback as a child, he or she might never be able to get enough compliments, or will be uncomfortable receiving compli-

26

ments. In either case, it is necessary for a leader to be aware of such a deficiency and provide sincere positive feedback.

Self-actualization is seen by Maslow as the highest or "peak" experience. This level results from having all of our other needs met while we are engaged in a satisfying job. According to Maslow (1954), self-actualization is "… loosely described as the full use and exploitation of talents, capacities, potentialities, etc. Such people seem to be fulfilling themselves and to be doing the best that they are capable of doing." He explains that we humans desire self-fulfillment and want to become everything that we are capable of becoming.

When our employees come to work because they take joy in what they do, they can also become self-actualized. Part of our job as leaders is to make sure, as much as possible, that our employees' other needs are being met so they can operate at this peak level of being.

One last point: Employees don't suddenly come in to work one day at their highest level of productivity and remain there forever. Suppose you are in the middle of an exciting, challenging, and joyful task. The phone rings, and it's your boss. She is not happy. She wants to see you in her office—now! Suddenly, you no longer feel self-actualized. You are now more likely concerned about your job (safety needs).

The Employee's Job

Frederick Herzberg interviewed many employees during the course of his research in the 1950s. First, he asked them to think of the times when they were happy on the job and to describe the events that made them feel happy. Next, he asked them to think of times when they were unhappy on the job, and to describe the events that produced those feelings.

From these interviews, Herzberg discovered something remarkable: the things that people experienced on the job that made them happy were not necessarily the same things that could make them unhappy! Herzberg learned that employees generally believed that only a few things brought them the most happiness and satisfaction on the job. He called these things "satisfiers":

- Achievement
- Recognition
- Work itself
- Responsibility
- Advancement

But the factors that caused the most unhappiness on the job were different, with the exception of recognition. Herzberg's "Dissatisfiers":

- Poor organizational policy and administration
- Technically incompetent supervisors
- Lack of recognition
- A salary that was perceived as being unfair
- Poor interpersonal relations with supervisors

Thus, Herzberg discovered that having good organizational policy, technically competent supervisors, and a fair salary didn't of themselves make people happy. Having these items satisfied just kept them from being unhappy. He believed that it is necessary to improve the way that each employee is treated if you want to eliminate dissatisfiers and use the satisfiers to motivate the employee.

One way of looking at dissatisfiers and satisfiers is to think about your garbage pick-up. Suppose that last Saturday you had a big party at your home. Sunday night you put all the garbage in the big cans and took the full cans to your backyard for the city to pick up Monday morning. You come home from work on Monday evening and discover that your garbage has not been picked up. To make matters worse, you see that dogs got into the cans, tipped them over, and scattered the remnants of Saturday's party all over the yard. You spend an hour in the gathering dusk cleaning up the mess.

When you arrive at work the next day, you call the city and raise heck about them not picking up your garbage on Monday. That evening, when you arrive home, you see the garbage is again strewn all over your yard—and your neighbor's yard. You pick up the garbage, muttering under your breath.

You call the city Wednesday morning and really let them have it. You also complain to several of your co-workers about the crappy city services. That evening, when you arrive home, you notice that the garbage had been picked up.

The next day, you do not arrive at work shouting "Halleluiah! My garbage has been picked up!" Not having your garbage picked up for several days made you very unhappy. When the city finally picked up your garbage, it didn't make you happy—it just meant you were not *unhappy*.

Dissatisfiers are like that: They are garbage. Your job, as a leader, is to clean up the garbage so that you can use the satisfiers to make your people happy.

You might have noticed that the items employees said made them happy were those that had to do with the job—i.e., achievement in the job, recognition for a job well done, the job itself, more responsibility, and advancement to a higher level. But the items that made people unhappy had to do with how they were treated. Only "Recognition" appeared in the top-five of both lists as a factor causing happiness (or, in its absence, unhappiness). That is why employee recognition is such a powerful motivational tool.

Application

These early theories of motivation can teach us a lot about how to motivate ourselves and our employees. In the following section, you will see how to apply motivational theory to the question of what you as a leader can do to increase employee motivation in three important areas—the employee's job, the organization, and your own actions toward employees.

The Employee's Job

We can make a significant positive impact on the morale of our employees by matching the job to the individual as much as possible. An effective leader modifies jobs to fit people, not people to fit jobs. Small changes in a job can result in large changes in motivation. We can look for ways to make our employees' jobs more interesting, create challenging and responsible jobs for them, reduce the stress level as much as possible, protect their status, organize the work so one task is completed before another is started, and make sure that we provide specific feedback on their results. Here are a few ways to do that:

Create interesting jobs for your employees. Granted, there are restrictions as to what can be done in restructuring an employee's job, but if you believe that there is nothing you can do to make a job more interesting for an employee, then that is exactly what will happen to his or her motivation—nothing. Take the time to talk with your employees to learn the kinds of things they like and don't like to do. It is quite possible to enhance an employee's job and make it more interesting.

One way is to use "reverse specialization" and combine tasks previously done by several people into one job. Also consider cross-training people within one section or department so there are new and more-interesting tasks. A key question to ask is, "What can this employee do uncommonly well?" Chances are that what an employee does well is also something that he or she enjoys doing. If you can modify a job so that the employee can better utilize his or her strengths, you will probably produce a more motivated employee.

Create challenging jobs for your employees. It is possible to have an interesting job that is not especially challenging. A job tends to be interesting because it is something that the employee likes to do, but a job is challenging when it allows the employee to work to his or her full potential. The best job for an employee is both interesting and challenging. To create a challenging job, assign tasks that provide opportunities for growth and development.

Create responsible jobs. Do everything you can to make the job of each employee in your section or department appear special in the eyes of all employees. Never say that an employee's job is simple or something that anyone can do, or is a "no-brainer" job. To the employee, the job may not be simple at all.

Think through the reasons why each employee's job is important to the organization. Then make sure the employee understands those reasons and why what they are doing is important.

Reduce the level of stress in each employee's job. Impossible deadlines, excessive workloads, and constant interruptions all create unhealthy stress for employees. If you are part of the stress problem, then it is up to you to become part of the solution.

Make sure that deadlines are realistic. If the workload is excessive, document the need for additional people or say no to unrealistic demands that require employees to do more than is reasonably possible. Help your people manage interruptions by having them keep a log of when and how they are interrupted. Then examine this log to determine if there are patterns that can be changed to reduce unnecessary interruptions.

In the long run, continuous stress is extremely unhealthy for any employee. It is up to you to monitor them to make sure that their job requirements are reasonable.

Protect the employee's self-esteem with co-workers. Reprimanding an employee in private for something he or she did is bad enough. Chewing out an employee in public is even worse, because it affects his or her image and status in the group. If an employee does something you think is especially bad, it is sometimes difficult to avoid reprimanding him or her on the spot. Unless there is a safety problem, it is usually better to wait until you can talk with the employee in private. When you do, take the time to find out why the employee behaved as he or she did *before* you reprimand. You might discover that the employee had a legitimate reason for the behavior. Leaders who don't take time to actively listen seriously undermine an employee's morale.

Another way to diminish an employee's status is to give him or her a task to do and then step in and do it yourself. If you take over a previously delegated task, you are demonstrating to his or her fellow workers that you lack confidence in this employee.

Organize the employee's work so that he or she can complete one task before moving on to another. One of the things that gives an employee good feelings on the job is to complete a task before moving on to another. If the work is set up so that this rarely happens, you are losing a great opportunity to motivate. As much as possible, try to arrange the workflow so that every employee can complete a task before moving on to the next one.

Provide specific feedback on the results of task completion. Try to structure the work-flow so that employees can see the results of their completed tasks. If they don't receive specific and immediate feedback on their efforts, it is not only detrimental to their morale, but it also prevents them from correcting their behavior.

The Organization

The organization's policies and procedures significantly affect employee motivation. The suggestions that follow can prevent many problems that hinder morale.

Make the value of organizational benefits clear. There is not much that a leader can do about an organization's benefits, but the way that they are presented has a great deal to do with how they are viewed by employees. Do you know how much employee benefits cost your organization? Do your employees understand what their benefits are worth? Most employees don't really know how much it costs today to fund their retirement and pay for their vacation time, holidays, sick time, and medical insurance.

In most cases it is fairly easy to find out the value of the employee benefit package. You can talk to human resource people, add up the figures, and make sure that your employees know exactly what their benefits cost the organization each year. It is usually true that employees won't fully value what they don't know the cost of.

Enhance opportunities for salary increases for deserving employees. You might not have complete control over your employees' salaries, but there are ways to compensate. You can carefully evaluate your people and develop them in areas where improvement is needed. Then, make sure that they are paid fairly for their developed talents. If there is not much chance of obtaining additional money for a specific employee, the employee will still feel more valuable to the company simply because you tried.

One of the best ways to make sure that employees are paid fairly is to document their accomplishments. Keep an anecdotal file for each employee and record key accomplishments during the year. Then, at the end of the year, you will have the information necessary to conduct a fair analysis of the employee's performance, and you will be able to suggest an appropriate salary increase.

The anecdotal file will also help you explain to employees why they did or did not receive raises, help you justify the amount of any salary increase, and suggest areas for needed improvement. The amount of the employee's pay increase is less important than the employee's perception of the fairness with which he or she has been treated. It is far easier for the employee to accept less than what they expect if there are clear reasons why it is less and the employee is not taken by surprise.

Encourage technological growth. In recent years, there have been tremendous advances in job technology. Innovation has produced faster computers, computer networking, robotics, electronic networking systems tied to computers, miniaturization, telecommuting, and e-commerce. These are just some of the changes that are having a major impact on our employees' jobs. Not only are the tools they use to do their jobs changing, but their jobs are changing, too.

One of a leader's key tasks is to make sure that employees are involved in lifelong learning. Make sure your employees have access to journals that publish articles relevant to their jobs. Consider sending people offsite for training, or bring in technical representatives and set up mini-training sessions where needed. Go to the training department to obtain needed resources.

Whatever it takes, try to keep employees up-to-date on the changes that they will encounter in their jobs.

Help your employees make a difference in the organization. The basic question that must be answered and communicated to your employees is this: "How does each person's contribution affect the organization's success?" Do your people clearly know how their jobs help make the organization prosperous? It makes no difference if the end result is a product or a service; your employees must feel that what they do or don't do makes a real difference. Your job as a leader is to determine the relationship between employees' jobs and the organization's final output— and then to share this information with each employee.

Make sure that co-workers are friendly and supportive. Work to establish a friendly and supportive work climate. For example, with new employees, first determine their outside interests or hobbies. Then, when you introduce them to their co-workers, establish "interest" links between the new employees and their fellow employees. Set up a "buddy" system by assigning each new employee to a senior employee. You can also ask workers to play a part in the selection of new employees who will be a part of their work team.

With existing employee groups, try to develop their team spirit by working with them to create overall team goals. When individuals within a team work together to develop their group's goals, they become much more motivated to succeed. Train your employees in interpersonal communication skills. Of course, it is nice when you can arrange for the training department to conduct a half-day communication program, but if you can't, do it yourself. Select a good book on interpersonal communication that contains information on how to paraphrase, summarize, ask questions, and listen. After studying these techniques yourself, look for opportunities to teach them to your employees, either individually or in small groups.

Last, for truly effective work teams, make sure that everyone on the team is taught problem-solving and decision-making skills. Problem-solving skills such as situational and causal analysis, and decision-making techniques such as force-field analysis, the herringbone technique, and identifying and analyzing alternatives can all help teams work together more cooperatively and effectively.

Leaders need to remember that long-term happiness and high morale are as much the result of employee interaction as how they are treated by their bosses. You can't just say, "Be happy!" Instead, you must create a climate where they can support and help one another. And you must teach them the skills to do so.

Arrange acceptable working hours. Today's workforce is vastly different from what it was in the past. Single-parent families, two parents who work outside the home, and different values all add up to the need for more-flexible work hours. You might not be able to change the working hours of your employees or allow them to work out of their homes using computers and modems because of the organization's policies, but if you can, consider doing so. It might make your job easier, because it can reduce the amount of time you spend in direct supervision, lessen over-crowding in a section or department, and provide you with the kind of employees you might not have been able to hire before.

But such options do have their drawbacks. It will be very difficult to pick up on good performance or problem areas. Employees who work out of their homes will have to have solid work habits and self-discipline to maintain productivity. Employees also have social needs, which they won't satisfy if they work alone. These unmet needs can result in lower morale.

Provide good physical working conditions. Inadequate temperature control, excessive noise, unpleasant surroundings, and an unsafe environment are just a few of the things that can create poor morale in a section or department. Even though working conditions are really an organization's responsibility, managers can often make improvements. With strong legal penalties for unsafe working conditions and many inexpensive ways to create more-pleasant work environments, it is often fairly easy to obtain funding for better working conditions. But it is still up to us to make this happen. Leaders are the ones who will need to outline the problems and prepare the proposals for upper management, as well as follow up to make sure that things get done. Remember: improving the area where people work will not make them happy—it will only keep them from being unhappy.

Help employees obtain deserved promotions. It doesn't take long for the word to get around that a leader is concerned about the future promotional opportunities of his or her employees. It also doesn't take long for workers to find out that their manager would rather not have them promoted because he or she might lose them to another section or will have to train their replacements. Think about what *that* does to morale and productivity!

So, spend time meeting one-on-one with each of your employees to find out their job goals. If promotion is a realistic goal for a particular employee, then your job is to do everything possible to help him or her to win that promotion.

There are many things you can do right now to help prepare employees for the future. You can have them lead a meeting, train a new employee, be the team leader on a special project, and so on. If organizational exposure is important in order to obtain a promotion, "volunteer" an employee to serve on a special organizational task force or committee. Assign special jobs to the employee that require him or her to interact with people in other departments within the organization.

Organizational restrictions on promotions might keep you from promoting an employee, even if he or she deserves it. But if you have demonstrated a genuine concern for the employee's future by doing what you *can* do, you keep the employee from getting too disgruntled with the company.

The Leader's Direct Actions

A manager's direct actions toward his or her employees often have the strongest effect on their motivation. Here are some recommendations:

Share your expectations. Employees usually live up (or down) to expectations. If you expect a lot, you will usually get a lot. On the other hand, if you don't expect much from an employee, that's what you will probably get. If you feel that your employees are not very creative, you're not likely to ask for their suggestions or ideas. But if you expect them to have ideas about their jobs, you will probably get some good ideas—simply because you ask for them. Leaders who ask for better ideas develop employees who think of better ideas.

Be fair. Employees expect to be treated fairly, but remember: what's "fair" is defined by them, not you. The problem of fairness is complicated by the tension between the need to treat all employees the same and the need to recognize that each employee is different. Nonetheless, there are important things you can do to increase the chances that you will be perceived as fair. Look at these two examples:

Joe works for you. He is one of the nicest people you know. He has been with the organization for about two years, and has a very positive attitude about his job, the organization, and you. You find that it is easy to give him a lot of time and attention because he is so nice to be around.

Betty works for you. She has worked for your organization for 35 years, and she is nearing retirement. You find it is similarly easy to give her special time and attention, since she has been a loyal and dedicated employee for so many years.

Your actions in both these situations seem fair, don't they? However, your other employees might feel that giving Joe so much of your time and attention seems unfair, yet still accept your preferential treatment of Betty, the 35-year veteran.

Keep in mind these basic principles:

- A leader simply cannot treat everybody the same. People are different and they have different needs. As manager, you should give each employee what he or she seems to need at the time, without playing favorites. Playing favorites to meet your needs is, in fact, discrimination.

- It's usually good practice to communicate the rationale to the group when you are giving particular individuals what looks like preferential treatment. Don't get trapped by the employee's argument "Well, you did it for Mary. Why can't you do it for me?" Mary has different needs, and different needs require different treatment.

- When resources are limited, rotate or use the laws of probability to determine who gets a desired resource. Flip a coin, draw straws, or pull slips of paper out of a box to find out who will receive a desired assignment, who must work overtime, or who has to cover the phones on Christmas or Hanukkah.

- Rules and policies are created to help make jobs easier, but sometimes you will have to change them in order to be truly fair in specific circumstances.

Involve employees in goal-setting. Effective leaders usually set goals *with* their employees, rather than *for* them. If you know your employees like what they do for a living, then you will more likely feel comfortable allowing them to determine some of their own goals. Theory X bosses who believe that their employees don't like to work are more apt to set goals for them.

Don't get me wrong: Sometimes it is perfectly appropriate to set an occasional goal for an employee. If, for example, an employee is new to the job and doesn't have enough experience to create his or her own goals, the leader will probably need to write them. You might decide to write goals for a problem employee who has demonstrated an unwillingness or inability to write his or her own, or you might have to give employees goals that are required by the organization. But the best advice I can give regarding goals is to trust your employees to work toward their full potential and give them the chance. Workers tend to be more committed to the goals they set than they are to goals given to them. And second, motivated employees will often write better and more-challenging goals than their leader.

Keep employees informed. Some leaders believe that since information is power, giving information to employees is giving away power. Not true! In fact, the benefits of sharing as much information as possible with employees are enormous.

Consider these facts: 1) Employees who know what is going on make better decisions. 2) They will be more accepting of management decisions and actions. 3) They will be more prepared for changes. 4) Most importantly, they will feel more a part of the organization. For these reasons, let your people know what is going on in their organization.

Listen to employees. It isn't enough just to keep employees informed. You also need to listen to them. And when you listen, you must listen without interrupting. Unfortunately, this basic rule of communication and courtesy is often violated: we get so interested in what we want to tell the other person that we forget to listen to what he or she is saying.

By listening actively, you not only communicate to the employee the fact that you care about him or her, but you also obtain new information. You discover what works or doesn't work—and why. You locate problems and solicit suggestions for solving them. When you help spread helpful information to other levels of management, you improve the organization as a whole.

If you don't understand the power of effective listening, you will not get important information you need to be a good manager. Remember, in a one-on-one discussion, it is the listener who controls the conversation, not the speaker! The listener can steer the conversation by interjecting, posing questions, stopping the speaker, ending the conversation, or allowing it to continue. Listeners have the power.

Consult employees about decisions that affect them. This powerful way of leading not only improves the quality of your decisions, but also increases your employees' acceptance of those decisions. Your decisions will be better. Employees might think of alternatives beyond the one that you proposed, identify additional factors that need to be considered while evaluating a decision, or even identify unanticipated risks. Employees naturally like to feel that they are a part of every decision that affects them. Asking for their input before making a decision will usually increase their acceptance of it when it is made.

Delegate appropriately. Delegating work has many advantages: It enriches employees' work experiences, develops better employees, gives leaders more time for tasks that only they can do, and, most importantly, increases employee morale.

Considering these clear advantages, aren't most managers good delegators? No! It seems that many managers don't delegate because they don't want to! Fear of losing power or control, having to spend additional time training employees to do delegated tasks, or having to burden employees with additional work are all common reasons why managers don't delegate tasks.

That fear can be overcome when you realize that delegating a specific task doesn't mean that you have lost control of that job. You won't be physically doing the task, but you will still be able to provide quality follow-up with the employee to ensure that the job is properly completed.

It is true that in delegating, you might be giving up parts of the job that you enjoy doing, but the payoff in terms of employee morale makes it well worth it. You will have extra time to spend on other tasks that will provide even more payoffs than the one you delegated.

Delegation will initially require more time, but odds are that you will soon receive a return on your time that far exceeds the amount you have invested.

If you are concerned about delegated tasks becoming a burden on your employees, remember that we are talking about *delegating appropriately*. You must be concerned not only about your needs, but also about your employees' needs. Placing too much responsibility on an employee or simply giving more routine work to him or her is not real delegation.

To delegate, you need to evaluate your own job by listing the major tasks in it. Then, determine your authority level in each of the tasks. Use this system:

"A" = I have complete authority to do the task.
"B" = I can do the task, but I must then report what I did.
"C" = I need to obtain permission from my boss before doing the task.

When you have listed each task that is part of your own job and have determined your level of authority for each one, you are ready to delegate a number of your "A" tasks.

After determining which tasks can be delegated, evaluate your people to see which of them would benefit most by assuming the responsibility for specific tasks on the list. Finally, set up mini-training programs for the tasks that you have delegated. (See the chapter on delegation for more detail.)

Avoid over-supervising employees. Here are some examples of over-supervising: delegating a task and then doing it yourself; training an employee in exactly how to do a task, but continually monitoring him or her; or giving an employee too much detail about how to do a task.

Leaders walk a fine line between being available for their employees and over-supervising them. If you delegate a task, you need to let the employee do it. Instead of giving an employee too much detail on how to do a task, define the end goals or results, and then ask the employee how he or she plans to complete the task. Avoid asking for unnecessary reports or too many reports.

Conduct career-development sessions with the employees. One important component in your effort to motivate your employees is to meet with your employees about where they want to go in their career. In years past, if an employee was willing to work hard, success would come almost automatically because of the many opportunities that existed within most organizations.

Today, this is largely no longer true. The idea that "hard work will ensure success" has become more myth than truth. Unfortunately, employees expect the same opportunities for advancement that their parents enjoyed. This is no longer realistic.

Help employees explore their strengths, areas of needed improvement, knowledge, skills, likes and dislikes, values, and career goals. Set up a meeting to learn what the employee wants to do in the future, what needs to be done by the employee to get there, and how well the employee's goals meet the needs of the organization. (See the chapter on career development for more information.)

Provide honest ongoing recognition for tasks well done. Frederick Herzberg proved that recognition is a major motivator and lack of recognition is a powerful demotivator. Recognition becomes even more important to an employee when regulations and policy restrict other rewards (such as pay).

The Power of Positive Feedback

We all know that recognition is important to most people, yet there are managers and supervisors who still don't take the time to give employees a needed pat on the back. They have nice words for their superstar performers, but very few people are superstars! Most employees fall somewhere in the middle of the performance range.

The key to motivating employees is to remember how natural it is to want and need recognition. If we don't receive recognition for what we do at work, we will put our energy into seeking it elsewhere—often to the detriment of our job responsibilities.

Fortunately, there are many ways to recognize employees. Here are three:

1. **Remember that an employee's performance is never absolutely consistent.** Like everyone, he or she has good and not-so-good days. Be alert to those times when an employee is performing at an above-average level, and provide rapid recognition for such performance.

2. **Offer positive feedback on the things the employee does well.** An employee's job is normally made up of a series of small tasks and some of these tasks will be done better than others.

3. **Recognize a person's talents or strengths that are not directly related to the job.** An employee who is only an average performer might consistently arrive early, be good at orienting new employees, or keep his or her workspace clean and orderly. Your job is to reinforce the habit of excellence with positive recognition wherever you see it.

Remember: An employee might be only "average," but there is nearly always something that the employee does well. Genuine recognition given for whatever that employee does well builds motivation and self-esteem.

How should you note slight improvement in a problem employee? Suppose you recently counseled an employee who has a job-related problem and only makes minimal improvement—perhaps to a "just acceptable" level. Do you immediately tell this employee how pleased you are with his or her current performance?

Some leaders will answer, "No! Why should I give an employee a pat on the back when his performance is only barely acceptable? Besides, it was only last week that I chewed him out for his sloppy work. It's still too soon to tell if he has really changed." How much improvement is necessary before feedback is given? And *when* should the feedback be given?

Suppose we turn the question around and ask, "Will recognition increase the chances that this employee will keep up improved performance?" The answer to this question is probably yes, simply because sincere recognition is one of the strongest employee motivators.

Don't allow an already-marginal employee to lapse into unacceptable performance. An insightful leader recognizes that it is not so much the amount of improvement necessary before positive feedback is given, but rather the direction of that change. If it's a change for the better, positive feedback will encourage the individual to maintain improvement.

The second point raised concerns timing. When should you give positive feedback? If an employee does something poorly, you're not going to wait several months to tell him or her about it. The same is true with positive feedback: If you want to reinforce an employee's positive behavior, give feedback as soon as you see positive change. An effective leader hopes for improvement, expects improvement, and quickly reinforces the positive change in the employee's performance at the first sign of improvement.

What if you give immediate positive feedback to a marginal employee who has improved slightly, and he or she gets worse? Now you are really disappointed—and maybe even angry! After all, you gave the employee positive recognition, and the employee let you down. Well, sometimes this happens, but not usually. Don't let one or two negative results prevent you from improving your "career average" as a motivating leader. You can continue to provide positive recognition to low-performing employees when they show small improvements. If you do it as soon as you see change, your batting average will start to climb.

Providing Positive Recognition

The way that you recognize employees is also very important. General compliments such as, "You did a good job" or "I'm proud of your improvement" are not in fact the best motivators. The suggestions that follow really work.

Describe the importance of genuine, specific, and positive feedback. Overly general compliments are sometimes perceived as being insincere. Be specific. Describe in detail the positive behaviors you observe. Don't just say, "You did a good job." Instead, spell out what you mean by "a good job"—and then watch the employee smile.

This approach works because the employee most likely knows that he or she did well and will think your recognition of the specifics is observant, accurate, and genuine. An example of such specificity: "Your desk looks great! All the extra files are put away and there's nothing out of place. Your whole work space looks organized."

You can add meaning to a compliment by emphasizing why what was done is important. The opportunity for high-impact recognition is lost if you say only, "You did a good job," because you aren't being specific and you haven't said why positive performance is important. You need to explain:

- Why the performance is important to the employee
- Why it is important to the section, department, or organization
- Why it is important to you as the leader

Build employee confidence. An employee who works for two different managers will often exhibit two different levels of performance because each manager expects something different. Leaders with high levels of expectation usually obtain better overall employee performance. When you tell an employee that you have confidence in his or her ability, you are communicating strongly your expectations for the future. By expressing confidence in an employee's ability right after you see improved performance, you increase the employee's motivation to continue to fulfill your growing expectations.

Track progress and head off problems. When an employee does something better today than in the past, he or she has made some changes, whether it is a matter of coming to work on time, organizing work more efficiently, or something else. And when an employee changes, even for the better, there is a likelihood that he or she will encounter some new problems and even get teased by co-workers about his or her improvement.

All kinds of problems can arise with changes. An alert leader anticipates problems and checks out the situation by asking the employee if there is anything he can do to help them progress.

Express appreciation. Express clearly and warmly your appreciation for employee efforts. If you feel good about what an employee has done, say things like, "I really appreciate your efforts!" or "Thanks! I'm very pleased with your progress!" Reinforce your acknowledgment of their efforts and end the discussion on the desired positive note. After the meeting, make a note of your conversation with the employee, and place it in the employee's anecdotal file.

We have included three tools to help you become a more motivating leader:

- A leader's checklist, which will help you provide recognition to your employees

- An employee motivation survey, which asks employees to rate you in the three major areas covered in the preceding pages. After you receive the completed surveys, review them to see if any employees have specific motivational needs. Then tally each of the responses to see if there are any group needs. After evaluating the results, refer to the text for ideas on how to take action to improve the morale within your area of responsibility.

- A "motivating others" worksheet, which will allow you to systematically plan the actions you will take to improve employee motivation.

A Leader's Checklist for Motivating Employees

☐ **1. Describe the positive effort or results you have observed (in detail).**

Focus your attention on the employee.
Be specific: Describe the who, what, where, when, and how.

☐ **2. Tell why the positive effort is important.**

Why is the performance important to the employee?
Why is it important to the section, department, or organization?
Why is it important to you?

☐ **3. State that you have confidence in the individual's ability.**

Example: *"It's a good feeling to know that I can count on your efforts in the future."*

☐ **4. Ask if there is anything you can do to support his or her efforts.**

"What can I do to help you further?"

☐ **5. Emphasize your appreciation.**

"I just want you to know how much I appreciate your efforts."

Employee Motivation Survey
(Anonymous)

Note: Do not put your name on this form.

Your manager's name: _____

Your section or department: _____

Date: _____

My job:

	To what extent is this need satisfied in your job?						**Indicate the importance of each of the following to you:**					
	Not satisfactory	Somewhat satisfactory	Satisfactory	More than satisfactory	Much more than satisfactory	Not applicable	Not at all important	Somewhat important	Important	Very important	Extremely important	Not applicable
The job is interesting.												
The job is challenging.												
The job is a responsible job.												
The job is not stressful.												
The job provides status.												
The job allows me to complete a task before moving on to the next one.												
When a task is completed, the results are visible.												

Employee Motivation Survey (continued)

What organizations routinely provide or should provide:

To what extent is this need satisfied in your job?

Item	Not satisfactory	Somewhat satisfactory	Satisfactory	More than satisfactory	Much more than satisfactory	Not applicable
Benefits (retirement, health, vacations, sick leave, etc.)						
Opportunities for salary increases						
Technological growth						
A chance to make a difference						
A contribution to society						
Friendly and supportive co-workers						
Good working hours						
Good working conditions (safety, temperature, noise, appearance)						
Chance for promotion						
Job security						

Indicate the importance of each of the following to you:

Item	Not at all important	Somewhat important	Important	Very important	Extremely important	Not applicable
Benefits (retirement, health, vacations, sick leave, etc.)						
Opportunities for salary increases						
Technological growth						
A chance to make a difference						
A contribution to society						
Friendly and supportive co-workers						
Good working hours						
Good working conditions (safety, temperature, noise, appearance)						
Chance for promotion						
Job security						

Employee Motivation Survey (continued)

Indicate the importance of each of the following to you:

My manager:	Not at all important	Somewhat important	Important	Very important	Extremely important	Not applicable
My manager has high expectations of me.						
My manager is fair.						
My manager gives me a chance to have a say in how I do my job.						
My manager keeps me informed about what is going on.						
My manager listens to me.						
My manager consults me about decisions that affect me.						
My manager delegates tasks appropriately.						
My manager doesn't supervise too closely.						
My manager meets with me to work on career development.						
My manager gives me ongoing recognition for tasks that I do.						

To what extent is this need satisfied in your job?

My manager:	Not satisfactory	Somewhat satisfactory	Satisfactory	More than satisfactory	Much more than satisfactory	Not applicable
My manager has high expectations of me.						
My manager is fair.						
My manager gives me a chance to have a say in how I do my job.						
My manager keeps me informed about what is going on.						
My manager listens to me.						
My manager consults me about decisions that affect me.						
My manager delegates tasks appropriately.						
My manager doesn't supervise too closely.						
My manager meets with me to work on career development.						
My manager gives me ongoing recognition for tasks that I do.						

Employee Motivation Survey (concluded)

How would you rate your immediate supervisor's morale?
(Place an "X" in the appropriate box.)

Very low	Low	Somewhat low	Neither high or low	Somewhat high	High	Very high	Don't know

How would you rate your own morale?

Very low	Low	Somewhat low	Neither high or low	Somewhat high	High	Very high	Don't know

(Do not sign this anonymous survey.)

Motivating Others

Directions to Manager or Supervisor: List the people who report to you in Column 1, and identify areas in which they have motivational needs in Column 2. In Column 3, identify specific actions that you will take during the next two weeks to improve each employee's motivation and morale. When you have completed each motivation task, put the appropriate date in Column 4. Then, in Column 5, make a brief note of how the employee reacted to your attention.

At the end of the two-week period, discuss the results with your own manager or supervisor. If you have no direct reports, you can select peers, your boss (he or she needs motivation, also), or spouse or close friends. Remember, this project is about MOTIVATION, not counseling.

Employee's name (You may use initials)	Motivational need (per Maslow)	Actions to be taken to improve employee's motivation and morale	Date completed	Employee's reaction(s)

5

Mentoring

Telemachus, young son of Odysseus: *"Mentor, how am I to go up to the great man? How shall I greet him? Remember that I have had no practice in making speeches; and a young man may well hesitate to cross-examine one so much his senior."*

Athena, disguised as Mentor: *"Telemachus, where your native wit fails, heaven will inspire you. It is not for nothing that the gods have watched your progress ever since your birth."*

– Odyssey 1.296

Mentoring is a great way for an experienced person to help another individual to grow and develop his or her life and job abilities. Police departments have done this for years: They assign a new officer, fresh out of training, to an experienced field officer. Most apprentice programs also follow the same format, assigning the new electrician, plumber, carpenter, or metal worker to a more-experienced person who passes on the knowledge necessary to become skilled in the job.

Mentoring is a personal, one-on-one connection between a respected leader or other senior or experienced person (usually not the direct boss) and an associate. The mentor helps an individual become sensitive to the organization's politics; establish networks with other key people; understand the "big picture" in terms of contextual or environmental culture and values; and develop an awareness of what senior leaders or society expect.

Coaching, as we will see in a later chapter, can be used in the mentoring process, but coaching is very different from mentoring. Coaching, usually done by the associate's leader, is almost always job-related and tends to be relatively short-term.

Mentoring, on the other hand, can be formal or informal, short-term or long-term, on the job or off the job. I've had a long-term mentoring relationship with the lady who used to clean my home. She is from Uganda. Shortly after I hired her, I asked what she did in Uganda.

"I was a school teacher," she replied.

"Why don't you teach here?" I asked.

"I can't. Teacher training in Uganda is like your technical schools here in the United States. I would need a university degree to be able to teach here."

"Do you like to teach?"

"Oh, yes!"

"Then why don't you go to night school, get your undergraduate degree, and become a teacher?"

"I couldn't do that."

"Why not? In this country, you can be anything you want to be."

"I just couldn't."

"Of course you can. Take just one course. See how you like it. I think you will be surprised at how much you enjoy classes here—and how well you can do."

As a result of this mentoring moment, she took one course. Many years later, she earned her undergraduate degree.

Mentoring is driven by personal values. It comes from a genuine desire to help another individual by taking time to listen and offer information or advice, and then to get out of the way.

The Mentor

Most of us can remember a time when a more-experienced individual (usually older) offered us meaningful advice and counsel. I particularly remember three mentors of my own: E. B. Dere, a man I admired and viewed as a model of what it meant to work hard; Vince Ruane, a brilliant man who guided me during my days at the 3M Company; and Paul Dinas, who showed me how to be a writer. All three of these men played different roles. E. B. was a role model, Vince was an advisor, and Paul was an expert in a subject I was ignorant about. But the important point here is that neither of these three men came to me and offered to be a mentor. I fervently wish they had. I would have deeply appreciated quality time, office door shut, and an "Okay, Dick. What's going on in your life, and how can I help?" conversation.

I would have welcomed a willing mentor, but I thought I would be imposing on the other person. Most of your younger associates today might also be reluctant to ask you to be their mentor. Yet like me, almost all would probably welcome that kind of relationship with you.

Mentorship is beneficial to both the mentor and the individual being mentored. First, it just feels good to have someone ask you to be a mentor. After all, the mentee would not have selected you if he or she did not think you were special (i.e., wise, experienced, respected, and a positive role model). Second, most senior leaders feel the need to leave a legacy prior to retirement. Mentorship is a powerful way to make a difference in the organization long after the mentor has retired or moved on to another career. Third, most of us have only a few real friends. Mentorship often leads to a deep friendship between the two individuals that lasts a lifetime. Finally, there is personal satisfaction when our mentee accomplishes important goals. I remember feeling a deep sense of pride when the Ugandan women mentioned earlier walked across the stage and was given her undergraduate degree. I have also learned from those whom I have informally mentored in the past. I learned more about their occupation and I learned more about life through their experiences. I have gained wonderful friendships, and I learned more about relationships by being with them.

Today, mentoring has become ever more important as we see individuals begin second, third, and even fourth careers. It's not so unusual to see a more experienced, younger person mentoring an older person who is embarking on a new profession.

Your organization may already have a full-blown mentoring program in place, complete with training for mentors and their mentees. However, formal programs are rare (and even rarer still are programs that are effective). What follows are a few of my own suggestions for those of you who are considering becoming a mentor.

Some Thoughts for the Mentor

Be willing to commit to quality time and a long-term relationship. Sometimes, a mentoring relationship lasts for decades. Other times, it is only a short-term relationship. Most mentoring relationships require a significant amount of time. A meeting where you close the doors and talk frankly with your mentee about a specific problem or goal can easily exceed an hour. You and your mentee might decide to meet once a week, or every other week, or even once a month. It all depends on the time you have to devote to mentoring and the needs of the mentee.

Identify someone whom you believe will benefit from your mentorship. Ideally, such an individual is motivated to succeed, is self-disciplined and can take responsibility for his or her own development, and is someone whom you like and would enjoy spending time with. Look for people you know have potential: individuals who seek opportunities to further enhance their careers, seek new job challenges, find ways to broaden their present jobs, have career-development plans, volunteer to take training courses, or attend evening classes to obtain advanced degrees.

Offer to be a mentor. The way you go about this is important. If you say, "May I be your mentor?" it would be hard for anyone to say no to this, even if they wanted to, because they are likely to be somebody you already know and have had some interaction with. Try this instead:

> *We have spent some time together here and there, and I have enjoyed that time. I see you as someone who has great potential. It might be that the amount of time spent with you is okay as it is, but I wondered if you would like to have more of my time. If so, I am open to creating a mentoring relationship. However, a relationship such as this requires a commitment of time you might not have. What are your thoughts on this?*

At this point, you can almost always tell if the answer is yes or no. Yes might suggest eagerness on the part of the other person to in fact spend more time with you. It might be an implied yes as he or she begins to ask questions about how the process of mentoring would work. On the other hand, if the person doesn't want or need a mentor, he or she is not likely to ask for your time.

Spell out your expectations. Ask your mentee if he or she sees your relationship as short-term, long-term, or something in between. Then, offer your thoughts on the length of time you see is feasible.

- Tell your mentee that you are interested in his or her life goals as well as occupational goals.

- As a mentor, you will likely learn personal and privileged information about your mentee. Trust is critical in a mentoring relationship. In order for you to be truly helpful, the individual must be able to confide in you. Tell the prospective mentee that an effective mentoring relationship is based on trust. State your code of confidentiality and ask the individual if he or she will agree to abide by this covenant. Such a statement could be something as simple as:

> *It is vital for the two of us to have a clear understanding of the confidential nature of our relationship. I will agree to hold all our conversations absolutely private, and I will not share what I learn about and from you without prior*

permission I will also agree not to share personal information that I would expect you to also hold in confidence. Will you agree to a code of confidentiality between us?

- State that either of you should be able to end the relationship without prejudice at any time. You could say:

My hope is to have a quality relationship with you that works for both of us. However, it is possible that mentorship with me won't meet your needs, or that I will become immersed in my present responsibilities and become less available for you. At that time, either of us should be able to end or suspend our mentoring relationship without feeling bad.

Ask questions to determine the mentee's life and occupational goals. It is important to see your mentee as a whole person, not simply one person on the job and another in life. Encourage your mentee to discuss goals in both arenas by asking questions such as:

- What life and/or occupational goals have you selected for today's discussion?
- Why is that goal important to you?
- What steps do you intend to take to reach your goal?
- What problems do you see occurring?

If you as the mentor hear mostly job-related goals, probe for life goals as well:

- As you consider your life outside of your job, what are some important goals for you in that arena?

And most important, ask how you can help.

Find out what the individual considers to be his or her strengths and possible areas for improvement. Ask questions like "What strengths do you have that will allow you to reach your goal?" "What do you see are your personal limitations as you strive to reach this goal?"

Listen. The best mentors are able to focus on the mentee and really listen to what he is saying. Use your active-listening skills. Nod your head as you listen. Paraphrase in your own words what you heard before you respond, and ask if what you hear is correct.

Avoid challenging the mentee's goals. If you have concerns about the appropriateness of a specific goal, ask why this goal is important to the mentee. The mentee carefully selected this goal to share with you. "Why in the heck do you want to do that?" or "You will never be able to accomplish that" are counterproductive responses that will likely make the mentee less willing to share other important ideas with you. Ask probing questions to help you understand the mentee's aspirations more clearly, and/or help the mentee see that the goal might need to be modified or dropped.

Ask questions such as "Why is the goal important to you?" or "How do you see yourself accomplishing that goal?" to see if the mentee's goal is actually feasible. After you learn the details of how the mentee plans to reach his or her goal, you might feel that the mentee has overlooked one or more important risks in reaching the goal. If so, ask, "In light of this fact [*the risk*], how will that impact your goals?"

Offer advice only when asked or when it is clearly needed. Effective mentors are able to determine when the mentee already has the knowledge to make the best decision and when the mentor needs to offer advice or feedback. Ask questions to help the mentee come up with his or her own answers. As a mentor, this is not easy; the tendency is for us to "help" the mentee by providing the information we already know. It is far better, however, to simply guide the mentee. If the mentee lacks the necessary knowledge to respond to your questions, then you can provide the information needed or tell them who to contact to obtain the information.

Help the mentee establish connections with others. Fortunately, mentors don't have to have all the answers. It is only important that you be able to help the mentee learn where to look for the answers. The mentor only provides direction. You will have an opportunity at follow-up meetings to share in the knowledge the mentee gained from others. This is one of the primary benefits of being a mentor—you have an opportunity to grow and develop yourself.

Focus on the mentee, not on the organization. You are not the mentee's leader. Your focus is to help him or her to become more effective. As a leader, your first responsibility is to all your direct reports—your team, and then to individuals on the team. Sometimes what is best for the team is not best for the individual, but when you are a mentor, your responsibility is first to your mentee and then to the organization.

End the relationship if it ceases to be of value. This should be a no-fault parting of the ways. If you see that your mentee doesn't follow up with his commitments, doesn't seem to spend much time preparing for the meeting with you, or seems to have lost interest in the mentoring process, it is best to end the relationship. You can do this tactfully by saying something like:

> *Relationships are often cyclic, in that there is positive energy in the beginning, but sometimes that energy fades over time. I think that we have reached that point. You seem to have a lot on your plate, and our association does not appear to be as effective as it should be for you. Therefore, I would like to end this mentoring relationship. When you have more time to devote to being mentored, I hope you will seek out a new mentor. I've enjoyed our time together and wish you well.*

Most of the chapters in this book focus only on the leader's behaviors—what the leader does or does not do with his or her associates. This chapter is a bit different in that it deals with the leader as a mentor as well as a mentee. Astute leaders who are mentors also seek the mentoring advice and support of others. They know that they can benefit greatly by having confidential, trustworthy, and wise counsel on specific issues they face on and off the job, as well as where they are going professionally.

Some Thoughts for the Mentee

Don't be afraid to ask a respected person to be your mentor. Consider a higher-level leader who is respected, trusted, and knowledgeable—and most importantly, someone you like and will enjoy spending time with. Look for established leaders who are "heroes" (almost every organization has at least one).

If you are selecting a leader within your organization, most researchers suggest picking someone who is at least three levels above you. This helps prevent any conflict or hard feelings with your direct supervisor, who might feel threatened because of your close relationship with his or her boss. (Your supervisor might also see you as a threat to his or her job.) If you have your eye on transferring to another section or department within your organization, pick someone in that area. Sometimes selecting someone outside of your organization makes sense, given your personal goals.

When you have carefully selected the one individual you wish to be your mentor, make an appointment and tell this individual that you would like him or her to consider being your mentor. Remember, it is almost always flattering to be asked, so don't be shy about approaching the other person.

Prior to meeting with your mentor, identify your own life and occupational goals. Take time to consider your most important goals. What knowledge, skills, and abilities will help you reach your goals? Are any of these goals a mismatch for your personality and/or values? What problems stand in your way? Specifically, what help do you need from your mentor? Your number-one task is to carefully assess yourself before you ask someone else's help. Write all this information down prior to meeting with your mentor; this will help clarify your thoughts and make it easier for you to stay on track in the meeting.

Tell your mentor what you want to accomplish on the job and in life. Prior to meeting with your mentor, you spent time thinking through your short-term and long-term goals. Share these goals with your mentor. Ask if your mentor sees the goals as feasible. Share your tactical steps in reaching your goals. Ask for help in the specific actions that need to be taken. Ask questions such as, "What else can I do to reach this goal?" "What have I overlooked?" "If I do this, what are the risks?" "How can I reduce the potential of any problems that will disrupt my efforts to reach my goal?"

Ask for feedback. As time goes by and you implement your plans to reach your goals, don't simply wait for your mentor to offer feedback. Share your progress and ask questions such as: "What do you think of this idea?" "How do you think I did in that situation?" "How could I have been more effective?" "What things did I do that you see as positive?"

Accept feedback gracefully and appreciatively when given by your mentor. A courageous and honest mentor will, from time to time, provide you with feedback on your attitudes and behaviors. This feedback could be perceived as positive or negative. The feedback that is not positive is difficult to process, so remember that your mentor cares about you. Honest feedback is part of that caring. Some feedback is difficult to take in, but a mentee who is committed to self-development should welcome this feedback. How else can we improve? It is your responsibility to listen, carefully consider your mentor's comments, and take action.

Take responsibility for your own development. Your mentor will be a great resource for you in achieving your goals, but his or her responsibility is *not* to do the work—that's your job.

Respect his or her time. Arrive on time for meetings. Turn your pager or cell phone off. Close out the meeting when your time is up. Respond to e-mails or phone calls promptly.

Act in trustworthy ways. It is critical that you both maintain confidentiality. Your mentor will likely share thoughts with you that must *not* be shared with another, and you will be doing the same. Trust and confidentiality are extremely important; if trust is broken, the mentorship will end.

Don't be afraid to end the relationship if it no longer works for you. If you find that your mentor postpones meetings or cancels them altogether, appears to be disinterested, or doesn't seem to remember what was discussed at your last meeting, it might be time to end the relationship and find another mentor. You can tactfully say something like:

I know that with your many responsibilities, it is often difficult to find the time to meet with me. I feel like I am taking too much of your time. I have found our relationship positive (here, you can almost always find things to say that are positive and honest). *That said, I do think that it is time for us both to move on. How do you feel about that?*

Think carefully about why you think it is necessary to bring the relationship to a close. Were you a cause of its demise? It is so easy to blame your mentor for the end of the relationship, but if you are going to find another mentor (and you must), you need to make certain that you can be the best possible mentee in your future relationship.

We conclude this chapter with a quick and easy step-by-step approach for the mentor and the mentee.

Mentor Checklist

☐ 1. **Determine if you have the time, skills, and attitude for a mentoring relationship.**

☐ 2. **Identify an individual you wish to mentor.**

☐ 3. **Offer to be a mentor.**

Sample language: We have spent some time together already—a few minutes here and a few minutes there. I have enjoyed that time, and see you as someone who has great potential. I wonder if you would like to continue our discussions. If so, I am open to the idea of entering into a mentoring relationship with you. However, it will require a commitment of time that you might not have. What are your thoughts on this?"

☐ 4. **Ensure privacy.**

Arrange to meet at a location and time that is private, and take steps to minimize interruptions.

☐ 5. **Spell out your expectations.**

- Decide together whether the mentoring relationship will be long-term or short-term.

- State that as a mentor, you are interested in helping the individual achieve life goals, as well as occupational goals.

- State your code of confidentiality, and be sure the mentee agrees to abide by this covenant.

  Sample language: It is vital for the two of us to have a clear understanding about the confidential nature of our relationship. I will agree to hold all our conversations absolutely private and not share what I learn about and from you without prior permission. At times, I will be sharing information that I expect you to hold in confidence, as well. Will you agree to a code of confidentiality between us?

- State that either of you should be able to end the relationship at any time.

  Sample language: My hope is to have a quality relationship with you that works for both of us. However, there is always a possibility that for whatever reason, mentorship with me won't meet your needs or that I will become immersed in my present responsibilities and become less available for you. At that time, either of us should be able to agree to end our time together without feeling bad.

(continued)

Quality Leadership Skills

☐ 6. **Ask questions to determine the mentee's life and occupational goals:**

- What life and/or occupational goals have you selected for today's discussion?
- Why is that goal important to you?
- What steps do you intend to take to reach your goal?
- What problems do you see occurring?
- As you consider your life outside of your job, what are some important goals for you in that arena?
- How can I help?

☐ 7. **What does the mentee consider to be his or her strengths and areas that need improvement?**

- What strengths do you have that will allow you to reach your goal?
- What do you see are your personal limitations as you strive to reach this goal?

☐ 8. **Listen.**

- Focus on the mentee.
- Employ active listening.
- Paraphrase what you hear, and confirm its accuracy.

☐ 9. **Try not to make judgments about any of the mentee's goals.**

Ask questions to help you understand the mentee's goals:

- Why is this goal important to you?
- How do you see yourself accomplishing this goal?
- What are the risks in doing that?

☐ 10. **Offer advice only when asked or when you believe it is clearly needed.**

☐ 11. **Help the mentee establish connections with others.**

☐ 12. **Focus on the mentee, not on the organization.**

☐ 13. **End the mentoring relationship if it ceases to be of value.**

Sample language: Relationships are often cyclic: There is positive energy in the beginning, but that energy sometimes fades over time. I think ours has reached that point. You appear to have a lot on your plate, and our association does not seem to be as effective as it should be for you. Therefore, I would like to end our mentoring relationship. When you have more available time and/or once again need a mentor, I sincerely hope you will seek out a new mentoring relationship.

Mentee Checklist

☐ **1. Select a respected person to act as a mentor to you.**

- Select an individual who is respected and knowledgeable, and perhaps even is a "hero" to others in the organization.
- Make sure that this is an individual you would likely enjoy spending time with.
- Try to pick someone who is at least three levels above you.
- Consider people outside of the organization.
- Ask the individual to be your mentor.

   Sample language: I have carefully considered my life and realize that I would benefit by having a mentor. I have thought about a number of individuals whom I respect and admire, and you are my number-one choice. I recognize that being a mentor requires a significant investment of time on your part, so I do understand that you might feel that you cannot take on this role at this time. However, if you have the time to establish such a relationship with me, I would be deeply honored. Would you have the available time to consider becoming my mentor?

☐ **2. Before your first formal meeting with your mentor, think about your life and occupational goals.**

- What knowledge, skills, and abilities will help you reach your goals?
- Are any of these goals a mismatch for your personality or your values?
- What problems might stand in your way?
- What help do you need from your mentor?

☐ **3. Tell your mentor what you want to accomplish on the job and in life, and ask him or her to help you achieve these goals.**

- Share your goals with your mentor.
- Ask if he or she thinks the goals are feasible.
- Share your tactical steps in reaching your goals.
- Ask for help in the specific actions that need to be taken.
- Ask questions such as:
    What else can I do to reach this goal?
    What have I overlooked?
    If I do this, what are the risks?
    How can I reduce the potential problems that might disrupt my effort to reach my goal?

☐ **4. Ask for feedback.**

- What do you think of this idea?
- How do you think I did in that situation?
- How could I have been more effective?
- What things did I do that you see as positive?

(continued)

□ 5. **Accept feedback gracefully and appreciatively.**

□ 6. **Take responsibility for your own development.**

□ 7. **Respect your mentor's time.**
- Arrive on time for meetings.
- Turn your pager or cell phone off during meetings.
- Close out the meeting when your time is up.
- Respond to e-mails or phone calls promptly.

□ 8. **Act in trustworthy ways.**

□ 9. **Don't be afraid to end the relationship.**

Sample language: I know that with your many responsibilities, it is often difficult to find the time to meet with me. I feel like I am taking too much of your time. I have found our relationship positive in many ways, such as_____. That said, I do think that it is time for us both to move on. How do you feel about that?

Part 2

Leadership Skills for Improving Performance

6

Establishing Standards of Performance

Before any improvement is undertaken, it is essential that the current standards be stabilized and institutionalized. In the kaizer philosophy, there can be no improvement where there are no standards.

– Michael Tushman and Philip Anderson
Managing Strategic Innovation and Change

Every employee has quite honestly said, at least once, "I didn't know I was supposed to do that!" Whatever the situation, there is usually one reason why the task didn't get done: someone failed to communicate exactly what was expected.

Sometimes it's a matter of the leader failing to communicate what the employee should *not* do. When workers find themselves in such situations, they often begin to play it safe by not seeking out additional tasks or responsibilities.

Leaders must also explain specific performance standards for each part of an employee's job so employees won't have to wonder what a "good job" looks like or how to know that they are doing a job well enough or if they are spending too much time and energy on a task. Communicating standards of performance is a critical part of organizational leadership.

Why Standards?

Performance standards are useful for a number of purposes. They can help you plan and schedule work, estimate budget needs, handle disciplinary problems, provide feedback, solve problems, change processes, and identify a need for additional staffing.

Planning and scheduling work. When standards properly define how much work is to be produced by an employee, it is possible to plan total output by combining the output of several employees. For example, maintenance work can be scheduled based on downtime of standby equipment (which might be based on production output over time).

Estimating budget needs. You can estimate the quantity of materials and labor you need if you know the amount of work to be produced by using data from performance standards. Then budgetary needs can be estimated by applying labor and material costs to quantity.

Handling disciplinary problems and grievances. Information obtained from standards that is compared with actual performance can provide proof that an employee is performing below standard.

Providing performance feedback. Comparing the performance standards to actual employee performance provides job performance feedback to both the leader and employee. The leader can use the information to provide positive feedback to employees who exceed standards, and the employee can use the information to monitor his or her performance.

Finding the cause of a performance problem. Because performance standards address each task, the leader can isolate a problem to one or two tasks. Task isolation will provide a starting point for problem analysis; it helps a leader avoid making vaguely worded observations such as "You're not doing as well as you should" or "Your production is not satisfactory."

Comparing and evaluating changes in methods. Improving methods and processes often improves quantitative and qualitative output over time. If standards are in effect, we can compare each change or suggested change to the standard, and obtain information on its relative value to the standard.

Determining staffing needs. Standards can be written up to indicate how much one employee is expected to produce in a given time. If increased output or workload is desirable, this is pertinent when considering additional staffing needs.

Working with Employees to Set Performance Standards

Now let's look at an approach that will help you and your employees establish performance standards together. Meet with each employee at least once each year to analyze the employee's job and mutually agree upon appropriate standards of performance. Here are the areas you need to cover:

Planning and conducting the initial discussion. The better prepared the employee is before a performance standards meeting, the easier it will be for him or her to discuss the job. Approximately one week before the standards meeting, meet briefly with the employee to:

a. Explain what performance standards are, and why they need to be established.

b. Ask the employee to provide information needed to establish such standards and to measure performance.

c. Help the employee begin by doing the following:

> Select a critical job task.
>
> Determine the standards that will measure performance, expressed in quality, quantity, cost, or time.
>
> Analyze any problems that will prevent optimum performance and explain the employee's authority level to complete this task.

d. Give the employee a copy of a *job standards worksheet* (such as the one at the end of this chapter), and ask him or her to complete it before the standards meeting.

The objective in this pre-standard meeting is to make sure the leader and the employee each have the needed information for the next meeting. Ideally, the employee should propose these standards. The employee should know what tasks the job includes and what he or she can do. The last part of this preparatory step is to set a time and place for the actual standards meeting.

Job standards. Describe what you see as the employee's job. You should also use the Sample Job Standards Worksheet provided at the end of this chapter. This will help you provide more-specific input during the meeting and to relate the employee's job standards to your own standards or unit objectives.

What the job entails. Begin the performance standards meeting by discussing and then agreeing upon the general description and content of the job. This has to be done before you can analyze and specify individual job tasks.

The employee's perception of the job. Ask the employee to identify the first job task and its relationship to the total job; how this task might be measured; any problems he or she has with the task; and his or her perceived authority to do the task. This step is the heart of establishing performance standards. The employee is telling you what he or she should do, how much, and how well.

This is the employee's opportunity to state how he or she perceives the job, so let the employee do the talking! But as the employee talks, be sure to listen carefully to make sure that suggested standards are stated clearly. Eliminate vague or unclear terms, and be especially attentive when the employee identifies quantity or quality. Help him or her be as specific as possible.

If the employee has problems while completing a task, your job is to help him or her develop solutions. Sometimes employees bring up an internal problem (i.e., one that is under the leader's control). For example, if the employee says, "I'm supposed to consolidate the manpower reports, but I can't figure out how to do it," you are dealing with a lack of knowledge, which is an internal problem that you can do something about. In the other case, the problem may be external (e.g., "The other department sends its reports in late every month. That means I can't make my deadline."). This is a problem-solving/decision-making situation; you might have to delay establishing this standard or temporarily set a low one.

Try to get the person who has the most information to make the decision. Listen carefully to what your employee says about authority level, because the employee may be saying that he or she can and wants to make some decisions without having to get prior approval. That might be a good idea! Sure, it's difficult at times to give up control. But remember: you are also responsible for training and developing your employees. By letting an employee take on more responsibility, you are encouraging him or her to become more valuable to the organization.

The manager's perception of the job. This is your opportunity to provide input by discussing and resolving any differences in the way each of you see the task. Your job is to reduce the employee's tension and to create a good climate for mutual development of standards, joint problem solving, and common agreement throughout the process. Here, you are both attempting to answer these questions clearly:

- What are the job tasks?
- Which tasks are most important?
- How will each task be measured?
- What problems impede task completion?
- What are possible solutions for these problems?
- Who has what authority in each task?

Reaching consensus. Consensus greatly increases the chance that the employee will feel that the performance standards are fair and thus become motivated to achieve them. It also tells the employee that if he or she meets a standard, then performance on that task is satisfactory.

Try to picture yourself as a troubleshooter, guide, coach, or facilitator. Don't get trapped in an evaluative, judgmental role; that will make the employee feel defensive, frustrated, and deceived. He or she will feel that, in spite of your request for input, you have your own preset agenda and it won't make any difference what he or she says.

Successful leaders believe that their job is to make it easier for their people to do their jobs. You can help your employees in these ways:

- Identify any job tasks that the employee omitted (particularly critical ones).
- Make sure that performance is measured quantitatively or qualitatively (preferably both).
- Clarify vague terms.
- Ask the employee for his or her thoughts and recommendations on problems that are identified.
- Clarify any confusion about authority levels.

Look at and listen to the employee carefully. Notice nonverbal communication—frowning, nervousness, hesitation, or relief and relaxation. Such nonverbal signals can tell us quite clearly whether or not we are really reaching agreement.

The final list. Ask the employee to prepare a composite list of the job standards you wrote and those that he or she wrote after the meeting. This puts the collaborative information into final form, and fosters a sense of ownership.

The employee has likely invested significant time, energy, and concern in preparing for this meeting, so end the meeting by sincerely thanking the employee for his or her efforts. You are expressing deserved appreciation, as well as reinforcing productive future behavior.

Following up. Follow up by reviewing the composite list of standards with the employee. Obtain a copy of the employee's composite worksheet, and briefly review it with the employee. This is an important opportunity for any final clarification and adjustments. Both of you should keep copies of the final agreement.

Agree upon a trial period and set a future meeting date and time for a review of the employee's standards. This will reduce tension if the employee feels irrevocably committed to an untried plan of action that he or she feels unsure about. It can also correct any problems that surface between the two of you before they become serious and communicate to the employee that standards are important to you and that you will be following up.

We close this chapter with a meeting checklist for the standards meeting and a Job Standards worksheet that you can copy and use to set standards with your employees.

Performance Standards Meeting
Checklist

Take some time to think about what you want to say to an employee in a performance standards meeting. Here are a few suggestions.

Prior to the performance standards meeting:

☐ 1. Plan and conduct an initial discussion with the employee. Explain what performance standards are and why they need to be established.

> **Sample language:** A performance standard is simply a statement that describes a job task and how well it is to be performed. I'd like you to propose the standards for your job. We'll discuss and agree on them at the next meeting.

> Analyze one key job task, explain criteria for good performance standards, and discuss authority levels. Go over your job standards form if you are using one.

> **Sample language:** This form will make it easier for you to write down your standards. Notice that I've written one job task as an example. Let's go through this task completely to give you a better idea of how to develop the rest of your standards.

☐ 2. Complete your own list of job standards.

During the performance standards meeting:

☐ 1. Review the job summary.

> **Sample language:**

> Let's go over this paragraph that sums up the job.
> Do you feel it is accurate?
> Is there anything you would like to add or change?

☐ 2. Ask the employee to describe each job task. Ask the employee to explain how he or she sees the task being measured, and ask them how they think you both ought to measure performance. Ask the employee to list problems he or she has with the specific task, and state perceived authority levels.

> **Sample language:**

> Okay, read your first critical job task.
> How do you think we ought to measure performance?
> Are there any problems that are causing slowdowns or trouble?
> Do you think this task requires my prior approval or that you should report to me after you complete the task?

(continued)

☐ 3. Share your perceptions of the task identified by the employee. Explain how you see the task measured and its relationship to the job. Describe problems and possible causes that might prevent the task from being completed. Propose solutions to any problems. State any differences in your perception of authority.

> **Sample language:**
>
> This task might be difficult to measure.
> What are some of the indications that the job is done the way it ought to be done?
> A concern that I have is....
> Another possible cause of this problem might be....
> Here is an idea you might consider.
> In this task, I feel that you have complete authority to do the task, but I would like to know how it turns out for you.

☐ 4. Reach a consensus.

> **Sample language:** If you agree that you can achieve this standard, I'll consider the standard, when achieved, to be satisfactory performance.

☐ 5. Ask the employee to combine both sets of standards into one list after the meeting.

☐ 6. Thank the employee for his or her efforts and end on a positive and encouraging note.

After the performance standards meeting:

☐ 1. Follow up by reviewing the composite worksheet on standards with the employee.

☐ 2. Agree on a trial period.

> **Sample language:** Okay, we'll use these standards for one month. Do you think that will give us enough time to test them thoroughly? We'll get together on the 16th at 10:00 a.m. to see if any changes are needed. Will that time be convenient for you?

Sample Job Standards Worksheet

Job summary: _____

Authority Levels
1. Complete authority.
2. Act and report.
3. Act after approval.

List the main tasks of your job	Importance of Task A = Highest priority B = Medium priority C = Lowest priority	What specific standards are used to measure performance? (Quality, Cost, Time, Satisfaction)	What problems exist that hamper optimum performance?	Authority level for the task
1.				
2.				
3.				
4.				
5.				
6.				

Establishing Standards of Performance

65

7

One-on-One Training Skills

"When my supervisor explains something to me, she knows the work so well. I wish she could get it across to me. She rattles it off and I'm not sure I have it."

"There was very little training because the work was heavy. I really wasn't trained—just a quick 'Do this, and here's how.'"

"I got off to a bad start. I came when they were really busy, so I just sat there and read books."

Job instructional training, on-the-job training, or even behavior modeling—whatever you call it, one-on-one training is probably the oldest kind of learning there is. Parents teach their children this way, and senior employees use it to teach skills to new employees.

The Beginning of Formalized One-on-One Training

World War I produced a critical need for almost half a million new workers. Charles R. Allen, a Massachusetts vocational instructor, was asked to develop a process for training urgently-needed shipbuilders. In 1917, Allen developed four-step, on-the-job training that consisted of showing, teaching, doing, and checking.

Time and again, this simple process has been used effectively to train new employees in all kinds of organizations. It works because it is just plain common sense.

Modern behavioral science indicates that Allen's four-step process can be enhanced by adding two additional steps for effective one-on-one training, so that it looks like this:

Prepare for the training.
Ask questions to determine the trainee's experience.
Tell the trainee about the task.
Show the trainee how the task is done.
Encourage the trainee to do the task.
Follow up to ensure that the trainee can do the task.

Let's examine all of these topic areas.

Preparing for the Training

One of the basic problems with one-on-one training is that we often do not take the time to prepare properly for the training session. Training preparation is indeed important, but is it "urgent"? Urgent tasks must be done today, but important tasks such as preparation frequently get postponed until later. Preparation ensures that our training is concise and realistic, and usually results in a more-positive experience for the leader and his or her trainee.

Most leaders conduct one-on-one training, but not all are effective at it. We tend to talk too much and tell the employee everything we know about the task, rather than just those things the employee needs to know. Wasted time, bored trainees, and frustration for everyone result from all this talking. To be an effective trainer, you need to analyze the job that will be taught; list activities; determine what you want the trainee to be able to do; and develop training plans and strategies.

Listing the activities. Effective training separates what the employee must know from what it would be nice for the employee to know. First, you should list the key duties of the job, and then put those activities in some sort of order. Then you can make intelligent decisions about what should be taught, what shouldn't be taught, and what can be postponed until later.

Let's say you are a new leader and it is my responsibility to train you. I would first prepare for the training by making a list of the major activities for your new job. This list would probably look something like this:

A leader's key responsibilities and tasks

Assign work.
Counsel problem employees.
Make decisions.
Write goals and objectives for the department or section.
Develop employees.
Conduct yearly performance appraisals.
Give positive feedback to employees.
Write reports.
Hold meetings.
Assist in selecting new employees.
Manage daily timecards.
Coordinate work with other sections.
Make reports to supervisor.

Chances are that you will already be familiar with some of these activities. You are likely to already have set your goals and objectives, so no one would need to spend time to teach you this activity. "Develop employees" is an activity you might not have had a chance to learn in your previous job, however, so I would teach this to you.

Determining the tasks. When we detail the key tasks of each activity, we can see fairly quickly the specific topics that need to be covered and those that don't. Let's say you are an absolute whiz at managing your time. Now, let's really jump off the deep end and pretend that I'm a whiz at scheduling my time. If I don't stop and remember that I don't have to teach him how to schedule his time because he's already a whiz at it, chances are that I'll bore you silly for two hours telling you how important it is to manage your training time!

Task detailing can also remind me to cover a key topic in our one-on-one training sessions. It tells me exactly what you and I need to do, because each task I've detailed that you don't already know how to do automatically becomes a training objective for us.

In the example that follows, I have selected "Develop employees," from the preceding list of activities, and then detailed all the sub-tasks you will need to do in developing employees.

Activity: Develop employees

Details of this task (sub-tasks):

Determine training needs of individual employees.
Schedule time for training.
Complete task listing on employee's job.
Complete task detailing on listed tasks of the employee's job.
Develop training plans.
Locate or devise training aids.
Train.
Follow up to determine whether or not training is successful.
Develop revised training plan to meet any needs that still exist.

Then, I would take each of the detailed tasks that you don't already know how to do and plan how the training will be done.

Plans and strategies. In this part of my preparation, I would take each topic that we'll cover and develop my strategies or plan for that topic. I broke down each step of the task in detail, and will use this to guide me in creating a training plan for your new job.

Planning is something you probably already know a good deal about, so I won't spend time here describing planning processes, but I will illustrate "Develop Training Plans" from the task detailing of "Develops employees," in order to show what I would do in this step if I were going to train you to be a leader.

Develop training plans:

Check the library for books on one-on-one training.
Go online and search for good sources of information on the topic.
Write out the best step-by-step training model I can find.
Develop a skit to demonstrate how a new employee is trained.
Reserve the video equipment to use while practicing.
Reserve the conference room.

This type of preparation—listing major activities, task detailing, and planning—will help to provide a smooth and effective training program. And note that all this essential work has been done with paper and pencil. I haven't yet even started the training!

Conducting the Training

After you have thoroughly prepared for the training, the next step is to conduct the training by asking questions, telling the trainee about the task, showing the trainee how the task is done, encouraging the trainee to do the task, and following up to ensure that the trainee can do the task.

Ask questions to determine the trainee's experience. Today, most one-on-one training models include the original "Show, Tell, Do, and Check" steps of the original Allen training model—along with additional steps such as preparation and introduction. However, I believe that the employee's previous experience should be considered as well.

Why ask questions? I always try to learn about the trainee's prior experience.

- It demonstrates a caring attitude on the part of the trainer, since he or she expresses interest in the trainee by asking questions and listening.

- Training time can be reduced if you identify what the trainee already knows.

- You can relate new learning to the employee's prior experience.

- Some of the employee's experience might interfere with new learning.

If I need to teach an adult how to make PowerPoint transparencies, I might ask first, "What's your experience with overhead transparencies?"

If the individual isn't sure how to respond or says "None," I will probably stop this particular line of questioning. Instead, I might ask, "What kinds of programs, if any, have you attended where PowerPoint or overheads were used?" or "What are some of the things you like about overheads? What are some of the things you don't like about overheads or PowerPoint presentations?"

I listen actively, without interrupting. Then I will ask clarification questions, such as "Can you be more specific?" "Could you give me an example?" or "How was that done?"

Types of questions. Generally, the best questions to use are so-called open questions which start with *What* or *How*. In addition, there are questions that are perceived by the employee as requests for more information (although, technically, they are "closed questions" that can be answered with "yes" or "no"). Closed questions such as "Can you be more specific?" or "Can you give me an example?" imply that we expect the individual to provide the information.

Other open questions that start with *When* or *Where* ask for specific details, and thus are less desirable for general probing of the trainee's experience. For example, if I am asking for a trainee's experience with overheads or PowerPoint, I first inquire, "What experience have you have with overheads (or PowerPoint)?" rather than, "When did you encounter overheads or PowerPoint?"

The least desirable questions seem to be personal *Why* questions (*"Why* did *you* do it that way?"). This type can produce defensive behavior, since it focuses on personal motives. Instead, ask something less personal, such as "Why did *they* do it that way?"

Describe the task simply and clearly. "Telling" is a step any leader should be able to do well, right? Wrong! It's so easy to tell employees everything they might ever want to know about a specific task, but too much talking is a problem. Carefully prepare, and don't go over tasks the employee already knows how to perform. Avoid "talking problems" by carefully asking key questions to determine the employee's experience. Talking too much can get the leader and the employee into deep trouble.

Avoid telling them what they already know. Focus on what the individual doesn't know and needs to learn, and try to relate it to what they already know. Give the employee an overview of *what* is to be done, and put it into the context of the job's environment. Next, tell *why* the job should be done, providing reasons that make sense. Organizational policy is not the "why." If you don't know the *why,* you need to find out, because reasons for doing a task give the trainee motivation to do it.

Last, provide specific information that describes *how* the task is to be done. Use sketches, pictures, and even illustrations with rough drawings to describe how the task should be done. Give the employee an opportunity to interrupt and ask questions. If the employee has none, ask questions about what they said: "How is this like your old job? What problems do you see in doing this? What questions do you have, at this point?"

Please avoid the time-worn, "Do you have any questions?" Ask, "What questions do you have?" The "What" implies that questions are expected. You can also ask questions about what you are going to explain next, but don't set up the trainee for failure by asking things that he or she has no way of knowing. During this "telling" portion of the training, ask questions that most people will be able to answer.

Demonstrate how the task is done. Physically demonstrate what you want the employee to do. As you demonstrate the task, provide a verbal explanation step-by-step. The employee should hear and see how it is to be done, and understand where, when, and why it is done.

Consider having the employee talk you both through the task. As the employee tells you what to do, step-by-step, do it. This technique gets the employee involved in the learning process and reveals exactly what the employee has or hasn't learned. Showing the employee how the task is done through modeling might feel a little awkward in the beginning, but making a mistake or two ourselves simply makes us more human. A little humor here goes a long way. The employee will be more relaxed when it's time for him or her to practice.

Encourage the trainee. We can read books about riding a unicycle, watch someone ride one, and even write an article on the joys of unicycle riding, but we can't learn to ride a unicycle until we actually ride that thing! Most employees can't learn how to do a task simply by reading about it, and they can't learn skills by watching us or anybody else. They have to do the task themselves—and receive feedback on their performance. That's your job as a trainer. Watch them perform in a practice session, and then provide helpful, constructive feedback.

If this is the employee's first job, he or she will probably be nervous and unsure. Look for opportunities to give positive feedback on what he or she has done correctly. Avoid using phrases such as "You did that wrong." "You made an error." "There were too many mistakes in your work." "You'll just have to try harder in the future." "You failed!"

Instead, focus your remarks on what was done improperly and how it can be corrected. Stay away from the personal attack.

One of the best ways to help trainees develop task skills is to have them tell you what they are going to do before they do it. This provides the opportunity to correct them before they make a mistake and help them perform the task properly the first time. The employee gains confidence in his or her own ability to figure things out, which leads to better retention of the correct way to perform the task.

Follow up. Following up does not mean concluding with the familiar statement, "My door is always open. If you have any questions, don't hesitate to stop by, and I'll help you any way I can." Employees who are apprehensive about their job and job environment won't feel comfortable enough to come to you with their questions.

Following up means *you* follow up. Take the initiative. Make time in your busy schedule to "visit" your employees on a regular basis. Good intentions don't count much here—action does!

Find out what the employee is feeling and thinking about the job. Second, determine how well the job task is being done, and identify any areas that need improvement. Ask employees how they feel about the task, what they like about it, what they don't like, and what they are concerned about.

Then have the employee complete the key tasks so you are sure that he or she is performing them correctly. When you see positive performance, say so. (Avoid "parental" responses such as, "I'm proud of you!") Then carefully analyze the performance and identify areas that need improvement.

One-on-One Training Skills
Leader's Checklist

☐ 1. **Prepare for training.**

- List the tasks.
- List the details.
- Develop training plans and strategies.

☐ 2. **Ask questions to determine the employee's experience.**

Examples:

"What experience have you had with jobs like this?"
"What have you done in the past that was similar to this?"

☐ 3. **Tell the employee about the task.**

Examples:

This is what you will be doing:
While completing this task, these are the people you will be dealing with…
This is where the job will be done.
This job should be done when…
The reasons for doing this job are…
This job is important because…

Then ask:

"What questions do you have at this point?"
"What concerns do you have about doing this?"

☐ 4. **Show the employee how to do the task.**

Example: *"Watch me as I do this task. I'll talk my way through it for you."*

☐ 5. **Encourage the employee to perform the task.**

Example: *"Now you do it as I watch. And why don't you tell me what you are going to do just before you perform each step?"*

☐ 6. **Follow up to make sure that the employee can perform the task.**

Example: *"Why don't we meet tomorrow and see how you are doing? I'll stop by your area right after break—say at about ten o'clock."*

Planning Worksheet

1. Prepare for the training:

   Note one key activity.

   List one detailed sub-task.

   Outline plans and strategies for the task.

2. Ask questions to determine the employee's experience.

   - What does the employee already know that will aid learning? Hinder learning?

   - What information do we need in order to teach this employee the specific unit of knowledge selected from our task-detailing sheet?

3. Tell the employee about the task.

   What specific unit of knowledge are we going to give this employee? Briefly write down what you will say. Don't try to write out a "script." (This should be in the form of notes.)

4. Show the employee how to do the task.

   What will you do?

5. Encourage the employee to do the task.

   What specific parts of the task do you think the employee will be able to perform correctly?

   When the employee performs the above item successfully, what will you say?

   - Describe what you say.

   - Tell why it was important.

   - Express your feelings.

   What specific part of the task might be difficult for the employee?

   What will you say if the employee does this incorrectly or has been doing the task correctly?

   What does the employee need to know about complicated, preventive, or corrective tasks and/or housekeeping that affects the performance of the task learned?

6. Follow up to make sure that the employee can do the task.

   What kinds of specific follow-up action will be necessary for you to take?

8

Improving Employee Performance through Coaching

Coaching is unlocking a person's potential to maximize their own performance. It is helping them to learn rather than teaching them.

– John Whitmore
Coaching for Performance

The words *coaching* and *counseling* are often used synonymously, but I believe they are two very different actions. Counseling refers to helping an individual correct his or her problems. Coaching is helping someone become even more effective by focusing on the whole person and his or her job.

A good coach is a partner. He or she wants peak performance from the people he or she has responsibility for. The coachee wants the rewards that come from personal effectiveness: extrinsically in the form of recognition, and intrinsically as a result of feeling competent. Both partners have an investment in accomplishment.

When people are motivated to improve, they have a stake in accomplishing the task the best way possible. Good coaching requires neither the carrot nor the stick: It requires good leadership.

It is a one-on-one interaction. The coach creates in the other individual an awareness of the possibility of change, explores with him or her various change alternatives, assists in selecting a key area for attention, and helps create action plans to accomplish the desired changes.

If you want to be an effective coach, you must do these things:

- Talk *with* the individuals, not *at* them (as is often done in one-on-one training).

- Make extensive use of the individual's prior experience.

- Focus on present performance, rather than on future career goals or the political climate.

- Help the person become more effective, rather than only address his or her performance problems.

- Respect the individual's knowledge and abilities, and consider him or her a capable contributor.

Why Coach?

Organizations are downsizing, rightsizing, restructuring, and reengineering. Whole layers of management have disappeared in many organizations. "Lean and mean" are the operational words in today's firms. Often, leaders are required to deal with wider spans of control (more employees report to them), increased workloads that were delegated to them from their bosses, and overworked employees who are expected to be even more productive.

In addition, employees' jobs are becoming more technical and complex. According to recent reports, the growth of technical workers as a job class has tripled, compared to the workplace as a whole. This means that leaders are now required to supervise employees who, in all likelihood, know a great deal more about their jobs than their leaders do. Helping such highly skilled employees requires that leaders coach their employees in order to enhance productivity. So it's no wonder that astute leaders are looking for (make that *hungry* for!) new ways to manage.

Coaching develops self-sufficiency, builds ownership and competency, increases motivation, results in better performance, ideas, and solutions, and increases personal and job satisfaction. It is something we do in all areas of our lives, whether we realize it or not.

A New Way

Socrates used questions to pursue Truth with the youth of ancient Greece. And Plato, a disciple of Socrates, also used this method of communicating. It became known as dialectic discussion: *dia* from the Greek word meaning "two" and "across," and *lectic* meaning "to lecture." People attained new knowledge by talking together and asking questions. Today, we use the word "Socratic" to describe this method of communication.

Many of us know what the words *Socratic* or *dialectic* mean, but not many of us have had a chance to acquire coaching skills. We might have been taught how to make presentations or give speeches or teach, but how many people have taken a class about helping someone become more effective by asking questions?

Discussion is a better idea-generator than a coach's monologue. There are things that the other person knows that the coach doesn't. If the coach simply tells the other person what to do and how to do it without engaging in a dialogue, he doesn't get to hear the other person's ideas. Likewise, if the other person doesn't bother to utilize his or her coach's experience and wisdom, he misses out on the coach's ideas. But if both can talk with each other, the end result is often greater than either thought possible.

Asking specific questions is a very effective way to find out what the coachee knows.

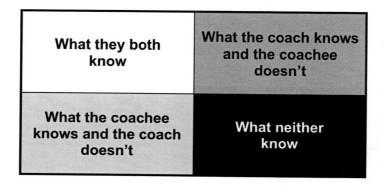

Guidelines for Asking Questions

Let's first look at some general guidelines for coaching. Then, later in this chapter, we'll present a step-by-step model in how to coach.

Ask. Don't tell. Most leadership tasks start with preparation. You have likely spent a significant amount of time either preparing to conduct an interview with a job applicant, thoroughly preparing to train a new employee, or preparing for a performance appraisal meeting, but a lot of coaching is done on the run, when there usually isn't time for extensive planning. We're coaching when we see someone doing a task and we take a moment to talk with that person about how the task might be done more effectively. We also coach when someone asks us for help with a particular task and we agree. Coaching doesn't start with preparation—it starts with questions.

Just ask questions. Sounds easy, right? Well, it is fairly easy to learn the different types of questions to ask, but *knowing* the questions and actually *using* them are altogether different matters.

Let me give you a real example. I was an independent consultant for a number of years before starting my business. During that time, I wrote a journal article entitled, "So You Want to Be a Consultant—It Isn't as Easy as It Looks!" In it, I shared all of the things that I had learned about starting a consulting business. As you might imagine, a number of fledgling consultants called for additional advice. I would talk, talk, talk, and talk, and they would become terribly impressed about how much I knew. But I talked *at* them, not *with* them.

I am now a little older and wiser. The last couple of people who have wandered into my office to talk about becoming a consultant weren't talked to, they were talked *with*. I asked questions, a lot of questions. And when they left, they had their own answers, not mine.

I recently talked with an individual who was in the process of being "reengineered" out of her job and was considering becoming an independent consultant. One of the many questions I asked was, "How long do you think it will take you to begin generating revenue?" Her answer was, "About four months."

I didn't want to just tell her that I thought her schedule was unrealistic. "Considering the time it takes to market your services, schedule work to meet the client's timetable, invoice the customer after the job is completed, and finally get paid, how do you see that happening in less than six months?" I asked. Her answer: "Oh, I didn't think of the collection problems. Maybe six months is more realistic." This seemed to me like a much more realistic view of the time it takes to become a consultant.

Next, I asked questions such as, "How do you plan to survive the six months it will take you to begin generating revenue?" "What is your fallback position, in case you haven't quite produced enough income to meet your needs?" "Who are your prospective clients?" "How will you identify them?" "How do you plan to reach these clients once you have identified them?"

Each succeeding answer leads to another question. Your follow-up question should be focused on what the other person wants or needs, rather than on what you think he or she might need. If others have answers to your coaching questions (and they might), you both learn something.

Ask the five W's. Questions that start with *What* or *How* yield the most information and help the individual think in detail about the situation under discussion. *Why, Where,* and *When* questions are useful for obtaining more-specific details, but are less helpful for acquiring general information. The question that can get us in trouble begins with the word *Why.* "Why are you having trouble doing this particular task?" will likely result in the person's becoming defensive. Less threatening is, "What are your major concerns about this particular task?" However, you could focus on the future by asking something like "Why is that step in your plan important to you?" It is less of a challenge and is not likely to make the other person feel uncomfortable. "Why" questions can also be used as follow-ups to determine facts and feelings.

Answer questions with questions that contain clues about possible answers. This is not a manipulative device to get people to come up with your answer, but rather a complex way of communicating that helps people think of new possibilities. Include enough additional information in the question to broaden the other person's vision, but not so much information that you limit their response.

Be quiet after you ask a question so the other person has an opportunity to respond. If you think you know what the other person should say or do, this will be difficult, but keep your mouth shut. The objective here is to give people time to come up with their own ideas, rather than yours. This fosters ownership and commitment. Ten seconds can feel like an eternity, but try counting to ten before asking another question or offering your ideas. Do, however, provide non-verbal responses (eye contact, head nods, and the like) to indicate to the other person that he or she has your undivided attention.

By listening actively, you communicate that you care about them, but you also obtain new information and discover what works or doesn't work—and why. You can locate problems and elicit suggestions for solving them. If you don't learn the power of listening, you will not get needed information. Remember, it is the listener who controls the conversation's outcome, not the speaker.

Avoid running two questions together. Ask one question and wait for a response before asking another question. Sometimes when you ask one question, you immediately think of a better one or a better way of asking the first one. Before you restate your question or ask a second one, give people an opportunity to think about the first question. Then take your cue from the other person as to whether or not you need to ask the same question in a different way.

If the other person has difficulty answering, say, "Let me rephrase the question" and ask another question that provides additional clues. Strike a balance between jumping in to lead others to the "right" answer and waiting too long for an answer. If you maintain a comfortable silence after asking a question and they are still unable to respond, simply ask the question in a different way to provide additional information concerning the original question.

If another person seems unable to answer a question, ask permission before directly providing information. Prefacing a suggestion by asking permission keeps the other person in control of the conversation. Ask, "Could I make a suggestion?" and the individual might respond by saying, "Wait. Let me think about it for a minute." Let them take responsibility for the direction of the discussion.

Create a conversation. If all you do is ask question after question, the other person may soon begin to feel that he or she is being interrogated. There are two things that a coach can do to prevent this: 1) respond, or 2) use self-disclosure (i.e., talk about the mistakes you've made on the job).

Responding. When the other person stops talking, the coach can respond in several ways. If the other person covered a lot of information in his or her response to the coach's original question, the coach can respond by summarizing. Make a statement that attempts to reflect accurately the content of what was said by the other person. This will indicate to the other person that you really did listen to what was said, and will help ensure that what was said was also understood.

The coach might want to pay more attention to the feelings expressed than to the content of what is said. If the other person has strong feelings about what he or she says, the coach can recognize and affirm those feelings by saying, "I can see why you might feel that way," or "You seem to have some strong feelings about that." Note that this is not agreement; it is only an empathetic statement by the coach that legitimizes the other person's right to have feelings. Statements such as "You shouldn't feel that way" or "I don't understand why you would feel like that" discount the other person and put up barriers.

Using self-disclosure. Where does it say that coaches have to always do things right, never make mistakes, and, above all, never have feelings? Good communication occurs when two human beings talk honestly with each other. A coach is not weak or incompetent when he or she confesses to having made a mistake or expresses feelings about an issue that is important. So, it's okay to say, "I've had difficulty with that, too," or "A similar thing happened to me." (Note that this is not a "Oh, you think you've got troubles—wait until you hear mine!" kind of response. It is only a sincere effort to connect with the other person, help break down barriers, and improve the flow of communication.)

Listening, responding appropriately by acknowledging either the content or the emotion, summarizing throughout, and opening up are things good coaches do to maintain a dialogue with the other person. The idea here is to have a discussion, not conduct a monologue.

Okay, so you now know a bit about coaching by asking questions, and you probably see value in doing it. But sometimes it seems that even though we know better, we still end up telling people what it is they need to do, how they should do it, and when it needs to be done.

The following fable illustrates some of the subtle reasons why coaching can be difficult.

Parchment, Brooms, and a Dragon

Once upon a time, in a land far away, in the Kingdom of Light and Shadow, lived Jenny. She was known throughout the kingdom as a marvelous helper.

Now the Queen of the Kingdom of Light and Shadow was having great difficulty with her court. The parchment work was not getting done, and what did get done wasn't done on time. The storerooms were a mess, and nobody could find anything when it was needed. The castle rooms were dusty, and guests from other kingdoms usually went home early. There were bugs in the flour, worms in the fruit, and to make matters worse—a dragon in the moat.

The Queen, being busy with queenly things, really didn't have time to deal with these pedestrian problems. So she called for the Wizard and asked what she should do. The Wizard thought for a moment and then wisely informed the Queen that she needed an overseer: someone to manage the court staff and whip things back into shape. The Queen immediately thought of Jenny.

The Queen had heard stories about Jenny's willingness to help anyone do anything and decided that Jenny should be placed in charge of the royal court. So she summoned Jenny and appointed her the royal boss.

Jenny was thrilled to be so recognized by her Queen, but she was a little frightened about taking over as the new Chief of Staff. She just knew that the staff would resent her and would make her life miserable. As she sat in her dusty room and thought about her new job, a crow flew to her window and cocked one beady eye at her.

"Oh, Crow," cried Jenny, "whatever shall I do?"

"Be a coach," squawked the crow. "Not a boss."

"What does a coach do?" asked Jenny.

(continued)

Parchment, Brooms, and a Dragon (concluded)

"A coach helps people realize their full potential," said the crow as he flew away.

"That I can do," said Jenny to herself.

So she began to make a long list of the things that needed to be done. First there was the matter of the parchment work. Next were the storerooms and the cleaning staff. Then that pesky dragon, and finally, the worms and bugs.

She set out that very afternoon to visit the Chief Scribe. When Jenny asked how she could help the scribing department get caught up, the chief said that he didn't have any idea. Good help was impossible to find, the parchment was just not up to standards, the ink they were using dried too quickly, and the quills wouldn't stay sharp.

"Okay," said Jenny. "Let me see if I can get you some good help. Then I'll set up a total-quality management system at the parchment company, and I'll contact the ink suppliers about the drying time of their inks. I'm not sure what to do about the quills, but I'll figure something out."

"Oh, bless you," said the Chief Scribe. "It is so wonderful to know that my troubles are over."

"No problem," said Jenny, as she left to visit the cleaning staff.

She found the cleaning staff sitting on their buckets, gazing at the sunlight as it streamed through the dusty windows.

"What's wrong?" asked Jenny. "Why are you just watching the dust?"

"The straw in our brooms disintegrates when we try to sweep, the handles break, and our buckets leak," cried the Chief Sweeper.

"Oh, dear," said Jenny. "How can I help?"

"Get us some new brooms made with straw that is not rotten, handles of oak instead of pine, and buckets made of metal, not leather," said the Chief Sweeper.

"Let me see what I can do," said Jenny.

"Oh, bless you," said the Chief Sweeper. "It is so wonderful to know that our troubles are over."

"No problem," said Jenny, as she left to visit the moat.

"Chief Moat Keeper," said Jenny, "I guess you've heard that I'm your new Chief of Staff. As your new chief, how can I help you do your job better?"

"Take care of that pesky dragon," replied the moat keeper. "It is driving us nuts. It keeps us awake with the noise it makes, it eats the royal fish, and it has burned the drawbridge in three places."

"Let me see what I can do," said Jenny.

"Oh, bless you," said the Chief Moat Keeper. "It is so wonderful to know that our troubles are over."

"No problem," said Jenny, as she left to find the dragon.

"Dragon!" shouted Jenny. "Where are you?"

There was a great churning of the waters, and with a loud sound like distant thunder, the dragon poked his head out of the water.

"Hey, lady, what's all the fuss? Can't you see I'm trying to get a little shut-eye here?" rumbled the dragon.

"This is the castle moat, not a dragon's bathtub," Jenny replied. "Get your sorry hide out of the moat and hit the road."

"But I'm hungry!" roared the dragon. "The fish are all gone. How can I hit the road with an empty tummy?"

"Don't worry, you can count on me to feed you," said Jenny.

"What a wonderful idea," said the dragon, as he gobbled her up.

What do you think is the point of this story? If you were asked to write a snappy one-liner that said, "The moral of this story is…" what would you write?

One of the best responses I've heard to the question is this one:

"The moral of this story is that coaching others by doing for them can get you eaten alive, and you'll never get your work done."

* * * * *

Over the years, I've talked with people about why they think some professionals in the field aren't very effective. Here are some of their reasons:

- Some coaches need to "help" others (like Jenny did in the preceding story).
- Some coaches tend to have dominating personalities.
- It's often a lot faster to just tell (especially when we think we know the answer) than to ask.
- It's good for the old ego to be seen as the expert.
- The other person may think we are incompetent if we ask rather than tell.
- We feel awkward about doing things differently.
- Sometimes we don't really know how to coach.

Let's look at each of these problems in more detail.

"Helpers." It feels good to "help" by telling rather than asking. There is a bit of the "caretaker" in most of us. Maybe we were nurtured by our parents or other significant people and learned that it feels good to have someone do for us, so we nurture others in turn. Some of us as children were placed in caretaker roles in our own families and received a lot of psychological payoffs.

Caretaker coaches seem to create dependency. They are overly helpful, take back work that the other person is having difficulty with, don't want to be the source of the other person's discomfort, and thus have trouble convincing their coaches that change is needed. Many do it because they need to be needed.

Once such individuals understand their behavior and get some coaching experience, they will see that true coaching is doing what is best for the individual. There are also many psychological rewards that come from watching people become more competent and self-sufficient.

Dominating personalities. A coach who is domineering might have learned that style from an old boss or from early-childhood experiences. They feel a need to control their surroundings because of their own fears, or they really are unusually intelligent or technically competent and thus believe that they are paid to have all the answers to life's questions.

These coaches, however, can learn more-effective ways of relating to others. They need to see that controlling others leads to dependence, and dependence leads to resentment. Intelligent and/or technically competent coaches can also learn that coaching allows them to integrate their own experience with the other person's experience in order to create richer ideas and better solutions.

It is easier to tell. It takes a lot more time to help others discover their own answers than it does to just tell them what they need to know. And most coaches today are stressed beyond belief in dealing with life—where can they find the time to coach? They make time. It's a question of priorities—and investment.

Astute coaches know that what needs to get done will get done. They also know that investing priority time in coaching others can return remarkable dividends: dividends in the form of time saved, and dividends because people will be better performers, more self-sufficient, and highly motivated and challenged in what they've been coached to do.

The ego. It's good for the old ego to be perceived as the expert, but it will feel even better when you have a truly productive coaching session. Wait until you try it! The personal satisfaction you get from coaching cannot be duplicated.

Trying something new is awkward. Most things that we try for the first time are. The first time I rode a bicycle felt awkward. The first time I drove a car felt awkward. And the first time I tried to coach using questions also felt awkward. It takes time and practice to become skilled in the Socratic method, but you can become proficient with application and practice.

In the next section, we'll look at a common-sense model of how to use the Socratic method of coaching.

Coaching Model

Coaching is a process—it has a beginning, a middle, and an end. One simple Socratic process can be used to initiate or engage in a coaching discussion. It consists of just six steps.

Six Steps for Effective Coaching

1. **Create awareness of the possibility of change.**

2. **Explore possibilities.**

3. **Choose a key area for attention.**

4. **Develop an action plan.**

5. **Conclude the session.**

6. **Follow up.**

Creating awareness of the possibility of change. It is not particularly motivating to be told to do my job better if I already think that I'm doing the best that I can. The implication is that whatever I do is never good enough, and that I should have seen opportunities for improvement. And since I didn't, *there must be something wrong with me. I'm just not trying. I'm not working hard enough.* That's the subtle and not-so-subtle message given by people who say, "You should just try harder."

But it is not simply a matter of asking people to try harder. The majority of people are conscientious and really want to do the task well. The key to greater productivity is not to focus on how hard people work or to see them as the cause of the "problem," but to ask them what they do and why they do it; analyze how they interact with one another to get the task done, examine and evaluate the processes used; determine if the tools and materials are right for the task, and help them discover better ways to do the task.

That is one reason why using questions is so effective. The coach is not pointing out a performance gap. He or she does not call people into the office and counsel them on their "problem." In reality, the coach may not be aware of any specific thing that could be improved. What the coach does know is that life has real, but unknown, possibilities. He or she knows that there is a possibility of further improvement in performance, and is willing to spend quality time exploring this possibility with the other person.

The true purpose of using questions to coach others is to create elastic yet permeable boundaries around their existing belief systems. Questions are used to help people see new possibilities in order to achieve higher levels of performance and superior results. Coaching is taking a proactive stance toward future crisis and change by helping others constantly look for ways to be even more effective.

People can move from their present level of performance to new levels through this exploration process. Probe the way people feel or think about what they are doing and the ways they behave while doing the task. As John Whitmore said in his book *Coaching for Performance*, there is a world of difference between exhorting a tennis player to "Keep your eye on the ball!" and asking questions such as "Which way does the ball spin after it strikes the ground?" or "Where exactly on your racket does the ball hit?"

Exhortation does nothing to promote awareness; it only causes frustration. But asking a question that requires self-analysis focuses the player's attention on the way he is playing; while thinking about the questions, he becomes aware of what he's been doing.

Some questions that the coach can use to create awareness in the three areas of feelings, thinking, and behavior are:

- Feelings:
    How do you like doing this?
    How do you feel about looking for ways to do this even better?
    What concerns do you have about doing this?

- Thinking:
    What are the reasons you do it this way?
    What reasons might there be to change the way it's done?
    On a scale of 1 to 10, how do you rate yourself on it?
    What parts of this are most challenging for you?
    What do you see are the reasons why this is challenging?

- Behavior:
    What do you do as you complete this task?
    What are the key steps to completing it?

It may be, however, that you won't need one or more steps in the model. (For example, if the other person initiates the conversation and asks for your help in exploring possibilities for improvement, then you will likely be able to start with the next step, "Explore Possibilities.")

Exploring possibilities. Exploring possibilities is a natural part of the process, but it is so natural that coaches often find that they start to do it without intending to do it. You must encourage people to develop their own ideas about the possibilities that exist for change and improvement. Jump in and provide suggestions only after the other person has had a chance to thoroughly think about and discuss his or her own ideas. Give the other person an opportunity to think about the situation. Then meet at a later time to hear his or her ideas.

There are several reasons why it's important to ask for the individual's ideas before sharing yours:

- They might think of a better idea than the coach's, since they often know more than the coach about the details of the task.

- They are more likely to be motivated to make needed changes if the idea originates from them.

- Coaches communicate that people are respected and trusted through their actions.

- Coaches help people become independent; they are better able to make appropriate decisions when needed.

Some coaches who have trouble letting the coachee come up with the ideas are assigned the coaching role because they are good at solving problems. Naturally, they will have some strong ideas about what a person should do in order to be more effective. However, if the coach jumps in to tell an individual what he or she should do to improve performance, the other person is likely to react by offering ten reasons why the idea or solution will not work. If a coach can get the other person to come up with the suggestions, there is a better chance that real changes will be made.

If one person can suggest several ideas for a specific situation, two people can come up with more. This is because one person's ideas trigger new thoughts in the other. Thus, when you have two people bouncing ideas off each other, you greatly increase the chances of creating better-quality and more-creative suggestions. Astute coaches have learned that always to jump in with "the" idea for every problem is, in the long term, not beneficial. As James Thurber said, "It is better to know some of the questions than all of the answers."

If after careful probing you see that the person cannot offer any ideas, feel free to offer your idea. In this initial step, we are looking for "divergent" thinking—that is, ideas that originate outside of the other person's experience. Therefore, it is appropriate to offer new suggestions that the other person might not have thought of. At this point, the coach can simply ask, "May I make a suggestion?" In most cases, people will respond by saying, "Yes."

Here are typical questions that can be used in this step to explore possibilities:

- Which things are the greatest challenge for you? Why?
- What bottlenecks exist?
- What changes would you like to see in the way it is done?
- What other changes could be made?
- How would you like to be different from the way you are now?
- What things, if any, prevent you from being more effective?
- Would you like some time to consider the situation?
- Would you like me to make a suggestion, or would you prefer to have more time to think of ideas on your own?

This kind of discussion encourages divergent thinking. Now let's look at how a coach can help the other person think convergently.

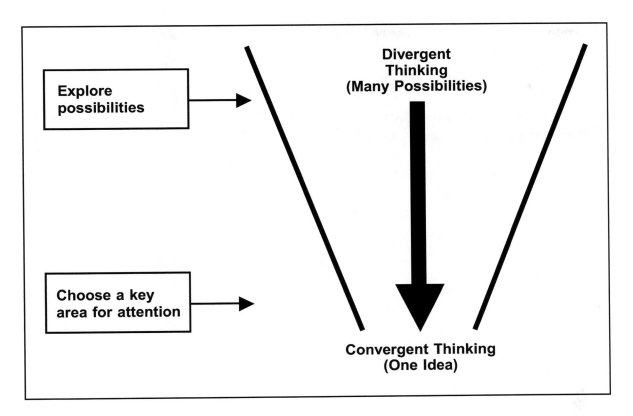

Selecting a key area for attention. While you are together exploring possibilities, your coachee might suggest a number of different ideas for analysis. Remember, the discussion in the preceding step encouraged divergent thinking. But in this step, the coach helps the individual think convergently; that is, the coach helps him or her focus on one key area. Attempting to look at many different ideas often results in the failure of them all.

The coach must also guide the individual, helping him or her consider any constraints to carrying out the suggestion (there might not be enough money to finance the idea, or maybe there isn't enough time to implement the suggestion).

When the key goal has been established, the coach helps the individual determine how the results will be measured.

Here are a few probing questions that the coach can use to accomplish this step:

- Which of these changes should be tackled first?

- What have you already done about this?

- What were the results of that action?

- What are the pluses and minuses of each option?

- What are the key factors that should be considered (time, money, personnel, supplies, resources, space, skills, personal effort required, chances of success, and so on)?

- What do you think should be the outcome or goal?

- Will this get you to your goal?

- How will you define and measure success?

But what if the other person selects an area for attention that is not the coach's first choice? Suppose the other person knows something that the coach doesn't that will make the coach's choice a poor alternative? Or conversely, maybe the coach knows something that the other person doesn't. Then what?

The coach can still ask questions, depending on the reasons why the coach felt his or her selection was better than the other person's choice.

Narrowing the Focus	Suggested Questions
The coach thinks one area of focus will provide greater benefit. (**Note:** It is possible that the coach will discover—through questions—that the employee's idea actually is better.)	• What are the benefits in doing it that way? • What were your reasons for choosing that idea? • Which choice would provide the greatest benefit?
The coach has information that the other person doesn't have that affects the coachee's selected area of focus, or the coach thinks that there is no way that the other person can accomplish the tasks he or she selected.	• What effect would selecting that area for attention have on_____? • If you consider_____, how would that affect your choice? • Given this concern, how would that influence your decision to select that area for attention?
The coach wants the coachee to agree to his suggested focus, or suspects that the other person's motivation to focus on another area might be best in the long run.	• How important is this to you? • How do you feel about this area that you selected?
The coach feels that the coachee will not get the results he or she expects, and that the coachee's choice will not be worth the effort.	• Considering the investment of time and effort required to do that, how do you see a return on your investment paying off?
The coach knows that the coachee's selected focus will not benefit the organization.	• How will this help the organization (or department) reach its objectives?
The coach believes that the coachee's selected focus will require too much of his or her time (the coach's).	• How much of my time will you need if you select that area for attention? • Given my present time constraints and the need for my continuous involvement if you select that area for attention, how do you see us making it happen?

Developing an action plan. After the individual chooses a key area for attention, the coach should then assist him or her in creating an action plan, step-by-step, with completion dates set for each step.

The coach should help the coachee identify any of the steps that might be problematic or of concern. If the coachee can identify problem areas before the plan is carried out, they can be solved early on. This greatly increases the chances that the goal will be achieved.

A coach can help reduce the coachee's natural anxiety and pave the way for the coachee by talking to others who will be affected by the plan. The coach can also interface with other departments that might need to be involved. By offering help, coaches demonstrate concern and show that they will do everything possible to ensure that the plans are successful.

It might not be possible to develop a complete action plan during the initial meeting. Ask the coachee if he or she needs more time to think through the plan, and agree to meet at a later time to review it.

In order to better understand the kinds of questions you need to ask as the coach, please read the case that follows and then answer the questions at the end.

The Case of the Careless Coach

Betty Ann was in the middle of a conversation about Joan's job. It started when Joan asked Betty Ann if she had a "couple of minutes," but dragged on for about an hour. The air conditioning wasn't working the way it should, it was hot and sticky, and the conversation up to this point seemed to have taken forever. Batty Ann managed to help Joan explore coaching possibilities, and Joan had even selected a key area for attention. Betty Ann sighed, surreptitiously looked at her watch, and realized that once again she would not be able to eat supper with her kids. She tried to move the conversation along.

"Joan," Betty Ann said, "I hate to cut this short, but it is getting late. I think that the area you have selected to work on will give you a good return on your investment of time. Why don't you now consider what steps you will need to take to develop an action plan? To start with, what's the first thing you need to do?"

"Okay, I think the first thing I need to do," replied Joan, as she began to write, "is to get upper management support. That's where I'll need your help."

"I agree that the executives need to support what you are doing, but I don't agree that that is the first thing you need to do. For example," asked Betty Ann, "what about the people in this section who have to play a part in making sure that the plan works? Don't you think that you should talk with them first?"

"Oh, I guess that makes sense. I'll talk to Bob, Dick, and Darleen tomorrow, show them what we've done, and ask for their advice."

"I think that makes more sense than sending this up the line and then being embarrassed later when the people who have to make it work don't support it," Betty Ann said. "What kind of reaction do you think you'll get from them?"

"My guess is that they will be excited," replied Joan. "I know that Bob has been asking for this for a long time, and it is right down Darleen's alley."

"Yeah, but maybe that's exactly why you might have a problem."

"What do you mean?"

"Since Bob has been asking for it, isn't he going to wonder why you didn't include him in this conversation? After all, it will affect his performance just as much as it affects yours. I'm curious as to why you didn't consider that before you came to me."

"I just didn't think about it," Joan said. "I know it sounds dumb, but I was so excited that I ran in here to catch you before you went home."

(continued)

The Case of the Careless Coach (concluded)

As Joan finished talking, Betty Ann glanced at her watch.

Joan exclaimed, "Oh, it *is* getting late. I'm sorry that I've kept you so long. Do you want to stop now and pick it up in the morning?"

"No," Betty Ann replied, "I've got a nine o'clock meeting with the VP, and then there's the department meeting at eleven. After that is the report that I was supposed to have finished this afternoon. So let's take a few minutes more and wind this up now so you can at least get started."

"Okay, if you're sure that's all right."

"Sure. Thinking again about your plan, what do you see as the next step?" asked Betty Ann.

"Well...I'm not sure. What do you think I should do?"

"One thing that occurs to me," responded Betty Ann, "is that you really need to consider the time constraints. That's going to be a critical factor. Let's see, you need to have it finished by the end of this quarter. Say, I've got an idea. Why don't you get Bob to help you do it? That'll solve two problems with one solution. Bob will feel more a part of the plan and you'll have the extra help in completing it. What do you think?"

"I guess so," replied Joan reluctantly. "Bob is just such a procrastinator. It's sometimes more work to get him to do something than to just do it myself. But if you really think that that'll help, I suppose I could ask him to help out."

"Great! Why don't you talk to him in the morning, review it with him, see if he has any additional ideas, and then ask him if he'd be willing to help?"

"One last thing, Joan. You also need to consider that your present system won't support the amount of memory required for the new program. What do you plan to do about that?"

"I think that my best bet is to get information services to either install a larger hard drive in my computer, or set up an outboard unit. Then, I can copy it onto the computer," replied Joan.

"Right! And since we don't have a license to copy it, we'll all end up in jail. You know what happened last year. How could you even consider such a thing, Joan?"

"Oh, I thought we had a license. A bunch of people are using it."

"No," replied Betty Ann, "we don't have a license. They wouldn't sell us one, so we had to buy it each time for each station. What a rip-off!"

"Could you see if you can get another copy, legally, for me?" asked Joan.

"I'll see what I can do. But for sure not tonight. Looks like we're finished up, so let's call it a night," said Betty Ann. "Let me know toward the end of the week how you are coming along."

"Okay," replied Joan.

Joan and Betty Ann said goodnight and left.

Try to answer these questions:

As Betty Ann helped Joan develop an action plan, what questions did she ask that were appropriate?

What questions did she ask that were inappropriate?

What questions could she have asked that she didn't?

She made several statements that could have been questions. What were they?

The following are typical examples of answers to the questions:

What questions did Betty Ann ask that were appropriate?

"To start with, what's the first thing you need to do?"

"What kind of reaction do you think you'll get from them?"

"Thinking again about your plan, what do you see as your next step?"

"What do you plan to do about that?"

What questions did she ask that were inappropriate?

"Don't you think that you should talk with them first?" This is a typical loaded question. It asks the other person to agree with the coach's opinion. It can also be said in a sarcastic or snide way. It puts the other person down because the silent and implied word that the other person hears is "Hey, *dummy*, don't you think that you should talk with them first?" Try to avoid asking loaded questions that can be misinterpreted.

"I'm curious as to why you didn't consider that before you came to me." This kind of query subtly implies that the other person did something wrong and that her motives are suspect. Again—it can be misinterpreted.

"Say, I've got an idea. Why don't you get Bob to help you do it?" The supervisor indeed received an implied "Yes, but..." response to her question. Far better would have been to ask Joan what thoughts she had about the situation.

"How could you even consider such a thing, Joan?" This question is usually a put-down.

"Why don't you let me know toward the end of the week how you are coming along?" This so-called follow-up action on the part of the coach is not specific. The coach can help the coachee by setting a specific time when the two can get together.

What questions could she have asked that she didn't?

"What else do you need to consider?"

"What additional support do you need?"

"How else can I help?"

Betty Ann made several statements that could have been questions. What were they?

"I agree that the executives need to support what you are doing, but I don't agree that that is the first thing you need to do." Better: "I agree that the executives need to support what you are doing. Who else needs to be a part of this action plan, and when should they be contacted?"

"Yeah, but maybe that's exactly why you might have a problem." Better: "Since Bob has been asking for this all along, what do you think will be his reaction to being excluded from the planning?"

This entire statement could have been a question. In the preceding paragraph, Joan said, "Well…I'm not sure. What do you think I should do?" Better: "I'm not sure exactly what the next step should be. Would you like to have more time to think this out, and then we can meet at a later time to review your plan?"

"Right! And since we don't have a license to copy it, we'll all end up in jail." Better: "In light of the fact that this program is copyrighted, how do you plan to obtain it?"

Here are some helpful questions to help the coachee create an action plan.

- What is the first thing that needs to be done now?
- When will it be done?
- Who else needs to be aware of what you are doing?
- If you do that, what could go wrong?
- What is the worst that could happen?
- Who could "deep six" your efforts?
- How can you prevent that problem from occurring?
- If the problem occurs in the future, what can you do now to reduce its seriousness?
- What additional steps should be in the plan?
- What do you think are the chances of pulling this off?
- What else you do need to consider?
- What other resources do you need?
- What support do you need?
- How do you anticipate obtaining that support?
- What is the best that can happen?
- How can I help?

Concluding the coaching session. One good strategy to use in concluding the coaching session is to summarize the discussion to ensure clear understanding. Misunderstandings result when two people think they clearly understand what was said, when in fact they don't. If the coach and the coachee each summarize the key points they made in the discussion, then both will have a solid feeling of accomplishment. The coach can ask "Because I don't always hear what was really said, would you mind summarizing what we have discussed?"

The coach can also ask questions like these:

- What else should we consider before we close out this discussion?
- What other questions do you have?
- When should we meet to discuss your progress?
- What will you have accomplished by that time?

Following up. "If you have any questions, don't hesitate to call" is not following up. Following up means that the *coach* follows up. The coach is the one who takes the initiative and meets with the coachee as needed. If the coach spends quality time in coaching and then fails to follow up, the coachee will have a legitimate reason to believe that the coach doesn't really care. The coach must follow through.

The coach must not over-manage the plan that the coachee has agreed to carry out. On the other hand, he should not abandon the coachee, either! There is a great difference between monitoring someone's efforts and breathing down his or her neck. A coach can walk this line by letting go of the nitty-gritty details of how the plan should be accomplished, and instead schedule times to review the other person's key activities and final results.

When the coach follows up, he or she should acknowledge the coachee for what he or she did that worked as planned. At this review meeting, the coach can ask what the coachee has learned from completing the plan, and what can be done differently in the future.

If things aren't accomplished as well as expected, don't blame the coachee. Instead, help him or her identify ways to accomplish what needs to be done, and look at your role in those plans that were not fully successful. If a coach believes that he or she was part of the difficulty experienced by the coachee, he or she should have the courage to say so.

Good questions to ask:

- How do you feel about your progress in carrying out your plan?
- What did you learn from this experience?
- In hindsight, what would you do differently if you had to do it all over again?
- How else could I have helped you?
- Now that you have completed your original plan, what is the next thing you would like to work on?

*   *   *   *   *

Asking such questions helps you assist the coachee to create better ideas, become more independent, take responsibility for future action, build self-esteem, and feel challenged by what he or she does.

If you coach by asking questions, you don't have to be an expert on what the other person is doing—another benefit!

To make it easier for you to use the steps and the question technique, I've prepared an outline and a simple planning worksheet, which conclude the chapter.

Coaching Questions

To create awareness of the possibility of change, ask three kinds of questions:

"Feeling" questions:

> How do you like doing this?
>
> How do you feel about looking for ways to do this even better?
>
> What concerns do you have about doing this?

"Thinking" questions:

> What are the reasons you do it this way?
>
> What reasons might there be to change the way it's done?
>
> On a scale of 1 to 10, how do you rate yourself on it?
>
> What parts of this are most challenging for you?
>
> What do you see as the reasons why this is challenging?

"Behavior" questions:

> What do you do as you complete this task?
>
> What are the key steps to completing it?

To explore possibilities, ask:

Which things are the greatest challenges?

What bottlenecks exist?

What changes would you like to see in the way it is done?

What other changes could be made?

How would you like to be different from the way you are now?

What things, if any, prevent you from being more effective?

Would you like more time to consider the situation?

Would you like me to make a suggestion, or would you prefer to have more time to think of ideas on your own?

To choose a key area for attention, ask:

Which of these changes should be tackled first?

What have you already done about this?

What were the results of that action?

What are the pluses and minuses of each option?

What are the key factors that should be considered (time, money, personnel, supplies, resources, space, skills, personal effort required, chances of success, and so on)?

What do you think should be the outcome or goal?

Will this get you to your goal?

How will you measure the success of your goal?

To develop an action plan, ask:

What is the first thing that needs to be done now?

When will it be done?

Who else needs to be aware of what you are doing?

If you do that, what could go wrong?

What is the worst that could happen?

Who could "deep six" your efforts?

How can you prevent that problem from occurring?

If the problem occurs in the future, what can you do now to reduce its seriousness?

What additional steps should be in the plan?

What do you think are the chances of pulling this off?

What else you do need to consider?

What other resources do you need?

What support do you need?

How do you anticipate obtaining that support?

What is the best that can happen?

How can I help?

To conclude the coaching session, ask:

What else should we consider before we close out this discussion?
What other questions do you have?
When should we meet to discuss your progress?
What will you have accomplished by that time?

To follow up, ask:

How do you feel about your progress in carrying out your plan?
What did you learn from this experience?
In hindsight, what would you do differently if you had to do it all over again?
How else could I have helped you?
Now that you have completed your original plan, what is the next thing you would like to work on?

9

Improving Employee Performance through Counseling

When Yen Ho was about to take up his duties as tutor to the Duke of Wei, he went to Ch'u Po Yo for advice.

"I have to deal," he said, "with a man of depraved and murderous disposition. How is one to deal with a man of this sort?"

"I'm glad that you asked this question," said Ch'u. "The first thing you must do is not to improve him, but to improve yourself."

— Taoist legend

Employees who are constantly late for work, keep cluttered work areas, and take too much time for breaks and lunch are a pain in the neck for their leaders. The employee usually knows better, so it's not a question of ignorance concerning policies or regulations. Perhaps the manager responds by saying "He is just lazy" or "She really should stop doing that." But somehow these comments—especially when they are expressed to the employee—don't bring about much change. We end up giving formal warnings, and even suspensions. And still there is little permanent change, if any. Why? Possibly it has something to do with us—the leaders!

Have you ever known a leader who had a special knack for addressing his or her employees' problems? A super leader who could take marginal workers and turn them around? Very likely you have. There are many effective leaders who consistently take performance problems and solve them so that they stay solved.

When we look closely at such leaders, we notice that there are certain things they all do—common-sense ways that they handle their "people problems." They seem to have an ability to tell the employee what is expected, get the employee involved in finding a solution, and develop with the employee a plan of action that really seems to work. We'll show you how they conduct counseling discussions with their employees in this chapter.

We'll use the term *"counseling"* to refer to a workplace discussion, initiated and conducted by a leader with his or her employee in order to correct a problem. In most cases, the employee is not meeting acceptable standards of attendance, work habits, or job performance. The leader then analyzes the situation with the employee by describing what is happening and what is expected, determining the probable cause(s), developing solutions, and implementing an action plan for improvement.

Preparation

If you wish to conduct a good counseling discussion with an employee, you must prepare. Counseling is too important to the organization, to leaders, and to the employee to just "wing it." As you will see, counseling is a complex process that requires solid preparation. Let's look now at the key areas you need to cover as you prepare to discuss an employee's performance.

The performance concern. The first thing we should do to prepare for the counseling discussion is to describe the employee's behavior in *specific* and *behavioral* terms. Avoid general statements such as "Jane is not performing satisfactorily," "Bill is not motivated," or "He or she has a poor attitude." Statements like these do not describe behaviors, nor are they specific. Also avoid "absolute" statements that are probably untrue, such as "Tom *never* completes his work on time" or "Joe is *always* late."

The key question to ask yourself is, *What is the employee doing or saying that needs improvement?* For example, consider these nonspecific thoughts:

> *"Her work is not completed in a satisfactory manner."*
> *"He has a poor attitude."*
> *"She talks excessively, and constantly interrupts others."*

You must actually write these things in specific, behavioral terms:

> She is 50% deficient in meeting work quotas, and 20% of her work contains errors (which resulted in 8 to 10 complaints per week).

> He was tardy 8 days out of 10, absent 4 days in the past two months, laid his head on the desk during his training, and made 10 errors this week.

> She interrupts her co-workers at least once every 30 minutes. Does 50% of work during a full work day.

You might find it will take more than one statement to adequately describe the employee's behavior.

Your expectations. The second step in preparing to conduct an employee-counseling discussion is to write out what you expect of this individual. For every statement written about what is going on, there should be a corresponding statement about what it is that you expect.

The key questions to ask yourself are these: What do I expect of this employee? What specific things do I want this employee to do differently? What are the requirements for this employee? Specifically what is 'good' performance? Be specific, and use numbers and/or examples to describe exactly what job performance is required. For example, if you describe the problem as *"The employee is tardy an average of 1 day per work week and has been absent 2 days during the past month,"* we could write a corresponding standard of performance something like *"The employee needs to arrive on or before 8:30 each morning 19 out of 20 times during any 4-week period for the next 6 months."*

Note that our written standards of performance should be realistic. Don't set up the employee for failure. Your job is to create realistic standards in order to help the employee achieve success.

Probable causes for the performance shortfall. A discussion about performance should cover probable causes. The operational work here is *probable*. The realities of the work world are that, in many cases, the leader does not know the real cause of the employee's difficulty in advance of the actual discussion. Therefore, it is important that you state what you think might be the cause of the situation and carefully analyze the possible causes. Just be sure to keep an open mind about what the cause actually is until you talk with the employee.

To gain a better understanding of the variety of causes we should investigate, consider one manager's description of the performance problem he has been asked to help correct:

The Case of the Enigmatic Employee

Betty Anne is 26 years old, married, and has two children. She has been with us for six years, and at one time was one of the best employees in the section. But recently, I have had nothing but problems.

She just seems to have a bad attitude. She will do what's required, but not a whole lot more. Some of the other employees are grumbling a little because she's not doing any extra work when things pile up. As a result, she doesn't seem to be getting along with them like she used to.

Several months ago, I was asked to take on the leadership job of our section. Betty Anne had been here about six months longer than I, but when the leadership job came up, she let everybody know that she didn't want to be a leader. I am almost certain that Betty Anne was asked if she wanted my new job, but I don't know for sure, as I haven't talked about it with my boss.

Getting to work has been a problem for her since the organization moved from downtown to the west end. I suspect that childcare has something to do with that.

Somebody must have said something about the situation to my boss, and now my boss wants me to appraise Betty Anne's performance and submit a plan of action. I'll bet her problem has something to do with arranging transportation for her children.

What do you think is the *one* most-probable cause of Betty Anne's performance problem?

Consider the three basic categories of causes: managerial and organizational shortcomings; the employee's personal factors, and outside influences. Any of the following could be legitimate causes of Betty Anne's performance problem:

- Managerial and organizational shortcomings

  "The new leader and/or management did not communicate appropriately with Betty Anne when the section's promotion was announced."

- The employee's personal factors

  "Betty Anne is not doing any extra work, which results in poor peer relationships."

  "Betty Anne really wanted the leader's job, but chose not to be 'up front' about her needs."

- Outside influences

  "The downtown move has resulted in child care/transportation problems for Betty Anne."

Which most-probable cause did you identify, and in which category does it fall? If you selected the *employee* as the primary cause of the problem, then you are not alone! Almost all of the leaders who have read this case suggest that the employee is the major cause of the problem, and that he or she needs to change in some way. But this case was carefully crafted so that any of the three causes could be selected equally. Why is it, then, that the vast majority of leaders identify causes that are related to the employee?

Could it be that, when looking at employee problems, we tend to focus on the employee rather than on the organization or ourselves? Probably true! But if we don't look at *all* the possible causes as objectively as possible, then we may be taking the right action on the wrong problem. Most employee problems are caused by managerial or organizational shortcomings, personal problems, or outside influences. A list of causes, arranged by category, is presented below.

Performance Shortfalls: Possible Causes

Managerial and Organizational Shortcomings

- Lack of motivational environment
  - No opportunities for advancement
  - No challenge in present job
  - Lack of knowledge of advancement possibilities
  - Not recognizing employee's changing needs
- Personality problems
  - Personal clashes between the employee and his or her leader and/or co-worker
  - Personal clashes with the "personality" of the organization itself
- Inappropriate job assignments
  - Employee doesn't know how to do the job
  - Employee feels it is necessary to take an undesirable job to avoid limiting his or her future chances
- Improper leadership
  - Leader doesn't know how to lead
  - Leader knows how to lead, but doesn't
  - Leader doesn't have time to lead
- Lack of training
- Failure to establish duties
  - Job tasks are not communicated
  - Goals are not set with the employee
  - There are minimal performance expectations

Employee's Personal Factors

- Lack of motivation in the right direction
- Limited goals
- Problem personality
- Dissatisfaction with job assignment
- Failure to understand duties
  - Didn't listen, didn't understand, or forgets
- Chronic absenteeism
  - Alcoholism or other drug-related problems
  - Chronic illness (mental or physical)

Outside Influences

- Family problems
  - Sickness (physical and/or mental)
  - Death of family member
  - Separation and/or divorce
  - Children "acting out"
  - Spouse lost his or her job
- Social morals (conflicts: social values/organizational values)
- Conditions of labor market

Lawrence L. Steinmetz. (1985). *Managing the Marginal and Unsatisfactory Performer,* Addison-Wesley. Reproduced with permission.

Leading theorists say that the leader and/or the organization is often the cause of employee problems. Douglas McGregor proposed that the leader's attitude drastically affects the employee's performance. Abraham Maslow believed that the leader is primarily responsible for creating an environment where the employee's higher-level needs can be met. Frederick Herzberg pointed out that a leader's positive affirmation, or the lack thereof, highly affects an employee's morale and motivation.

The quality of the solution implemented to "fix" the employee's problem is directly dependent on the accuracy of the identified cause. Therefore, it is critical to spend time thinking through probable causes when preparing for and conducting the counseling discussion.

Explore probable causes by thinking through the situation in detail before meeting with the employee. Then determine what facts you have and what facts you need. Be clear about the specific questions you should ask during your discussion with the employee.

Look at past records. Is there an observable pattern? Has the problem always existed? Or is it recent? Do you have enough information? Do you need to talk with others? What is the employee's record, compared with others in your section? In the department? In the organization?

It is remarkable how often we think the cause of a performance problem is one thing, and then we find out during a discussion with the employee that it is something else. The "problem" hasn't changed. We have! New information from the employee can greatly alter our understanding of the problem.

Few things are more frustrating to an employee than to be told to "work harder" when the real cause of a problem is something he or she can't control. You will learn much about what the real difficulty is by taking the time to explore the cause. Any solution that's going to be effective must be based on a sound understanding of the problem and its cause. Therefore, before the meeting, think through possible causes by asking yourself the following questions:

- Is the employee aware of his or her below-standard performance?
- Does he or she know what is expected?
- Are there any factors this employee cannot control?
- Does he or she lack ability or knowledge?
- Is there a lack of motivation?

Thinking through probable causes before the meeting will give you a chance to get additional information if it is needed, but again, remember that these probable causes are only tentative. Your information is incomplete until you talk with the employee.

Tentative solutions. The last step in preparation is to develop a "real world" solution for each of the most likely causes identified. To do this, seek out ideas from other respected leaders and brainstorm a list of possible solutions for each major cause. Then, when you evaluate the quality of the options, you can analyze them before destroying them with sixty-nine reasons why they won't work. Select specific and practical *tentative* solutions for the key causes that you know you can implement or help implement.

The solutions selected are *tentative*. You really won't know for sure what *the* best solution is until you have had an opportunity to talk with the employee. Both the leader *and* the employee need to spend time thinking about what should be done to improve the employee's performance.

In the next section, we will explain how to use the information you have gathered to conduct a counseling discussion with an employee.

Conducting the Counseling Discussion

Having spent quality time in preparing for the counseling session, we are now ready to meet with the employee. Like all meetings of this sort, you should conduct it in private. Set aside a solid block of time so that you will be able to devote your efforts to the meeting without being interrupted.

Some leaders tell the employee the day before, usually in the late afternoon, that the meeting is scheduled for the following day. These same leaders ask the employee to carefully consider the specific situation and come prepared to discuss the cause and suggest solutions. This gives the employee a chance to think about the issue and sometimes seems to improve the quality of the discussion.

The performance concern. Your employee has arrived and is now seated in your office. First, don't expect the employee to improve until he or she knows what is being done incorrectly. In some situations, of course, the employee will not realize that his or her performance is poor. Chewing out an employee who honestly doesn't know a rule or regulation or what you require doesn't make much sense. It would be more appropriate to chew yourself out for doing a poor job of communicating or training in the first place.

When you discuss a situation with the employee, you must focus on performance—not the employee's personality. Stay away from statements such as "You don't work fast enough" or "You have a bad attitude." "Fast enough" is not really specific, and "bad attitude" attacks the employee, rather than giving him needed information about his performance.

Say, "I'm very concerned about this situation," rather than "You have a problem." After all, if you are the leader, it's *your* problem, too!

Then, talk about performance, and in specific terms: "I am concerned because the number of errors has increased 6% during the past month." "Today was the third time this week that you were over five minutes late coming back from break."

This is not always as easy as it sounds. Maybe you know what is wrong but find it difficult to express the "wrongness" in words. It's just easier to make a general statement about "poor attitude" or "poor performance" than to be specific, isn't it?

Stop and ask yourself questions like these: Why do I think this employee has a bad attitude? What has he or she said or done that makes me feel this way?

Questions like these help us understand what an employee says or does. Defining the behavior specifically is a big part of solving the performance problem. But this means you must do your homework by giving the performance problem sufficient thought before you meet with the employee.

Expected performance. Next, describe the required performance specifically. By telling the employee exactly what we expect, we have clearly defined the *performance gap.*

Here, as before, you must be very specific. Avoid making statements like "I expect better performance," "You really need to work harder," or "You ought to change your attitude."

You should know what you expect from this employee. Phrase it simply but specifically. Here are some examples of clear performance expectations:

- "Under standard operating conditions, the maximum error rate allowed is zero."
- "Breaks are ten minutes long."
- "Horseplay of any kind is not allowed."
- "All employees are expected to be here before 8:00 a.m."

Importance of expected performance. Here, you tell the employee why the required performance is important. "Because it's organizational policy" is not a very good justification for a performance standard (at least not from the employee's point of view). It's all right to indicate that something is organizational policy if you explain the rationale behind the policy. Most policies exist for good reasons—and if you don't know the reasons, you had better find out before the meeting!

Consider the regulation or policy from the employee's perspective. Why should the employee arrive at work on time? Why should he or she want to keep the work area clean? Why is it important for the employee to return from breaks on time? Why is it critical that employees earn a return on the organization's investment in salary and benefits?

Why are we concerned about the employee's performance? Our reasons might be things like increased production, looking good to our own boss, a better raise for us in the future, and so on. But these are not the employee's reasons! His or her motivation to do better might be concern about losing a job or wages; pressure from fellow workers; the threat of disciplinary action; or even recognition and praise from you, the boss.

Your objective has to be to foster an internal desire within each employee to improve his or her performance. You can, of course, impose external force to require him or her to change ("You *will* change if you want to keep your job!"). In some cases, this may be necessary, but far better results come when employees decide to improve their performance because of clearly perceived reasons that make sense to them.

Your concern. After you tell the employee why the required performance is important, you now express your expectation that the employee's performance will change. It is important to tell employees that you are personally concerned about their poor performance. After all, you are their leader. If employees feel that substandard performance is no big deal to management, they probably won't take the situation very seriously.

In the press of our duties as leaders, we don't often take the time to spell out how we feel. So how are they supposed to know we are concerned?

This is the time to explain clearly that their poor performance is serious. "I'm deeply concerned about your performance. It's important to the organization, it's important to me, and it should be important to you."

Identifying the cause of the problem. One basic rule in troubleshooting is this: Do nothing until you have identified the probable cause of the problem. This also goes for performance problems.

After you describe in specific terms the employee's performance, state what you expect, spell out why the performance is important, and express your concern, the next step is to help the employee discover the cause of the problem. Ask questions to explore possible causes, but try to ask *open* questions, because they draw out more information than "closed" questions (which can be answered with a simple yes or no—getting you nowhere).

The question, "What relationship do you see between absenteeism and performance?" is likely to generate much more information than "Do you see any relationship between absenteeism and your performance?" We need information to determine causes, and open questions are best for getting it.

- When do you think this situation first started? When was everything okay?
- Where is the problem occurring? Where is it not occurring?
- What do you see is the cause of this situation?
- Why do you think this is occurring?

To help the employee look at all sides of a problem, we can also ask, "What other things might be causing this situation?" Solutions (the next step) only work if they fit the cause, however. That's why spending time to identify the cause is so important. Take your time on this step. The cause of the problem must be accurately identified before you have any chance of really correcting the performance problem.

The employee's own ideas. After you and the employee have identified a probable cause of the situation, you are now ready to determine a solution. Here, the employee might think of a solution that you have not considered that's even better than yours. But more importantly, the employee is more likely to change behavior when the solution comes from him or her.

You were probably promoted to leadership because you are good at solving problems, so this step might be a hard one. Naturally, you will have some strong ideas about what the employee should do in order to improve. Nonetheless, don't share them now. Instead, ask the employee for theirs.

Remember: What is important is not so much what the employee says at the meeting, but what he or she does *after* the meeting to improve performance. If the employee suggests the solution or is a part of the solution plan, he is more likely to view the idea as workable and accept the responsibility of making sure that the solution is implemented on the job. So we ask questions in the meeting:

- "What do you think we should do about this situation?"
- "What other things can we do?"

Note: It's sometimes easier to change the environment around a problem than it is to change the employee. If the employee has a trashy work area, the solution might be as simple as putting a trash can closer to the employee's work area.

Ask the employee to be specific about what should be done. "I guess I'll just have to try harder" isn't enough. Ask "How are you going to do that?" or "What are you going to do to improve your performance?" If he says, "I'll try to improve my performance," ask "How much can you improve?" The more specific the improvement target or goal, the better the employee's chances of producing real results.

Initially, few employee ideas are perfect. On the other hand, completely useless solutions are also rare. Most ideas and solutions fall somewhere between perfection and "zero," as can be seen in the shaded area of this diagram:

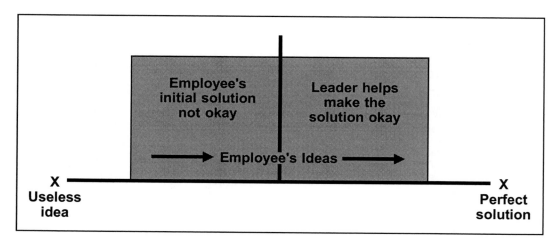

Quality Leadership Skills

If the employee's solution is not acceptable as first suggested, you can ask "How to" questions to help enhance the employee's solution ("What would that accomplish?" "How do you see this being done?" "What can you do to help make that happen?") Your job in this step is to first help the employee develop a specific solution by asking key questions, and then to help them refine and improve it. Keep in mind, however, that effective leaders focus on the positive aspects of employee suggestions and refrain from immediately jumping to what's wrong with an idea. Once you both have discussed the positive aspects, suggest ways to improve the quality of his or her solution.

Follow-up action. Close the discussion by summarizing what you have agreed on to seal the employee's commitment and reduce the possibility of later misunderstanding. Make clear your expectations by communicating to the employee the specific action that you expect to take.

Some leaders make notes on their calendar in the presence of the employee about a follow-up date and the improvement expected. Other leaders have the employee write out a short summary of what he or she will accomplish during the improvement period, with both parties keeping a copy. Whatever method you use, be sure to summarize. And then follow up!

A "Leader's Checklist" that will help you plan and conduct your next employee performance counseling interview closes the chapter.

Performance Counseling Discussion
Leader's Checklist

☐ 1. **Start the discussion by describing the performance problem that you are concerned about.**

- Make sure you have gathered all the relevant facts (from supervisors, co-workers, and so on).
- Use the "We" technique ("We have a situation that concerns me.")
- Be specific. State what the employee has done or not done or said or not said, that makes you believe that he or she is performing poorly.

    "Today was the third time this week that you were over five minutes late coming back from lunch."

- Describe the poor performance only. Do not get personal.

    "The number of errors has increased 6% during the past month."

    "The records show there have been ten days of absenteeism during the past three months."

    "The area around your work station is messy, and material spilled on the floor has not been picked up."

☐ 2. **Describe the performance you expect.**

- Tell the employee exactly what is expected of them.

    "Under standard operating conditions, the maximum allowed error rate is 1 error per 1,000."

(continued)

Improving Employee Performance through Counseling

"Breaks are ten minutes."

"Material should not be on the floor."

☐ 3. **Explain why the expected performance is important.**

- Provide the reasons behind a policy, regulation, or performance standard.

- Provide "employee" reasons, if possible—reasons that relate to the employee's personal interest.

  "This much absenteeism causes a real hardship for the rest of the people in your section."

  "The policy of 'no horseplay' is for your protection. It could prevent you from having an accident that might cripple you for the rest of your life."

  "We must meet performance standards so that the organization will continue to stay in business and so you will continue to have a job."

☐ 4. **Express your concern.**

"I am and always will be deeply concerned about performance. It's important to the organization, it's important to me, and it's important for you. To me, excellence is a way of life. The organization believes in it; and my employees must not only believe in excellence, but practice it!"

☐ 5. **Identify the cause of the situation.**

- Before and during the meeting, gather information relevant to the problem:

  How this employee's record compares with the records of others in the section or department

  Any observable patterns in this employee's poor performance (Mondays or Fridays, holidays, particular time of year, etc.)

  How long this problem has gone on

  When it started

  Where the problem is occurring

  The time when this isn't a problem

  Changes that might have caused the problem

  Other symptoms of this problem

- Ask the employee:

  "What do you feel is causing this situation?"

  "What other major reasons do you see?"

  "What are the things that interfere with your performance?"

(continued)

Remember: You are both looking at the problem and its likely causes, but it isn't up to you to decide what caused it. Let the employee develop insight into what has happened and what can be done about it.

☐ **6. Ask for solutions.**

- Discuss the employee's solution first.

   "What are your ideas about this situation?"

   "What suggestions do you have for improving your performance?"

   "What can you do to resolve this situation?"

   "What else can you do?"

- Focus on specific solutions, not general ones.

   "What would that accomplish?"

   "How do you see thing being done?"

   "What can you do to help make that happen?"

   "What can be done to make this work?"

   "Do you see any roadblocks to prevent you from carrying that out?"

- Offer your assistance.

   "How can I help?"

☐ **7. Agree on specific action for follow-up.**

   "This has been a good discussion. I appreciate your ideas and solutions. We have agreed that you will... and I will... (summarize the solution). Is that correct?

   "Good. We'll get together in two weeks (make a note of the date and time on your calendar) and discuss your progress. I feel good about your commitment to improve, and I know you can do it."

Counseling Discussion: Self-Assessment

Immediately after the employee leaves your office area, fill out this form. Then meet with your supervisor to discuss the results.

Name of Employee: _____ Date of Discussion: _____

The performance concern:

How well did I describe the employee's situation?

Did the employee get defensive? ☐ Yes ☐ No
If yes, why do you think that was the case?

The expected performance:

How well was I able to describe the expected standard of performance?

What reasons did I give for its importance?

Were these the employee's reasons, or my reasons?

What could I have done or said that would have been more effective?

Your concern:

How did I show my concern?

The cause:

What questions did I ask?

Did I get to the root cause of the situation? ☐ Yes ☐ No
If not, what do I think is the real cause?

Solutions:

What solutions did the employee come up with?

How successful was I in getting the employee to do most of the talking?

How specific did we get in the final solution?

What assistance did I offer?

Counseling Discussion: Self-Assessment (continued)

Specific action for follow-up:

Summarize the action steps agreed upon.

General thoughts/questions about the discussion:

How do I feel about the discussion?

How do I think the employee feels, as a result of the performance discussion?

What do I think are the chances for improvement?

What else can I do?

10

Handling Employee Concerns

It's no accident that your maker created you with two ears and only one mouth.

– Unknown

When an employee storms into a manager's office furious about something, it is hard to remain calm. Some leaders assert their authority and chew out the employee for being disrespectful or out of control. But look at the cost of this approach: An employee who has a chip on their shoulder can create ill will among co-workers and negatively affect morale and efficiency. He or she might even be an accident looking for a place to happen.

One of a leader's responsibilities is to protect the organization, and angry employees present a safety risk. Deal immediately with the employee's feelings before you take any action.

In this chapter, we present a method that works.

Listening

Real listening is hard work! Do not under any circumstances jump in and cut the employee off, and do not tell him or her what you think or feel. Hold your tongue and listen, without interrupting, in order to:

- Learn more about the situation.
- Demonstrate that you really care about the individual.
- Give yourself more time to think about how the situation can best be handled.
- Give the employee an opportunity to express his or her feelings, thus reducing the emotional level.

Stop doing whatever it was you were doing and attend, make good eye contact, nod your head appropriately, and respond minimally. Encourage the employee to vent as long as is necessary.

Summarize

After the individual has finished, use your own words to summarize what you think you heard. Then ask if what you heard was correct. This accomplishes three things:

- You will confirm that what you thought you heard was what was really said.
- It shows the employee that you care.
- It lets the employee know that you really do understand what he or she is upset about.

109

It's sometimes hard to listen to even one or two minutes of emotional statements without interrupting, and it's even harder to remember all that was said. But when we know that we will have to sum up and repeat what we just heard, we tend to listen better. And when we summarize, we show the employee that we care enough to pay attention.

Acknowledge the employee's feelings. You do not have to agree with what the individual is saying, but you do have to show that his or her feelings are real. And he or she needs to know that you respect his or her right to have such feelings. This is a very critical step.

Before moving on to the next step, please read the scenario that follows and answer the question at the end.

The Case of the Wrathful Worker: Part 1

Jodi, the section's supervisor, leaned back in her chair, looked out the window, and thought about her day so far. It had not been good. Everyone seemed to want a piece of her time. "Jodi, would you be willing to help me design this report?" "Jodi, I can't get my computer to save this document. What do I do?" *Jodi do this, Jodi do that.* She sighed as she considered all of her own work she had yet to do because she had to help others.

Suddenly, she heard an angry voice in the hallway. As she looked up, Bill stormed in. Jodi knew that her day was not going to get any better!

"Somebody opened a personal letter that was addressed to me!" shouted Bill, waving an envelope in her face. "Nobody, but nobody has the right to open and read my personal mail! If a letter is addressed to me, then I am the only one who has the right to open it."

"Well," Jodi replied, "I can see that you're really angry that your private mail was read. I would be angry, too, if someone had read mine. But in this case, it was probably just opened by mistake in the mail room."

"Then somebody needs to raise hell with those jerks in the mailroom," Bill replied angrily.

"I'll tell you what," Jodi said. "I will make a point to talk to the mailroom supervisor and ask her about it." Jodi reached for her notepad. "Who was the letter from?"

Bill looked embarrassed. "Well, uh, it's a final late notice from the finance company about my car payment. I don't know why they sent it to me at work, but in any case, it should never have been opened."

"You're right," Jodi said, "It should *not* have been opened! I'll talk to the mailroom supervisor and make sure that it doesn't happen again."

"Thanks, Jodi," Bill replied. "It's downright embarrassing for this to be read by others. Let me know what you find out."

"Okay, Bill," she said. "I will make sure that it doesn't happen again."

As Bill left, Jodi could hear him muttering about those incompetent, brain-dead people in the mailroom.

Question: What action would you take now, if you were Jodi?

The Case of the Wrathful Worker: Part 2

Jodi sighed as Bill left her office. *Oh well,* she thought. *What's one more thing in an otherwise lousy day?* She took the elevator down to the mailroom, walked in, and asked for Betty, the supervisor. "She's on break," one of the clerks said.

Jodi took the elevator back up to the third floor and looked in the break room. Spotting Betty at one of the tables with a group of other supervisors, Jodi walked over and asked, "Betty, can I see you for a minute?"

"Sure," Betty replied as she got up from the table. "I'm finished here."

The two women walked over to the corner of the room. Jodi told her about what had happened with Bill.

"I remember that letter," Betty responded. "It was not actually addressed to Bill. It was addressed to the accounts payable department. They sent it back to me after they opened it, and I sent it on to Bill."

"I'm confused," replied Jodi. "Who was it addressed to?"

Betty rubbed her chin. "Well, if I remember correctly, it was a little confusing. I *do* know that it was addressed to the accounts payable department, but referenced Bill's name on the envelope. Evidently they opened it, saw that it was actually supposed to go to him, and sent it back through interoffice mail. But we definitely don't open anyone's personal mail! It irritates me that someone would think we did!"

Jodi looked at her watch. "Okay. I'm sorry to have bothered you about it. Let me go back and talk to Bill and find out what happened."

Jodie took the elevator back up to her area and walked over to Bill's desk. "Bill, can I see the envelope to that letter?"

"Sure," he replied. He opened one of his desk drawers and handed her the letter.

She looked at the address:

> Reference: Mr. Bill Williams
> Accounts Payable
> The Sorata Organization
> Box 299012
> Richmond, VA 23235-9012

"Bill," Jodi exclaimed, "I've wasted almost forty-five minutes complaining to the mailroom about a letter that was obviously addressed incorrectly. Look at this address. It was sent to you at your work address, and was supposed to say 'Mr. Bill Williams, Reference Accounts Payable. And why are they sending this notice to your work address?"

"Oh," replied Bill sheepishly. "At the time, I was planning to move to a new apartment, so I had everything sent to me here. Sorry I put you to so much trouble."

What should Jodi have done before she went to the mailroom?

Jodi's mistake was jumping to some sort of action before first identifying the *cause* of the problem.

Ask diagnostic questions. An effective leader is also a good troubleshooter. And good trouble-shooters ask questions to diagnose the cause of a problem.

In some cases, you will already know the full details of the situation. The employee might not know that you know, however. Asking questions at this point might generate additional information, but it serves another purpose as well: The employee will also know that you really do understand the situation.

Be sure to ask *open* questions that begin with the words, "Who," "What," "Where," "When," "How," and "Why" because you want information.

Ask for the employee's suggestions. Get the employee to tell you what should be done. Employees are usually more open to their own ideas than to ours. And if their solution is in line with yours, why not let them suggest it? Leaders who use this technique say that many times, the employee's idea or solution turns out to be better than their own.

Present your position. If you agree with the employee's idea or solution to the problem, say so. If you don't, clearly state your position and give your rationale. Avoid the "It's organizational policy" kind of answer. Employees respond better if we give common-sense reasons for our position.

Agree on an action plan. At this point, the leader should summarize the discussion and agree on any action that will be taken. This helps to prevent later misunderstandings by making sure the leader and the employee agree on what will happen after the discussion.

Thank the employee. Be sure you thank the employee for coming in. What? Thank an employee who barged into your office and raised his or her voice? Yes!

Angry or upset employees are poor workers. They can cause reduced production and create lower morale. Thanking the employee for coming to see you sends the signal that they should feel comfortable coming in again. It also improves your image as a leader who cares about every employee, and ends the meeting on a positive, morale-building note.

This eight-step method for handling complaints comes from the experience of leaders who care about their employees—leaders whose main responsibility is to get the job done through others. Effective leaders know that organizations don't run by themselves. Using this method will help you be a better leader, not just a "boss."

Now, here are the steps to addressing employee dissatisfaction:

1. Listen.
2. Summarize what you think you heard.
3. Acknowledge the employee's feelings.
4. Ask diagnostic questions.
5. Ask the employee for suggestions.
6. Present your position.
7. Decide on specific follow-up action.
8. Thank the employee for calling your attention to the problem.

Handling Concerns:
Checklist

☐ 1. **Listen.**

> Focus your attention on the employee.
> Nod your head to show understanding.
> Say "Yes," "I see," or "Uh-huh" as the employee talks.

☐ 2. **Summarize what you think you heard.**

> "Let me see if I understand. You are upset because…

> Repeat in your own words what you heard. Then ask, *"Is that correct?"*

☐ 3. **Acknowledge the employees feelings.**

> "I understand how you feel."
> "I can appreciate your concern."

☐ 4. **Ask diagnostic questions.**

> "Who is and isn't involved?"
> "What has occurred?"
> "Where is the problem occurring?"
> "Where is the problem not occurring?"
> "When did it start?"
> "When was everything okay?"
> "Why do you think it happened?"

☐ 5. **Ask for the employee's suggestions.**

> "What do you think we should do about the situation?"
> "What other suggestions do you have?"

☐ 6. **Present your position.**

> If the employee's suggestion in Step 5 is acceptable, say so. If the suggestion does not seem appropriate, present your position.

> "I'm sorry; I really wish we could do that. But we can't, because… What I suggest we do is…"

☐ 7. **Decide on specific follow up.**

> "Now let's see. I will… And you will… Do we agree?"

☐ 8. **Thank the employee.**

> "I really appreciate your coming to me with your concerns. And if you have any other questions about this, please feel free to talk with me about them."

Handling Concerns: Self-Assessment

1. How well did I listen to the employee?

2. What was the employee's original complaint?

3. How accurate was my summary?

4. What did I say to show empathy for the employee's feelings?

5. What (if any) questions did I ask?

6. What ideas did the employee have?

7. If the employee's suggestion was okay, what did I say?

8. If the employee's suggestion was not okay, how did I handle it?

9. What follow-up action was agreed to?

10. How did I thank the employee and express my appreciation for their participation?

Part 3

The Process of Leadership

11

Delegation

Do you take work home at least twice a week? Do you often feel overworked and over-stressed because you have too much to do? Do you keep missing your important deadlines? Do you have to deal with constant, recurring crises? Do you find that you don't have time for important issues, such as long-range planning? Do you spend significant time putting Band-Aids on symptoms of problems, rather than fixing the problems themselves? Do you think that if you don't do it, it won't get done? Do you enjoy doing things for others (especially your employees)?

If you answered yes to one or more of these questions, you may have a problem and possibly a very serious one—a problem that can kill you figuratively and literally!

Not being able to delegate is a killer. The stress from it can stop your heart. And even if you survive the stress, it can kill your chances of ever being considered suitable for more responsibility.

The more responsibility we are given as we move up the promotional ladder, the more important it is to delegate. It's just an organizational reality. In fact, a promotion is a formalized, ritualistic way of delegating, because the organization takes all of our work and delegates it to someone else. So if you can't delegate, your chances of being promoted are slim.

Of course, there are some tasks that can't be delegated. It's hard to delegate a task that can't be taught or to delegate leadership aspects of our jobs that only we can do or tasks that have an unacceptable risk of failure. But in most cases, we not only can delegate—we *should*.

Why delegate?

There are many important reasons why leaders need to delegate work to their subordinates. Leaders delegate work because...

- They are so overworked that they have no choice but to delegate.

- They're ambitious and know that the higher up they move in the organization, the more they will have to delegate.

- They need to free themselves to do more critical and important tasks.

- They don't want to do a task. In fact, they can't stand doing it!

The first four reasons listed above focus on the leader—that is, why the leader benefits from delegating tasks. The following reasons are why the employee benefits:

- It might make more sense to delegate the task to the employee because of the relationship of the task to the employee's job.

- The employee might be better suited to do the job.

117

- The task might provide the employee opportunities for recognition.

- Delegation usually increases the motivation of employees in that their jobs become more challenging.

- The task is specialized, and someone else has skills to do it that the leader doesn't possess.

Let's look at how we can delegate effectively, with a high probability of success.

How to Delegate

There is a logical, step-by-step way for new leaders to learn how to delegate. If you are a veteran boss who doesn't delegate much, use the information to enhance your leadership skills!

Preparing to delegate. The first step in delegation is to identify the key tasks in your job, as well as your authority level for each task. Suppose I am the director of program development in my old company. The first thing I would do is to list all of the major tasks in my job on a job analysis worksheet like this one:

Job Analysis Worksheet

1. **Task List**

    Write proposals and reply to proposal requests.
    Make presentations to key potential clients.
    Attend training shows (two per year).
    Attend professional meetings (monthly).
    Research content for training modules.

Next, determine your "authority level" for each of these tasks. Since I am here playing the role of program development director, I will imagine that I had a kind, lovable, wonderful boss named Dick Leatherman, who was terrific at delegating. As Dick's employee, I will review my task list to decide which of the following authority levels I have concerning each task:

Level 1 = I have total authority to do the task. It is a routine part of my job.
Level 2 = I can do the task, but *after* it is done I need to let Dick know that I did it.
Level 3 = I need to check with Dick *before* I do the task.

Then, I carefully evaluate each task to determine 1) if it's a task that I can delegate, and 2) whether or not I want to delegate it. I might also choose not to delegate a specific task for one reason or another.

Here is a sample of how I might look at my delegating option:

Task	Authority Level			Delegate?			To Whom?	Notes
	1	2	3	No	Maybe	Yes		
Write proposals and reply to proposal requests.		X			X			
Make presentations to key potential clients.		X			X			Consider doing this as a team with Jack until he learns.
Attend training shows (two per year).	X					X	Matt	
Attend professional meetings (monthly).	X			X				
Write training modules.	X					X	Mary	Delegate only the content research at this time.

Tasks such as "Make presentations to key potential clients" or "Write training modules" are ones that I might be able to delegate, but probably only portions of them. I should be able to delegate several other tasks when I have the time to invest in training and the employees who can take on the responsibility.

After completing a job analysis worksheet to decide which parts of your job to delegate, think about how these tasks should be delegated and to whom. Ask yourself these questions:

Which tasks can be done better at a lower level? What is the lowest level that can handle the task?

Which tasks are leadership tasks that cannot be delegated (for example, taking disciplinary action, handling confidential matters, or giving rewards and recognition to others as the leader)?

Are there any problems that stand in the way of delegating a task?

- Is there time to delegate the task?
- Does my boss have a problem with my delegating this task?
- What is the risk if the employee fails in the delegated task? Is the risk acceptable?
- What is the complexity of the task (i.e., can the task be taught in a reasonable amount of time)?

Who is best suited to take on the task?

- Is there someone who can do it better than I can?
- Will the individual be overloaded if he or she takes on this additional responsibility? If so, are there aspects of his or her work that could be delegated to others?
- Does this individual want this additional responsibility?
- Will performing this task help the individual grow and develop?

Is it better to split up the task into several subtasks and assign each part to a different employee (thus lightening the load, and giving each person a chance to show what he or she can do)?

What should the employee's authority level be for the delegated work?

- What is a successful performance of the task? How will you and the employee know that the delegated task has been done well?
- What will a specific training plan look like for this employee on this task?
- Who else should be informed that this task is going to be delegated?

At the end of this chapter you will find a delegation planning worksheet that you can copy and use as a guide in thinking through these questions. And as you make decisions about tasks to be delegated, you can note this information on your job analysis worksheet, as I did in my example.

You should develop complete training plans for more-complex tasks before meeting with your employees. Here is an example of a plan that I, as the hypothetical director of program development, could use to train one of my employees:

Task to be delegated: Attend training shows (two per year).

Employee Training Plan

Activities	Date to be Completed
1. Order booklet: "Working the Show"	Today
2. Review and list our show objectives	1 June
3. Design a check sheet for the show	3 June
4. Schedule a meeting with Matt	4 June
5. Meet with Matt to:	6 June
• Discuss show objectives	
• List items to bring (books, video-player and monitor, training modules, catalogs, business cards, etc.)	
• Review list of workshops to attend	
• Review list of distributors' booths to visit	
• Discuss making face-to-face client contacts	
• Set follow-up meeting to review Matt's progress	
6. Hold a follow-up meeting with Matt	1 July

Describing the task. After you have identified what to delegate and to whom and have designed a training plan, set up meetings with these employees to discuss the tasks that will be assigned. In this step, tell them:

- What needs to be done
- Why it needs to be done
- How the delegated task fits the overall objectives of the section or department
- *Suggestions* as to how the task could be completed

- Whom he or she needs to contact to complete the task
- Expected results
- Priority of this task relative to other tasks in the employee's job
- When to start on the task, and by what date it should be finished
- Any other needed information—especially things that we know but do not have in writing

Providing training if necessary. If the employee does not know how to perform the task, you might need to provide additional training. First plan out the training using the Delegation Planning Worksheet. Then, meet with these employees individually and tell them how to do the task. Next, *show* them how to do it. Finally, let them *do* the task while you observe them doing it, showing respect for their efforts throughout.

Offering help. Good leaders recognize that employees will feel a little anxious about taking on a new responsibility. Reduce your employee's natural anxiety by offering to help pave the way by talking to co-workers who will be affected by the delegation of this task. You may need to delegate part of the employee's old job to someone else in order for this employee to have time to perform the new task. Show that you care about the employee and will do everything possible to ensure his or her success in the new task.

However, do not over-manage a delegated task. It is far better for the employee if you allow him or her to handle the new assignment. Don't "abandon" the employee, or breathe down his or her neck. Just let go of the nitty-gritty details of how the task should be done, and schedule times when the two of you can get together to review the employee's key activities and final results. This will significantly increase the employee's self-confidence. The employee might even figure out a way to do the task better than you did.

Dennis LaMountain, an internationally known organizational consultant, has an interesting way of looking at this issue. He believes that most people have delegation style tendencies that affect the way in which they help others. Read each of his situations on the following pages that typify what leaders encounter on the job.

In each of the cases, there are four possible ways of handling the situation. While none of the ways may be exactly the one you would choose, select one of the four statements following each case *that most nearly describes the way you would handle each situation.*

SITUATION #1: "No One Else Is Available"

You've been preparing a statistical report every month for the past several years. You finally decide to have one of your employees do the monthly reports in order to free up your time for other things. It would be an important learning experience for someone. But for whom? The only person who has time available and knows something about statistics hasn't been on board very long. But you decide to try him. After explaining the task to him, however, he seems a bit overwhelmed. He says:

"Well…, yes. It sounds like a challenge. But I'll have to tell you that I haven't done anything quite like this before, and it sounds pretty important to get it right. Are you sure you want me to do it?"

* * *

Assume that you would begin by telling him you have confidence that he can do the report. Then, you would most likely do what? (Give your first choice 4 points, second choice 3 points, third choice 2 points, and last choice 1 point.)

_____ A. Show him step-by-step how you have been preparing the report and the way you want it to look.

_____ B. Say that although you are available if absolutely necessary, you would prefer that he take the initiative of preparing a first draft of the report on his own.

_____ C. Show him samples of previous reports, and ask him questions to get him to think through the process for himself.

_____ D. Get him started doing it while you watch, making suggestions or correcting him as necessary.

SITUATION #2: "The Missing Shipment"

You have just finished reading a note from Jane, one of your more experienced and reliable employees. The note says that the BMI shipment has not yet arrived at its destination and Jane is having trouble tracking it down. Both of you know that this shipment will provide the basis for a key demonstration at 8:00 a.m. tomorrow morning. You still have the note in your hand when Jane appears at your door, out of breath and looking a little panicky. She exclaims:

"Good! I'm glad you saw my note and I caught you in! I'm afraid we won't find the shipment in time. That meeting tomorrow is very important. Maybe you should take over."

* * *

Assume that you would first obtain more information on the problem from Jane. Then, you would most likely give 4 points, 3 points, 2 points, and 1 point to which of the following:

_____ A. Remind her that it is her responsibility, and that you are confident that she can handle it.

_____ B. Ask her what she plans to do to correct the situation, and help her think through the resolution of the problem.

_____ C. Tell her exactly what needs to be done to correct the situation in time for the demonstration.

_____ D. Leave her in charge, but explain how she should handle the more-critical aspects of the problem.

SITUATION #3: "The Great Idea"

One week ago, you interviewed and hired a new employee. It was clear to you at the time that she had all the necessary skills and capabilities for the job, as well as all kinds of ideas about the way that things should be done. Although you liked her enthusiasm, you did not agree with all of her ideas. Just now, she called to say she wanted to see you about a great idea. You invited her into your office, and she said:

"I have a great idea for reformatting the monthly report—really give it eye appeal, and make it easier to understand the numbers. I'm sure I know how to use the computer graphics program well enough to generate some really snazzy charts and graphs before our Tuesday deadline. What do you say?"

* * *

You would most likely:

_____ A. Tell her that you have had some similar thoughts, and that you would like to work with her on the graphs. Coach her on the best appearance and rule out any unworkable ideas.

_____ B. Commend her for having a good idea. Tell her you will give it some thought and then show her how you would like the graphs and new format to look.

_____ C. Ask her some general questions to see how well she has thought this idea through. If she is on the right track, give her a "go-ahead," but ask to see the final draft.

_____ D. Commend her for her idea, and tell her to go ahead with the project. Then tell her you are available if she needs any help. Ask to see the final draft Monday afternoon.

SITUATION #4: "Sloppy Documentation"

Pat is one of your more experienced and trusted employees. He came to you recently to say that he has some time on his hands and wondered if you have any special projects that he could take on. For some time, you had been thinking that documentation in the department is far too haphazard and inconsistent in quality. You call Pat in, explain your concern to him, and tell him that you would like to see the department prepare and stick to one format for documentation. You ask him if he would be interested in that kind of a project. He responds:

"Yeah, I would. Should have suggested that myself. I agree with you about our documentation, and I've seen a lot better formats. Sounds like an interesting project!"

*   *   *

You would most likely:

_____ A. Ask Pat what specific criteria he thinks the format should include, offer suggestions if necessary, and then ask him to prepare a sample of the kind of format he would recommend.

_____ B. Outline for Pat the general characteristics of the format that you would like to see, and then ask him to prepare a sample that would meet the criteria you have suggested.

_____ C. Ask Pat to go ahead and prepare a sample of the kind of format that he would like to see become the standard for the department.

_____ D. Explain to Pat the format you have in mind, and ask him to make sure that all other documentation conforms to this format.

One of the major considerations in effective delegation is the leader's selection of the most effective level of involvement in the delegated assignment. In each of the situations you just faced, we asked you to experience these kinds of decisions, forcing you to choose between four different levels of personal involvement in the delegated assignment. These levels of involvement are often referred to as delegation styles: Tell and Instruct; Reason and Persuade; Question and Involve; and Assign and Monitor.

Leaders who "command and control" have total personal involvement and essentially keep the responsibility for the project. At the other end of the spectrum are leaders who have total lack of involvement in the project. Of course, these are two extremes; it is unusual for any leader to actually delegate in this way.

A leader's willingness to accept risk or uncertainty will determine his or her delegation style. If I am willing to accept a high degree of risk, then I am more apt to be less involved with my employee. Conversely, if risk is scary to me, then I am apt to be more controlling.

This relationship is illustrated in the following graph showing the impact of various delegation styles as a result of the leader's need to avoid risk and his or her involvement in the delegated task.

Involvement and Delegation Style

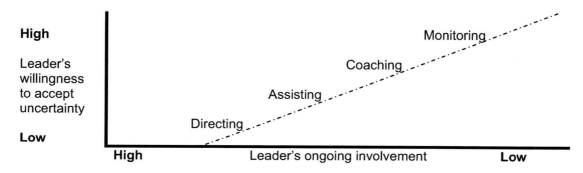

At the four points along the graph's diagonal line, we have indicated delegation style. Note that these labels do not imply that the leader has a fixed style that does not change. On the contrary, effective leaders move up and down along this diagonal line in order to use the approach or style that best suits the individual who is assigned the delegated task and the specific task that is assigned.

The four styles can be described as follows:

Directing. Here, the leader delegates the assignment, but tells and instructs the delegatee exactly how the assignment is to be done. This style of delegation is especially appropriate for new employees or when we assign a new task to a less-experienced employee.

Assisting. The leader assumes that the delegatee is capable of handling some of the assignment without specific instructions. The leader, however, thoroughly explains the more difficult or risky aspects of the task.

Coaching. The leader defines the expected end result, and then asks a few questions to see if the employee has a good idea about the way that the assignment could be completed.

Monitoring. The leader defines the expected end result, and then allows the employee to reach that end in his or her own way.

I believe that most of us have a natural delegation style that we feel the most comfortable using. Knowing which style we tend to use most often and most effectively has a positive impact on our leadership performance. Nevertheless, we are capable of learning to use other styles effectively when needed.

Following up. Follow up when the task is completed so you can give the employee feedback on performance, good and not so good. At this time, you can let the employee know specifically what he or she did that you liked and what you didn't like. You can suggest concrete ways in which the employee's performance could be improved, or explain how a satisfactory performance can be made even better. Finally, you can ask the employee what he or she learned from the experience and what he or she intends to do differently in the future.

Remember, also, that more often than not, you bear some of the responsibility for the employee's performance if things aren't accomplished as well as expected. Therefore, when providing feedback, be sure to let the employee know when you think you are part of a particular problem. Avoid blaming an employee for what goes wrong. Instead, simply make sure that the employee knows how to do it properly the next time.

Summary

Delegate every day. When an employee asks, "What should I do?" respond by asking, "What do you feel you should do? What do you think is the best thing to do?"

Stop rubber-stamping. Are you signing documents just because you're the *boss?* Do you make your employees come to you for approval because you are the boss? Do you make all the contacts with people outside the organization? Do you make all the presentations to others in the organization? If this is you, then you are a *boss,* not a leader! And you need to begin delegating.

Here is an example of poor delegation:

At a university that shall remain nameless, competent adjunct teachers are trusted with the awesome responsibility of teaching adult students and helping them with their journey to obtain a degree. Yet these teachers are required to obtain approval for the customary $50 honorarium paid to guest speakers. They are required to obtain written approval before approaching the possible guest speaker. When they have official approval, the teachers must return to the guest. If the guest says "yes," he or she also signs the form. Finally, the teacher is required to submit a formal request for the $50. What a waste of time! What a degrading process to require these mature, experienced teachers to endure. This is a typical example of bureaucracy at its worst, and it destroys morale. Far better would be to allow the teachers to authorize the $50 honorarium and then submit the paperwork only after the speaker completes his or her task. If there was concern about the budget, the teachers could be given a limit on guest speakers per semester.

At the end of this chapter, you will find three forms:

- A Delegation Job Analysis Worksheet for you to use to evaluate your job for delegation possibilities

- A Delegation Planning Worksheet that you can use to plan exactly how a specific task should be delegated

- A Delegation Evaluation Worksheet that you can use as a guide in evaluating your performance on a delegated task

Ask your employees, if you have the courage, how you can improve your delegation skills.

What could you have done that would have made it easier for them to do the tasks that you delegated?

Should you have provided more training?

Met with them more often? Less often?

Did you provide them with the authority to do the task?

Did you let them do it?

Did you take over, or take back, the job?

Ask your employees for feedback on what you did well in delegating and how you can improve the next time.

Delegation: Job Analysis Worksheet

Task	Authority Level			Delegate?			To Whom?	Notes
	1	2	3	No	Maybe	Yes		

Delegation: Planning Worksheet

Task to be delegated: _____

Task assigned to: _____

Date task assigned:	Date task to be started:	Date task to be completed:
_____	_____	_____

1. **Is this person best suited to take on this new responsibility?**

   How well can the individual do the task?

   How willing is the individual to take on the additional responsibility?

   How will doing this task help the individual grow and develop?

   How does this task play to the employee's strengths?

   What problems might this employee have in completing this task?

   How overloaded will the individual be if he or she takes on this additional responsibility?

   Can any of his or her present responsibilities be delegated to others? If so, what work should be delegated, and to whom?

   Would it be better to split up this task into several subtasks and assign each part to a different employee (lightening the load, and giving several people a chance to show what they can do)? If so, what are my plans to accomplish this?

   Is there someone else who could perform this task better?

   If so, who?

   State the reasons why the task is assigned to the above-named person.

2. **What problems stand in the way of delegating this task?**

How much time (training and follow up) is required to delegate this task?

Is there time to delegate this task?

If not, how will I be able to find the time?

Does my boss have a problem with my delegating this task?

What is the risk if the employee fails in this delegated task?

How acceptable is the risk?

How could the risk(s) be reduced?

What is the complexity of this task (i.e., Can the task be taught in a reasonable amount of time?)

What should be the employee's authority level for the delegated task?

3. **What is a successful performance of this task?**

How will you and the employee know that the delegated task has been performed well?

What things should not happen in doing this task?

4. **Who else should be informed that this task is going to be delegated?**

5. **Employee training plan (if needed):**

Activities	Date Completed:

Delegation: Leader's Evaluation Worksheet

To be filled out by the *leader* on his or her employee.

Employee: _____ Date form completed: _____

Individual completing this form: _____

Delegated task:

What was the quality of the completed task?

What did this employee do well in completing this task?

What could have been done more effectively? How?

Was the task accomplished within the allotted time?

    If not, why not?

How was the employee's other work affected by the delegation of this task?

Was this the right person to do this job?

    If not, why not?

Delegation: Employee's Evaluation Worksheet

To be filled out by the *employee* for feedback on how well the manager did delegating the tasks.

To: _____ From: _____

Re: Feedback on my delegation of the following task: _____

_____

Date: _____

Dear (Employee):

Please provide me with feedback on my delegation skills by honestly answering the following questions. When you have completed this check sheet, please return it to me. After I have read your comments, I would like to meet to discuss them in more detail so I can become a better delegator.

1. What did you like about the way I delegated this task to you?

_____

_____

_____

2. How could I have improved? Consider such things as:
    - Did I select the appropriate person to do this job? Should I have selected someone else?
    - Did I tell you whom to see and who else needed to be contacted?
    - Did I explain what results I expected before you began the task?
    - Should I have provided you with more training? Less training?
    - Should I have met with you more often? Less often?
    - Did you feel that I was available to answer your questions as they came up?
    - Did I provide you with the authority to do the task?
    - Did I let you do it? Did I take over or take back the job in any way?
    - Did I provide you with positive and/or corrective feedback when you finished the task?
    - Did you encounter any problems that I should have foreseen?

Please explain below how I might delegate better in the future. Be specific. Note examples where possible.

_____

_____

_____

_____

_____

Thank you for giving me this feedback!

12
Problem Solving

Making the right decision on the wrong problem is usually a disaster. Making the wrong decision on the right problem one can usually fix!

– Peter Drucker

Some people seem to have a knack for coming up with the best solution to a problem. Others with the same intelligence and experience propose solutions before they are even sure what the problems are! We've all seen examples of disasters that occurred when the cause of the problem wasn't analyzed before expensive action was taken: decisions that resulted in wasted time, materials, and money or plans that looked perfect on paper, but failed in real life.

I remember attending a problem-solving meeting in which one participant asked five times in the course of an hour, *"Yes, but what is causing the problem?"* Another person kept saying, "Let's *do* something! Anything! We need to take action now!" Someone else continued to push his own solution to the "problem." I had no idea why I had been invited to the meeting. The guy next to me wanted to tell me about a fishing trip he had taken, while someone else kept trying to get the group to explore different alternatives in order to obtain a better solution. The big boss showed up ten minutes late for the meeting and left after fifteen minutes. The key person who had most of the data was paged twice and had to leave the meeting. Nobody took minutes, and no one used the easel or whiteboard to obtain group focus. And I ended up with a headache!

Most of us have been to meetings like this, and they're always a waste of time. Part of the problem is that people do not know the basic principles of problem solving. Therefore, a great deal of time is wasted as people run off in all directions. Besides correcting the obvious problem of meeting interruptions and late arrivals, there are some very simple things we can all do to make problem-solving meetings more productive.

This chapter will help you develop skills in problem solving. It will show you logical but simple ways to become a more effective problem solver.

Put the Problem in Writing

It is amazing how important a simple thing like writing down information can be. You don't have to have a clipboard in your hand; just take a minute to make the problem "visible" by writing it down somewhere.

If problem-solving is only taking place in your mind, no one can help you. Others are kept from pointing out oversights, errors, or faulty assumptions. "Visibility" will help keep a group on track and focused.

Writing down the problem also helps us see the whole problem rather than just some parts and pieces of it, and can keep a group on track and focused. It also gives us a reliable way to review the process and see where things have gone wrong. Finally, part of our job as a leader is to help our people develop. We may be outstanding problem solvers, but if we can't make what we think visible, how can we teach our subordinates how to solve problems? In this chapter, we provide two common-sense tools for solving problems: Situation Analysis, and Diagnosing Causes.

Situation Analysis

Situation Analysis is a useful tool for problems that are big, complex, and bulky, with lots of parts and pieces: you can break the large and even messy situation down into manageable pieces. These pieces become the problems, decisions, plans, and even new problem situations to be analyzed. High turnover, low morale, dirty facilities, and even sky-high costs are often thought of as problems, but technically they are not problems at all. They are statements about symptoms of problems.

Let's set up a messy situation and examine how situation analysis can be used to break it down into manageable chunks.

Situation Analysis: Scenario

Old Jake, a senior manager with ITA, went to see his friend for some help with a problem. Here is what he said to his friend:

"I just don't understand those leaders. Back when I was a foreman—excuse me, I mean foreperson—an employee took a lot of pride in the fact that he or she was a leader at the best darn organization this side of the Mississippi. But now, if morale were any worse, I'd have to jack my people up with a hydraulic lift. They are grumbling and complaining worse than a bunch of workers who just got an across-the-board pay cut.

"Now, because I've been here longer than anyone else, the boss wants me to come up with some bright ideas to make the morale problem disappear. I don't even know where to start on this one. It's a real mess, because so many things are causing the problem. Maybe it's because every time there is a dispute between a team leader and a worker, the team leader gets shot down by the personnel department.

"Of course, it could be that the team leaders just aren't as tough as they used to be in my time. I mean, after all, each of us was a 'foreman.' We had respect! And it seems like the workers can sense when a foreman—I mean 'team leader'—is weak. And then they needle him or her constantly until something blows.

"The low morale might also be a result of some team leaders not being able to make that big transition from being a worker to being a leader. I've seen several like that. Tom is a good example. He's the most miserable human being I've ever seen. He loved doing what he was doing, and was good at it. Then he was promoted to leader, and now he can't keep his hands off the equipment.

"Another problem is that there's so much pressure to get high production. A team leader who achieves high production gets a lot of recognition from everybody. But sometimes things happen outside a leader's control that hurt his or her production. Then we've got a morale problem.

"I don't know. Maybe the problem of low morale is caused by the new 'work team' program. Delegating authority and responsibility to workers is fine—I'm all for it. But it seems like the workers really weren't ready for all that authority and responsibility. Now the team leaders are having fits trying to get their people to work together as a team—to take charge of their own goals and objectives, and at the same time keep up production. They're having meetings about having meetings! Why can't the organization spend some of its dollars on giving the workers some training, before dumping a new way of operating on them? It's crazy!

"What a mess! I'm usually an optimistic kind of person. But things aren't going well. Something needs to change."

Let's look at the way to solve Jake's problem with situational analysis.

Write down the problem. Situation Analysis begins when you make the problem visible by writing it down:

Separate the problem into its related parts. Then you must separate the problem into its related parts. Separating the pieces of a problem allows us to focus our energy on those areas that most affect the initial problem, and lets us see the problem as a whole. At this point, we don't have to analyze or conclude anything. We just jot down as many parts and pieces of the problem as we can think of. In the example, Old Jake would ask himself this question: *What are the things that make me think that we've got low team-leader morale?*

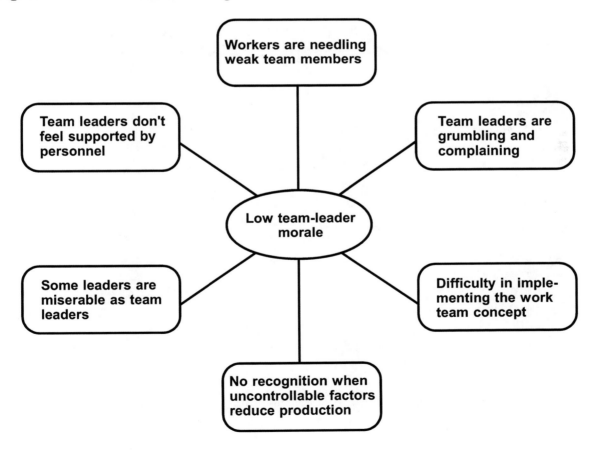

Determine which parts are causes and which are results. It is important to find out which parts of the problem are probable causes and which are probable results. Decide which of the separate pieces are causes and which are results of causes. To fix a mess, we must attack the causes, not the results. When four people who work for you suddenly quit their jobs, you do have to replace the people, but you can't stop there. In order to fix the cause of the problem, you must find out why they quit—the probable causes. Then take action on them first.

We can indicate a probable cause by drawing an arrow pointing toward the problem situation and indicate a probable result with an arrow pointing away from the problem. Then we cross out the "results," and focus our energies on the causes. Here's our example:

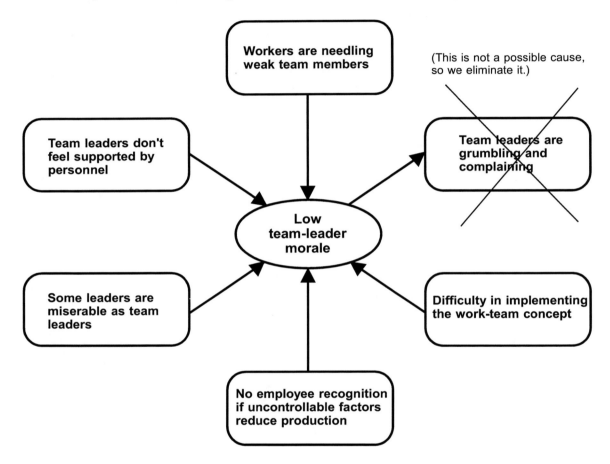

The grumbling and complaining is probably a result of low team leader morale. Eliminate it as a cause. If a piece of the situation seems to be both a probable cause and a probable result, treat it as a probable cause.

Set Priorities. Many problems have a number of related causes, some major and some minor. To be effective, devote your time to the major causes that can be changed. With today's tight schedules, you won't have time to do everything, so fix the things that matter the most. Make them visible components, determining causes and results. Then, assign priorities only to the causes, not to the results.

A simple way to assign priorities is to look at three things in turn: "Seriousness," "Urgency," and "Growth."

Seriousness:

- How serious is this cause in relation to the other causes?
- How big is it?
- How bad is it?
- How frequently is it occurring?
- Dollar-wise, how important is this part of the problem?

High seriousness, medium seriousness, or low seriousness?

Urgency:

- Do I have to drop everything else and take care of this today?
- Can I do it just as well next week?
- Can this part of the problem wait until next month?

High urgency, medium urgency, or low urgency?

Problem Growth:

- If I don't take care of this cause now, will it get worse?
- Will it soon spread out of control?
- Does it have a growing financial impact?

High priority, medium priority, or low priority?

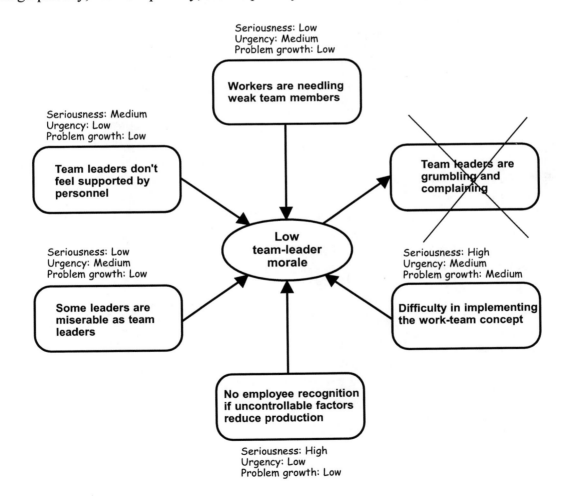

At this point, note that Old Jake rated two parts of his problem as "high" in seriousness: "No employee recognition if uncontrollable factors reduce production," and "Difficulty in implementing the work team concept." But his urgency rating for these two causes was not "high," but "low" and "medium," respectively. You may feel that if the seriousness of a problem is high, then the urgency must be high and the growth factor will thus also be high. But we need to be careful not to allow a high-seriousness rating influence our ratings of urgency and growth. In Old Jake's case, "Difficulty in implementing work-team concept" was serious to him. But he also felt that the urgency of this cause was only medium, and that the growth factor was also only medium.

Likewise, even though he rated "No employee recognition if uncontrollable factors reduce production" as high in seriousness, he rated it low in urgency. Jake's management needs to do something about this part of the problem. But realistically, it is not something that must be handled today—or even this week. In fact, it might be better to give this cause some time and solid thought before talking to management about it. Jake wisely rated this piece of the problem as low in growth. Yes, the problem is bad. But, no, the problem is not likely to get any worse. It is probably as bad as it is ever going to be. Therefore, it has low growth potential.

Analyze each major cause. Decide which of the situation's causes are either problems to be diagnosed, decisions that must be made, plans to be implemented, or new situations to be analyzed. Then, label each box in your diagram accordingly.

For example, "Difficulty in implementing the work-team concept" may be a problem to Old Jake because he doesn't really know what the cause is. He thinks it might be lack of worker training, but that is only an assumption at this point. He needs to discover why the teams are not working out. Only when he determines why this is occurring is he ready to take some kind of action to address the problem.

Jake knows why there is no recognition when uncontrollable factors reduce production. And since he knows the cause of this situation, his next step is to make some decisions about fixing it.

He also knows why some leaders are miserable as team leaders. He even knows what needs to be done about it. But he feels that determining how to do what needs to be done will require some planning.

Finally, Jake may have a new problem situation that must be further broken down. For instance, team leaders not feeling supported by the personnel department may represent a new situation to be analyzed, with its own set of causes and results.

Situation analysis will not produce a solution to the problem, but it will help make the various parts of the problem visible and help you evaluate each part in a meaningful way and decide where to focus your energy.

Think of a high- or medium-priority cause as an opportunity to do something differently and better.

Situation Analysis Worksheet

☑ 1. Write down the problem.

☑ 2. Separate the problem into its related parts.

☑ 3. Determine which pieces are probable causes and which are results. Draw arrows into the center for "cause," out for "results."

☑ 4. Assign S.U.G. priorities for each cause (H = High, M = Medium, L = Low).

  Seriousness: How bad? How big? How much money?

  Urgency: Must it be taken care of today?
       Will next week be just as good?

  Growth: Is the cause getting worse?
       Or is it already as bad as it is going to get?

☑ 5. Label the major causes: Problem, Decision, Plan, or New Situation Analysis.

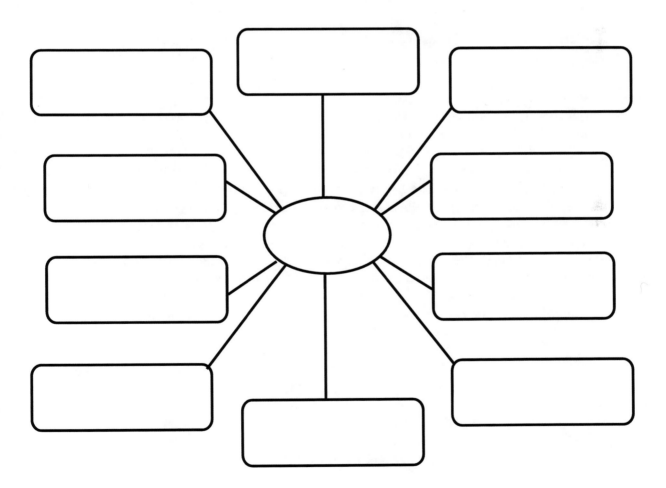

Diagnosing Cause

Don't just jump into action when you have a problem. Taking action without thinking, no matter how unproductive, can become a habit—and it will cause more problems for you in the end. Before you take action to solve a problem, you must look for causes. Then fix the cause that is most clearly connected to the problem.

When we problem-solve, we are finding the cause of a problem, not analyzing a situation, making a decision, or implementing a plan. We are problem solving when there is *a deviation from the standard;* when *we are uncertain why there is this deviation,* and *we are concerned.*

We can find the cause of a problem by doing these seven things:

1. Develop and write a specific problem statement.

2. Describe the problem by stating what, where, and when the problem is occurring, and what, where, and when the problem is not occurring.

3. Examine the differences between what, where, and when the problem is and what, where, and when it is not.

4. Look for changes in and around the environment of the problem.

5. Construct "probable cause" statements.

6. Test each probable cause.

7. Verify the most likely case.

Let's look at each part of the analysis process.

Step 1. Write a problem statement. Write out the problem statement and make it specific. Write "Poor morale in the data processing section," not just "Poor morale." This not only helps pinpoint the problem, but also highlights what the real issue is.

Step 2. Describe the problem. A cause can be identified more quickly if you clarify what is not the problem, as well as what is. The better we define the boundaries of a problem by specifying where the problem isn't occurring, the easier it is to determine the most probable causes.

Here you need to also specify the extent of the problem: that is, how bad or serious it is. This information can keep you from developing a $500 solution to fix a $3.00 problem.

These "what, where, when and extent" questions help you locate and isolate the problem area, and thus show you where to look for causes. An electronics technician calls it "trouble-shooting"; a doctor calls it "diagnosing." We might say it's "working smarter, not harder."

For example, suppose I have a bad pain. What kinds of questions would my doctor ask? "Where does it hurt? When does it bother you? When did you first notice it? How much does it hurt?"

But good doctors don't stop there. They also ask questions about what the problem is not. "Have you been experiencing pain anywhere else? Have you ever had this pain before? When don't you notice the pain?"

The doctor might discover that my problem is only in my right elbow, and not in any other part of my body. It hurts all day, not just at certain times of the day. The pain first started six weeks ago. And I didn't have it before then, except when I was in high school.

Step 3. Closely examine the differences between the "is" factors and the "is not" factors. If a problem exists in one area and not in another, the differences between the two areas can produce clues to help locate the cause. So we ask, "What peculiar differences exist between where the problem is occurring and where it is not occurring? What is different about when the problem occurs and when it doesn't?"

By specifying what, where, when, and to what extent the problem is and is not occurring, my doctor is able to identify the particular differences. When I see my doctor about the pain, the doctor might learn that I'm right-handed and that I was a pitcher in high school. Then, by determining the peculiar differences between what, where, and when the problem is and is not, he or she is then able to look for changes in and around the differences.

Step 4. Look for changes in and around the differences. Changes can cause problems. In fact, problems by definition are always caused by changes. Problems where no change has occurred are not truly problems; they are decisions that must be made or plans that should be implemented. For example, guess what my doctor discovered I was doing with my child every night after supper for the past six weeks. Right! My child joined the local little league baseball team, and needed practice in catching.

Step 5. Develop probable cause statements. Develop a probable cause statement for each change you notice. In the example of elbow pain above, a probable cause statement could be:

> "Pitching softball with my child each night after supper has resulted in tendonitis in my elbow."

Step 6. Test each probable cause. Test each probable cause statement against all of the IS and IS NOT facts, in order to determine the most probable cause. For example, my doctor might ask himself:

> *If it is tendonitis, would that account for the fact that the pain is in the right elbow and not the left? Yes.*

> *Would it account for the fact that it hurts constantly, and not just certain times in the day? Yes.*

> *The pain first started six weeks ago. Did the patient have it before, except when he was a pitcher in high school? Yes.*

Since tendonitis checks out against the known set of facts, my doctor would then move to the next step—verifying that this really is the cause.

Step 7. Verify. Is what you think is the cause really the cause? In the case of our example, my doctor can verify the cause of my pain by gently probing my elbow, or by taking X-rays.

Note that these seven steps of problem solving are usually inexpensive. They involve only paper and pencil mental analysis, and sometime phone calls to gather confirming information. Taking action to remedy the problem, of course, may involve financial commitment and many lost dollars if we fail to follow the problem-solving process above. Unfortunately, many people start solving a problem by throwing money into an ill-conceived solution before thinking through the problem. They jump in with both feet to take action—any action. They often end up spending much unnecessary time and money—and the problem still isn't solved.

Diagnosing Cause: Template

Use this template to help you diagnose a cause in seven steps:

1. Problem statement: _____

_____

2.	Is Occurring?	Is not occurring?	3. Difference between the "is" and "is not" columns	4. Changes in the problem's differences
What defect				
What object				
Where?				
When?				
Extent?				

5. Write probable-cause statements.

    1) _____

    2) _____

    3) _____

6. Test the probable-cause statements against the initial set of "is" and "is not" facts.

7. Verify the most-probable cause.

Now let's illustrate the seven-step problem-solving technique with a real-life example:

The Case of the Rejected Promotion

Tom Swift, Director of Marketing, shook his head in amazement. Jean Williams, one of his best telephone salespersons, had just turned down a promotion to be an outside salesperson. Of course, it would have meant a move outside the close-knit telemarketing group, but the possibility of a substantial increase in salary should have been tempting. It wouldn't have been so bad, except that this was the second person to turn down the position. Tom had asked Sue Atkinson first, and, after thinking it over, she said no.

Tom later asked both of them why they turned down the promotion. Jean and Sue both had similar responses. Jean said that she was happy where she was and didn't want the stress of taking on new responsibilities. "And besides," she explained, "I really enjoy the relationships that I have established over the years with my customers." Sue similarly said that she enjoyed her work and the people she worked with, and said that she, too, had made many friends among her customers, and didn't want to give them up.

A couple of years ago, Tom would have had to beat off outside sales applicants with a stick! Now, even though the opening had been posted for three weeks, not a single person had applied for it. Since there was a strong policy of promoting from within, it would be difficult to get approval to look outside the organization for a salesperson. Other departments in the organization had no problem finding applicants for promotions to other jobs.

I don't know, thought Tom. *Maybe it's Betty.* Betty had been Tom's outside sales manager for three years, and had a reputation for being the toughest taskmaster in the organization. "Firm but fair" was her motto. And was she firm! Betty set high goals, and saw to it that her salespeople met the goals year after year. *Maybe that's the reason I can't get anybody to take this job,* Tom thought. *Betty is just too hard to work for. She's not like Bill, the old manager who retired. He was a great leader and his people really liked him.*

Tom thought that perhaps the telemarketers might be afraid to make sales calls in person because face-to-face is a whole lot different than talking on the telephone. In some ways, he considered, it's actually easier because you can see the customer's non-verbals and respond to them. Outside salespeople have better call-to-sales ratios than do telemarketers.

He remembered why it's harder to make calls in person. The salesperson feels rejection more keenly in a face-to-face situation than on the phone. Since neither Jean nor Sue has ever done this, maybe they are afraid to face rejection in person.

Tom recalled more differences: An outside salesperson usually works alone. The telemarketers work alone on the phone, but they have lots of opportunities to talk with each other during the day.

The other big difference between in-person and telemarketing sales is the amount of time required on the job. The outside people make more sales, and as a result make more money. But it's definitely not a nine-to-five job like telemarketing. The outside people spend more evening and weekend time preparing for their calls. And they leave home earlier, and usually get back later.

But neither Jean nor Sue has a family, Tom recalled, so the extra time shouldn't have been that much of a problem—considering how much better the money is. Sue once said she would like to be considered for the telemarketing leader's job if it ever opens up. Surely she knows that it is definitely not a nine-to-five job.

(continued)

The Case of the Rejected Promotion (concluded)

> *I just don't know what the problem is,* thought Tom. *I do know that the telemarketers feel really good about working together, ever since the three team-building training workshops. They're such good friends. And it's great to see the way they support each other.*
>
> Tom knows that his boss will ask him at the afternoon managers' meeting how he is doing filling the outside sales job. At this point, Tom doesn't know what to say. He doesn't want to jump to conclusions or do anything until he is sure about what's causing the problem. But he suspects Betty is the problem. Maybe he should think about what he can do to help her become a more congenial supervisor to work for.

As we examine the above example, we can see many possible reasons why the two telemarketers turned down this promotional opportunity: a tough supervisor, more responsibility, working alone without a support group, extra time required in an outside sales job, and fear of face-to-face rejection. As with most actual cases, there are a number of possible causes. Each cause requires a different solution; if action is taken on the wrong cause, not only will the problem not be solved, but also there is a chance that the problem will get worse.

So Tom's first job is to get paper and pencil and write out a problem statement.

1. "Two telemarketers have turned down a promotion to outside salesperson."

2. He lists what the problem is, followed by where, when, and to what extent it is occurring.

3. After Tom has written what, where, when, and the extent of the problem, he then notes what, where, when, and the extent to which the problem is not occurring. The analysis so far looks like this:

2.	Is Occurring?	Is not occurring?	5. Difference between the "is" and "is not" columns	6. Changes in the problem's differences
What defect	Telemarketers refusing promotion	Telemarketers' job		
What object	Promotion to outside salesperson	Promotion within telemarketing department		
Where?	Telemarketing department	Other departments		
When?	Now	Prior to two years ago		
Extent?	Serious: two people rejected for promotion No applicants	Okay (both telemarketers accept the promotion) A number of applicants		

He determines the difference between the situation in which the problem is occurring, and where it does not exist. That is, what are the important differences between each set of IS and IS NOT facts?

4. He now looks carefully for changes that have taken place or would take place that might affect the thinking of the telemarketers concerning the promotion.

After Tom identifies situational differences and critical changes, he is now ready for Step 5.

5. He lists the *probable causes of the problem* (called "probable cause statements") related to each of the change factors. For example, "longer hours" is one of the changes involved in the promotion. Thus, Tom would write a probable cause statement that relates this new change factor to his initial problem statement, as follows:

"Because a promotion to outside salesperson entails longer hours, two tele-marketers turned down the promotion."

Change ⟶ Link ⟶ Problem

Longer hours	may require telemarketers to give up too much personal time, thus resulting in	their rejection of the promotion
Greater responsibility	could be a hassle, thus causing	their rejection of the promotion
Loss of established customers	might be too upsetting, leading to	their rejection of the promotion
Tougher supervisor	could be very difficult to work for, therefore causing	their rejection of the promotion
Closer relationships with peers	as a result of the team training program may be the reason for	their rejection of the promotion

6. **Tom numbers his six pairs of "is/is not" facts** concerning the what, where, when, and extent of the problem, and prepares to test his probable cause statements against these known sets of facts.

7. Tom looks at his probable causes and the facts, if any, that do or do not support the probable cause.

Change ⟶ Link ⟶ Problem			Set of facts numbers:					
			1	2	3	4	5	6
Greater responsibility →	could be a hassle, thus causing →	their rejection of the promotion	✓	A	A	A	✓	✓
Longer hours →	may require telemarketers to give up too much personal time, thus resulting in →	their rejection of the promotion	✓	A	A	A	✓	✓
Loss of established customers →	might be too upsetting, leading to →	their rejection of the promotion	✓	✓	✓	A	✓	✓
Tougher supervisor →	could be very difficult to work for, therefore causing →	their rejection of the promotion	✓	✓	✓	A	✓	✓
Closer relationships with peers →	as a result of the team training program might be the reason for →	their rejection of the promotion	✓	✓	✓	✓	✓	✓

Tom takes the first probable cause statement and asks, "If greater responsibility could be a hassle, thus causing their rejection of the promotion, does this explain why the telemarketers are refusing promotions and there is no problem that is apparent with the telemarketers' job? If Tom considers *only* this first set of facts, then his answer must be "Yes." So he puts a "✓" mark in the first box under "#1," as shown on the chart.

Using this same probable cause statement, Tom tests it against each of the other five sets of "is/is not" facts, and records his answers in the first row of the chart. Because this probable cause statement makes sense for only set of facts #1, #5, and #6, it is therefore answered "Yes" in these three sets of facts by recording a "✓" in each of the boxes shown.

If a specific probable cause statement doesn't check out against a specific set of facts, he records an "A"—which stands for "Assumption." In other words, he assumes that something else must account for that set of "is/is not" facts.

Tom checks out each probable cause against each set of "is/is not" facts, recording "✓'s" when the cause statement checks out, and an "A" when it doesn't. (If we don't have enough information to know whether one of our statements accounts for a set of facts, we can use a "?" to indicate this.)

After Tom checked all of his cause statements against all six of his sets of "is/is not" facts, only one cause appeared to account for every set of facts concerning the problem: "Closer relationships with peers as a result of the team training programs."

It is time to verify the most probable cause statement. Until he verifies that closer relationships resulting from the telemarketers' team training is the key reason for their rejection of the promotion offer, he cannot say that "closer relationships" is *the* cause, only the most probable cause.

Tom's probable cause grid analysis has not yet eliminated any causes, but rather tells him the cause to try to verify first: "Closer relationships due to team training." If he finds, after verifying, that this not the cause of the problem, he will then attempt to verify the next most probable cause or causes—in this case, "Loss of established customers" and "Tougher supervisor."

This problem-solving approach is based on recognizing that a problem situation involves effects that, upon analysis, indicate a most probable cause. The effects point to a very particular kind of cause—one that would produce just the unique effects (problem) that have been observed.

The cause of any problem leaves a telltale imprint of clues (effects) that can be investigated along four lines. The first is *identity*. In "The Case of the Rejected Promotion," the problem's "identity" was the telemarketers' refusal of a promotion to an outside sales position. The second clue is *location*. The problem occurred in the telemarketing department, and not in other departments. The third clue is *timing*. The problem occurring now was not present prior to two years ago. And the fourth line of investigation is the *extent* of the problem—its size and severity. With two people rejecting promotion to outside sales and no other applicants for the job, the problem is serious and needs attention. But because this problem was carefully analyzed, probable causes were identified for verification and any action will be directed to a verified cause.

Try using the seven-step problem-solving grid on the last page of this chapter to solve a problem you have. Note that when you complete this grid on a real problem, you may have some blank spaces in the grid. Don't let this frustrate you: The grid process protects us from jumping to conclusions and taking the right action on the wrong cause.

One final point. The criteria for a real problem are: 1) There must be a deviation from the standard. 2) The cause must not be known. 3) There is concern about the problem. A problem that meets all three criteria won't be a problem for long, because we will be motivated to find the cause and fix the problem. When we identify a list of existing problems, however, we will often find that our list includes a number of old problems. These old problems frequently have known causes, but haven't been solved—simply because we have not made decisions about them. These are not true "problems" at all; they are situations requiring decisions.

Summary

It is important to think through a problem before you attempt to solve it. First, make the problem visible in writing by creating a problem statement. Use a problem-solving process, and be sure you don't jump to conclusions and take premature, costly action before you have analyzed the problem and its possible causes.

The problem-solving technique we have reviewed is as useful in the hands of a group as it is for the individual problem solver. As a participative leader, you can use this process with your employees in group meetings, and with your co-workers in team meetings. Here are the seven steps again:

1. Specify what is wrong. Write a problem statement.
2. Describe the problem.
3. Specify the differences.
4. Specify all the changes.
5. Identify all the probable causes.
6. Test the causes.
7. Verify the problem's possible cause.

This seven-step diagnostic process will help you resolve problems quicker, correct causes (not just effects), solve problems so they stay solved, and prevent new problems.

Problem Solving: Worksheet

A problem exists when (1) a deviation from an expected standard has occurred, (2) the cause of that deviation is uncertain, and (3) the deviation concerns you.

1. **Problem Statement:** _____

2. **Problem...**

	IS	IS NOT	3. Difference (between "is" and "is not")	4. Changes in the "difference"
What is the Defect?				
What is the Object? (who/what failed)				
Where?				
When?				
Extent? (seriousness)				

Steps in Diagnosing Cause

1. Write a specific, negative problem statement.
2. Describe the problem by writing what, where, when, and to what extent the problem IS and IS NOT occurring.
3. Determine any peculiar, pertinent differences between what the problem *is* and what the problem *is not*.
4. Look carefully for changes that have occurred in and around the differences.
5. Write a probable cause statement for each change discovered in Step 4 above.
6. Test each probable cause against each specific set of *"is"* and *"is not"* facts, and identify the most probable cause.
7. Verify the most-probable cause statement, take appropriate action, and monitor results.

Problem Solving: Worksheet (concluded)

5. Probable Cause Statements
(one for each change from column 4)

Change	Link (to problem)	Problem	6. Test each probable cause statement against each set of *"is"* and *"is not"* facts. Probable cause *does* explain facts = ✓ *Does not* explain facts = A								
			(1)	(2)	(3)	(4)	(5)	(6)	(7)	(8)	(9)

7. Most-probable cause (statement): _____

- What can be done to verify that this is the cause? _____
- Given this cause is verified, what actions can be taken to correct the initial problem? _____
_____
_____
_____

13
Decision Making

Decision-making would be easy if it were always a choice between good and evil or right and wrong. In the real world, leaders have to make decisions that are multidimensional, usually between two or more imperfect remedies, on criteria that encompass long-range goals and plausibility.

– Rudolph Giuliani

Changes in organizational attitudes about top-down management and the consequent elimination of layers of management are forcing leaders to delegate ever more responsibility for making decisions. From non-exempts to department heads, employees who actually do the work are making decisions that have greater impact on their working environments. This is by and large a good thing, as long as everyone understands that poor decisions can have costly consequences. Selecting the wrong new employee, promoting the wrong person, or deciding on the wrong procedure can, in the long run, cost hundreds of thousands of dollars to remedy. Not only is money wasted, but time is lost and morale suffers.

Force Field Analysis and PERT charts are widely used, but proven, step-by-step decision-making processes are not widely known. Happily for us, two individuals, Charles Kepner and Benjamin Tregoe, conducted extensive research and wrote a now-classic book called *The Rational Manager*. In this book, they detailed a process for effective decision making and planning. The ideas that are presented here result from their earlier work and continued application by many professionals.

Making good decisions requires two separate processes: 1) selecting the best alternative, and 2) planning and implementing that decision, and anticipating problems. Both steps are crucial; a decision that doesn't factor in contingencies is as likely to fail as a plan that is based on a poor decision.

These decision-making processes can be learned in one setting and then easily applied to another. In this chapter, we will include a few examples of decisions that have little to do with a job, because they are often easier to relate to. Remember: It's all about the *process*.

In this chapter, you will learn how to 1) write open decision statements, 2) determine the underlying objectives in making decisions and identify the difference between *must* and *want* objectives, 3) create alternatives, and 4) evaluate the risks involved before you make a final decision. You will see a logical, step-by-step method that will help you make more-effective decisions. We'll begin with some important ideas on how to write a decision statement.

Decision Statements

The first step in effective decision making is to take the time to write an *open* decision statement. This will force you to think through the decision before it is made, make it easier to get help from others, keep you from making snap decisions, put your false assumptions on the table, and allow you to learn from your past written decisions.

In addition to making decision statements visible by writing them out, you also need to examine the way you write the statement. If your statement has only two parts, such as "Accept or reject that proposal," "Go to San Francisco or not," "Vote 'yes' or 'no' on gun control," or "Quit my job or not," you might make a premature decision because you are comparing only two alternatives.

To make more-effective decisions, keep decision statements open for more than two alternatives. For example, "Accept or reject that proposal" can be rewritten to give you other alternatives. If you start decision statements with the words "Select the best...," you can almost guarantee an *open* decision statement. "Go to San Francisco or not" becomes "Select the best city to visit." Now you are free to choose to go to San Francisco, New York, or even New Orleans.

How would you turn "Vote 'yes' or 'no' on gun control" into an open decision statement? Gun control is one possible solution to at least two different problems: reducing crime and preventing gun accidents. As Peter Drucker said, "Trying to solve two problems with one solution very seldom works." In this case, identifying the underlying reasons for gun control allows us to examine two entirely different problems: 1) reduce crime, and 2) prevent gun accidents.

Rather than limiting your decision statement to only one solution, it seems far better to determine the primary problems involved, and put each problem in a decision statement. This will allow you to develop a whole list of different alternative solutions for each decision statement. For example, the "reduce crime" and "prevent gun accidents" problems could generate a whole list of solutions as follows:

Problems:	High Crime Rate	Gun Accidents
Decision Statements:	Select best way to reduce crime.	Select best way to reduce gun accidents.
Alternatives:	1. Gun control 2. Stiffer penalties 3. More police 4. Better security	1. Gun control 2. Education 3. "Safety" ammunition 4. Childproof guns

Note that making the decision statements *open* now makes many different alternatives available. We can still implement gun control if we wish, but by transforming the initial gun control statement into two pertinent open statements, we have a variety of possible choices.

Objectives

The next step in decision making is to decide what you want to do—your goals, objectives, desired results—before creating alternative solutions. Developing objectives before alternatives counteracts the tendency to choose only those objectives that fit your pre-selected solutions.

Objectives come from questions such as:

"What factors should I consider?" (time, location, approvals, etc.)

"What results do I want?" (efficiency, productivity, safety, recognition, saving money, satisfaction, high morale, etc.)

"What resources are available?" (people, equipment, skills, budget, materials, knowledge, etc.)

"What restrictions are required?" (law, standards, ethics, policy, values, culture, etc.)

Try and include all-important items that are considerations in making your decision. The more sound data you have here, the better your final decision will be.

Take a look at the following example. Read the case study, noting what you feel are the important objectives in this situation.

The Case of the Home Purchase

Matt and his wife, Cathleen, sat down at the kitchen table to talk about their plan to purchase a home. Their lease will expire in four months, and Matt knows that Cathleen is looking forward to leaving the cramped, three-bedroom ranch. With four children—two girls ages 16 and 5, and two boys 15 and 9—it has been difficult for everyone. It is hard on their teenage daughter, who has to share a room with her little sister. It is also hard on the boys: they fight constantly, each blaming the other for messing up the room. Neither will accept responsibility for the mess. Fortunately, the house has a large yard for the dogs.

Matt hopes that they will get a 90% mortgage. They could just manage to put $40,000 toward a down payment and closing costs. It would wipe out their savings, however. With no way of borrowing extra money for emergencies, it would be risky, but well worth it.

Matt wants to get a garage for the boat, as he hates having to leave it out in the rain. Cathleen said they need at least two bathrooms. In fact, she told him that if a house doesn't have two full baths, she won't consider it. She was sick of "Grand Central Station," as she called their single bathroom. Public water, sewer, and gas were musts (all their appliances were gas, and Matt swears never to have a septic system again). It would be nice to be located within one mile of a shopping area. That is the one redeeming factor about their present home—it is only two blocks from a small shopping center.

Fortunately, schools are no problem; the school system in the area is excellent, no matter where you live.

To get the size house they need for the money they have to spend, Matt and Cathleen know they will have to buy a considerable distance from town. They don't mind the drive, as long as the house isn't more than 20 miles from work by the expressway and they don't have to drive with the sun in their eyes in the morning and evening.

Now decide which objectives are "must" or required, and which are desired ("want") objectives. By definition, a must objective is 1) important to the individual writing the objective, and 2) quantifiable to everyone. (When you develop alternative solutions, each solution must meet the required "must" objectives or it won't be acceptable. Save time by only considering alternatives that meet the required objectives.)

"Must" objectives reflect your basic needs (budget, time, policy, rules, or law). Examples are:

- "The fourth-quarter budget clearly restricts us to a maximum of $24,000 for that project."

- "The plan must absolutely be implemented by January the 5th of next year."

Although the budget is not to exceed $24,000, it would be great to bring the project in under budget and in less time. And even though it must be completed by January 5th, it would be nice to have it in less time. These are "want" objectives. "Want" objectives are often comparisons (low cost, least time, largest, nicest, best, biggest, etc.). An objective might be extremely important, but if it can't be measured, it is only a "want."

Now, considering the objectives in the case, which of the following do you think are "must" objectives, and which are only "wants"?

> Available in 4 months
> Minimum of 4 bedrooms
> Large yard (approximately ¼ acre minimum)
> Maximum of $40,000 out-of-pocket
> Garage for the boat
> Two baths
> Public utilities (sewage, water, gas)
> Near shopping area (within 1 mile)
> Not more than 20 miles from work
> Not west of town

Note that "must" objectives are not desirable unless they are absolutely necessary. There is a human tendency to put in lots of "must" objectives, but the more "must" objectives you have, the fewer options you will have as well.

Your must and want objectives in this scenario probably will be different from Matt and Cathleen's if you are making this judgment for yourself. In the scenario, the "must" objectives are: "available in 4 months; minimum of 4 bedrooms; maximum down payment and closing costs of $40,000; two baths; and public utilities.

Is there an alternative below that doesn't meet the objectives that Matt and Cathleen established in the decision to purchase a home?

1. A new tri-level home with a tiny yard, 4 bedrooms, 2-1/2 baths, is available for only $400,000. It is approximately 15 miles from work, no shopping area nearby. Public gas, water, and sewage are available. They can get a 90% mortgage with immediate possession. The builder, who is quite anxious to sell, will pay all the closing costs.

2. A new house that Cathleen really likes has 4 bedrooms and a two-car garage. In addition, it has two baths and the shopping area is only four blocks away. The yard is very small. The home has public utilities, including gas. It is only 10 miles from work, and will be available in three months. It is listed at $380,000, a 90% mortgage is available, and the builder will pay 1% of the 2% closing costs.

3. This house is Matt's choice. The house is about six years old and is in a beautiful neighborhood. The huge yard has many trees and a chain-link fence for the dogs. There is a large tool shed, which includes the owner's old John Deere garden tractor (with a

48" belly mower as part of the deal at no extra cost). Matt likes the fully developed yard, the fact that the house location is only six miles from work, and the large two-car garage with extra room for a workshop. A 90% mortgage is available, and the owner agrees to pay all closing costs. There is a shopping area only three blocks away, and the elementary school is only four blocks from the house. Gas and public sewer are available. The house has 5 bedrooms and 3 baths. The older couple who kept the house spotless is moving to an assisted living facility in two months, and at only $490,000, it is a bargain.

Obviously, Matt and Cathleen just don't have the funds for the third alternative. In real life, they looked at this house three times before they regretfully determined that there was no way they could purchase it. They wasted their time, the owner's time, and the real-estate broker's time, all because they didn't take the time in the beginning to establish their objectives and specify which were "wants" and which were "musts."

Let's look more closely at "musts" and "wants." Read the list of objectives and decide if each statement is important to the writer and measurable to everyone who reads the statement. Place a check in the first column if the statement is very important to the writer and put a check in the second column if the statement is measurable. Then indicate which statements received both checks. These will be "musts."

Objectives	✓ Important to the "writer"	✓ Measurable to everyone	"Must," or "Want?"
I'll only hire someone who's really easy to get along with.			
My new home must be all brick.			
It would be nice to have the meeting in building 220, but we could go elsewhere.			
I'd like to work in an office with a good view, but I really don't care too much.			
The only car I will consider is a van that seats a minimum of 6 people.			
It's imperative that we find a hotel that's comfortable.			
According to our estimate, we shouldn't pay more than $50 for a new wombat, but we can go over that if we have to.			
If the restaurant doesn't have a private dining room that accommodates 35 people, we can't consider it.			
For us to accept that new product, it must be feasible.			
I *must* be able to get along with the person I report to.			

The correct answers to the *Is it a must?* exercise are as follows:

Objectives	✓ Important to the "writer"	✓ Measurable to everyone	"Must," or "Want?"
I'll only hire someone who's really easy to get along with.	✓		Want
My new home must be all brick.	✓	✓	Must
It would be nice to have the meeting in building 220, but we could go elsewhere.		✓	Want
I'd like to work in an office with a good view, but I really don't care too much.			Want
The only car I will consider is a van that seats a minimum of 6 people.	✓	✓	Must
It's imperative that we find a hotel that's comfortable.	✓		Want
According to our estimate, we shouldn't pay more than $50 for a new wombat, but we can go over that if we have to.		✓	Want
If the restaurant doesn't have a private dining room that accommodates 35 people, we can't consider it.	✓	✓	Must
For us to accept that new product, it must be feasible	✓		Want
I *must* be able to get along with the person I report to.	✓		Want

The key learning points from these "must and want" exercises are 1) You don't want to have "must" objectives unless you really need them. 2) You, as the writer of the objectives, determine how important the objective is. 3) Everyone should agree on the measurability of the objective.

Let's look at another example. Note what you feel are the important objectives in this situation.

The Case of the Complex Choice

Bill, maintenance team leader for the Wonder Wombat organization located in Craigsville, Virginia, needed to hire a new employee for his section. He called a meeting of his team and began by writing out this decision statement on a flipchart:

"Select best entry-level employee for our maintenance team"

"You know that we have been authorized to hire a new entry-level maintenance person," he told his team. "This is the first time we have been given the authority to select our own team member, so let's do it right."

"The first thing we need to do is to generate a list of the things we want in the new employee. In other words, what knowledge, skills, and abilities does the new person need to do the job? What ideas do you have?"

After a moment's silence, Joan, the electronics technician, said, "It would be good if he or she already has a fundamental understanding of basic electricity. You know, if he or she could do things like change a lamp fixture; replace a florescent ballast; install a socket or switch; and most important, read an electrical schematic."

Tom, the pipe specialist, said, "Yes, it would help if he could read a schematic, but how about using simple tools? He should be able to solder using a gun or torch, use basic hand tools, know a voltmeter from a pressure gauge, and be willing to take on the nasty jobs that sometimes have to be done. I don't want a prima donna who's too good to fix a problem with a toilet!"

"Yeah," said Rick, another member of the team. "Handling tools is important. But we can teach him what he doesn't know. It seems to me that what's more important is that whoever we hire has a good attitude. You know, gets along well with people."

"And with a good attitude," responded Tom, "is the need for good work habits. We need somebody whom we don't have to pick up after, who gets to work on time, and who doesn't hold up the rest of us. In other words, let's get somebody who's a hard worker and doesn't goof off!"

"Say," suggested Joe, a technician. "What about my brother? You all met him at the picnic last month. He's a hard worker and a great guy! I know he is tired of driving a beer truck. He'd fit right in with the rest of us."

Bill, who had been writing objectives on the flipchart with a magic marker, paused and said, "Hiring your brother is a good idea, Joe, but human resources won't let us because he is your brother. So let's hold off considering alternatives until we've had a chance to finish the objectives, okay? So what other factors should we consider in hiring a new employee for our section?"

"How about reading and writing?" asked Rick. "I know it sounds stupid, but there are people in the job market who can't read and write. Any maintenance person we hire must be able to read!"

"Good point," said Bill. "I'll add that to the list. What else? How about you, Chuck? Any other ideas?"

Chuck, who hadn't said anything up to this point, thought for a minute and said, "I don't know. The only thing I can think of is that whoever takes this job has to be willing to work for the money we pay."

(continued)

The Case of the Complex Choice (concluded)

"Okay, good suggestion. 'Accepts salary limitations.' Anything else?"

Bill waits for a moment, and then shares his own ideas. "We need to hire someone who is available now, or at least within the next few weeks."

"Hey, I've got another," exclaimed Chuck. "You know that we are getting more and more requests for hard wiring of computer networks. Joyce, you can do it, but you don't have time. Getting that outside contractor in here is a pain. It would be great if the guy we hired knew something about computer networks!"

At this point, the team had developed the following objectives to use to make its decision:

- *Understands basic electricity*
- *Knows how to use hand tools*
- *Is willing to do any type of task*
- *Gets along with others*
- *Has good work habits*
- *Is able to read and write*
- *Meets salary requirements*
- *Is available to work in 3 weeks*
- *Can hard wire computer networks*

Bill then explained "must" and "want" objectives to his team. The team spent considerable time discussing the measurability of objectives. They felt that "Available to work in 3 weeks," "Meets salary requirements" (which they specified), and "Reads and writes" were their musts. They realized that the objective "Reads and writes" was not a "must" the way they wrote it, because it isn't yet quantifiable. Thus they developed a simple reading and writing test based on the forms and text that they used within their section. They showed this test to the human resources department and received permission to use it in their evaluation of applicants. Because of their discussions, they rewrote this objective to state, "Passes reading and writing test."

Some "Want" objectives are more important than others. In this example, understanding basic electricity may be a great deal more important than knowing how to use hand tools. Teaching someone who doesn't have a clue about Ohm's law, series and parallel circuits, and so on is difficult; showing someone how to use hand tools is likely not as hard.

Always assign higher weights to more-desirable objectives to reflect their greater relative importance. Using a scale of 1 to 10 and giving the highest number to the most-important "want" objective, the list might look like this for the decision statement:

"Select best entry-level employee for our maintenance team"

Objectives:

- *Understands basic electricity*   a want = 9
- *Knows how to use hand tools*   a want = 8
- *Willing to do any type of task*   a want = 6
- *Gets along with others*   a want = 7
- *Good work habits*   a want = 5
- *Passes reading and writing test*   a must

- *Meets salary requirements*   a must
- *Available to work in 3 weeks*   a must
- *Can hard wire computer networks*   a want = 2

Note that the team didn't assign a "10" to any of the want objectives. Try to avoid assigning "10's" to your objectives—you need to save them for extremely important objectives that can't be "musts" because they aren't measurable.

"Must" objectives may also have a corresponding "want" objective. For example, if it had been important to Bill's team, they could have written a new "want" objective, "Can start work at any time over the next 3 weeks" and maybe rated it a "2." Here, they felt that it wasn't very important that somebody start immediately, so they did not rewrite the "must" objective. However, they looked at "Meets salary requirements" and added a new "want" objective: "Satisfaction with salary." They rated it a "4."

Assigned weights will differ, depending on the raters. In a group, go for consensus. If you are doing this process by yourself, seek help from others by asking, "How important do you think this objective is, compared to that one? And why?"

Alternatives

Think of alternatives in the following classifications:

- *Corrective* alternatives that solve the problem
- *Interim* alternatives that don't remedy the problem, but do buy time
- *Adaptive* alternatives that allow you to live with the problem

Corrective action is normally the best type of alternative for fixing specific problems because it is the least expensive. (For example, if the problem is a fire, I can either take corrective action by putting the fire out with a fire extinguisher; take interim action by doing something to restrict airflow to the fire; or take adaptive action by deciding to let the fire burn out. By being aware of all three of these classes of alternatives, you significantly increase the number of available approaches.

To develop creative alternatives, first brainstorm a list of possibilities, and then evaluate and combine them to create workable solutions. Talk to people whose opinions and judgment you trust, and people who are involved in the decision or play a role in carrying it out. Show others the decision statement and the alternatives you are considering, and ask them for additional ideas.

It is much easier to make good decisions after clarifying our objectives and creating alternatives. For instance, in our previous example, should any of these prospective employees be eliminated because he or she fails to satisfy at least one of the "must" objectives?

Applicant #1: Female. Great personality. High school graduate. Attended a two-year electronics technical school after high school. New to the job market. States that she is willing to do any type of work. Little knowledge of work habits, as she has not been employed since school years. Fourteen years ago, she worked part-time after school as a maintenance person for a local grocery store chain. In the toolbox test that was devised by the team, she correctly identified 15 of the 16 tools that she was shown (missed the spanner wrench). She says that she was seldom late for work. Unable to check references, since the grocery store is now out of business. Reads and writes well; meets the salary requirements. Has no knowledge of computers or computer networks. She is unemployed and can come to work tomorrow. Said she really needs the job, and the money is fine.

Applicant #2: Male. In the interviews, seemed quiet and withdrawn—almost depressed. His job was eliminated when there was a major reorganization at his old company. He has been out of work three months and is having difficulty obtaining employment. He is a highly skilled maintenance person with 20 years of experience in carpentry, hydraulics, and electricity. He correctly identified all 16 tools in the toolbox test. His references check out. He has good work habits, but a history of sickness. His old organization would not specify type of illness. He said he needs a job and would be satisfied with the starting salary, though it is far less than what he had been making. He also stated that he doesn't mind doing any type of work, no matter how disagreeable. Reads and writes well. High school education. Could start tomorrow. Doesn't know anything about computers or computer networks.

Applicant #3: Male. High school graduate. Worked for his father during the summer while in high school. Father runs a small electrical contracting business out of his home. Father says his son is a hard worker, has good work habits, and never missed a single day from work. Applicant states he is not too proud to do any task that needs to be done. Reads, but writing skills are marginal. His writing sample, full of errors in basic grammar, had many misspelled words, and his handwriting is barely legible. When questioned about his writing, applicant stated that he has always had difficulty with his spelling. Correctly identified all 16 tools in the toolbox test. He meets salary requirements, and would like to start immediately. Seems like a nice guy, but very serious. Did not laugh or joke during any of his interviews with members of the team, even when it would have been appropriate. He is, however, a computer whiz. Has his own computer. Talks computer talk. Is familiar with computer networks, although he has never hard wired a system.

Do you think Bill's team has to eliminate any one of these three applicants from consideration because he or she fails to meet a "must" objective?

They have a difficult decision. They cannot consider applicant #3 because he doesn't meet one of their "must" objectives: "Passes reading and writing test."

We have pointed out that it is not desirable to have "must" objectives that are not absolutely necessary, because they eliminate alternatives. So, unless the team can find a way out of their dilemma by making "reading and writing" a "want" objective, they cannot select candidate #3, and must confine their attention to applicants #1 and #2 (both of whom meet all their required "must" objectives).

Decisions turn out better when we follow these steps:

1. Determine objectives.
2. Rank them.
3. Create several alternatives.
4. Rationally evaluate each one in terms of "musts" and "wants."

This process produces good decisions, because it helps us determine what is really important.

The team is now ready to write down information on how well each applicant meets each objective. Usually, it is probably best to first write in the data, noting "Yes" or "No," for the must objectives. As discussed, applicant #3 was eliminated because he did not meet the "must" reading and writing requirement.

1. **Write an open decision statement.**

"Select best employee for our maintenance team"

2. Develop objectives.		3. Create alternatives.		
Objective	Weight	Applicant #1	Applicant #2	Applicant #3
Understands basic electricity	9	Two years technical school	Highly skilled	
Knows how to use hand tools	8	Part-time maintenance person 14 years ago. Scored 15 of 16 on tool test	20 years experience. Scored 16 of 16 on tool test	
Willing to do any type of task	6	Says she is willing to do any kind of work	Was a senior crafts-man, but indicates would do any task	
Gets along with others	7	Great personality	Quiet and withdrawn, seems almost depressed	
Good work habits	5	Can't verify work habits	Good work habits, but has a history of illness	
Passes reading and writing test	M	Yes	Yes	No (eliminated because he could not pass reading-writing test)
Meets salary requirements	M	Yes	Yes	
Available to work in 3 weeks	M	Yes	Yes	
Satisfaction with salary	4	Satisfied	Salary may not meet his needs	
Can hard wire computer networks	2	No experience with computers or networks	No experience with computers or networks	
		Total 274	**Total 318**	

Notice that the team could have written "yes" and "no" answers for their objectives, but later, when they compare the alternatives with each other, it will be very difficult to weight a series of yes's and no's. By writing in data or information, they can later judge which alternative is best. (Of course, must objectives always include *yes* or *no*, or *go* or *no-go*, *meets* or *doesn't meet* the objective.) For example, in the objective, "Gets along with others," they could have written in yes or no for both applicants, but the team chose to write down more-detailed information.

Having previously compared and weighted their "want" objectives using a value scale of 1 to 10, the team will now do the same for each alternative. For each objective (each row), they will automatically give the best alternative a "10," and the other alternative something less then 10. (This will keep them from double-weighting an objective.) They will not weight the "must" objectives, since these objectives are really screening devices that eliminate alternatives that cannot be considered. (Note that the column for Alternative 3 has been deleted.)

2. Develop objectives.		3. Create alternatives.	
Objective	Weight	Applicant #1	Applicant #2
Understands basic electricity	9	2 Two years technical school	10 Highly skilled
Knows how to use hand tools	8	2 Part-time maintenance person 14 years ago. Scored 15 of 16 on tool test	10 20 years experience. Scored 16 of 16 on tool test
Willing to do any type of task	6	10 Says she is willing to do any kind of work	8 Was a senior craftsman, but indicates would do any task
Gets along with others	7	10 Great personality	4 Quiet and withdrawn, seems almost depressed
Good work habits	5	10 Can't verify work habits	8 Good work habits, but has a history of illness
Passes reading and writing test	M	Yes	Yes
Meets salary requirements	M	Yes	Yes
Available to work in 3 weeks	M	Yes	Yes
Satisfaction with salary	4	10 Satisfied	3 Salary may not meet his needs
Can hard wire computer networks	2	10 No experience with computers or networks	10 No experience with computers or networks
		Total 274	Total 318

As shown on the next page, the team multiplies the weight of each want objective by the weight of each remaining alternative (applicants #1 and #2), and records each product (objective weight x alternative weight) in the table.

2. Develop objectives.		3. Create alternatives.	
Objective	Weight	Applicant #1	Applicant #2
Understands basic electricity	9	x 2 = 18 Two years technical school	x 10 = 90 Highly skilled
Knows how to use hand tools	8	x 2 = 16 Part-time maintenance person 14 years ago. Scored 15 of 16 on tool test	x 10 = 80 20 years experience. Scored 16 of 16 on tool test
Willing to do any type of task	6	x 10 = 60 Says she is willing to do any kind of work	x 8 = 48 Was a senior craftsman, but indicates would do any task
Gets along with others	7	x 10 = 70 Great personality	x 4 = 28 Quiet and withdrawn, seems almost depressed
Good work habits	5	x 10 = 50 Can't verify work habits	x 8 = 40 Good work habits, but has a history of illness
Passes reading and writing test	M	Yes	Yes
Meets salary requirements	M	Yes	Yes
Available to work in 3 weeks	M	Yes	Yes
Satisfaction with salary	4	x 10 = 40 Satisfied	x 3 = 12 Salary may not meet his needs
Can hard wire computer networks	2	x 10 = 20 No experience with computers or networks	x 10 = 20 No experience with computers or networks
		Total 274	Total 318

The team added the product scores and had a tentative first choice—alternative #2. But note that at this point in their analysis, that choice is only tentative, because they must now consider the potential risks involved in choosing this candidate.

Analyzing risk. The fourth and last step in the decision process is to consider carefully the risk involved with each of the leading alternatives. This is the most neglected step in decision-making, because we all tend to look at life's new possibilities and beginnings enthusiastically. However, you must examine the risks in any decision before you make it. To do this, simply ask, "What can go wrong?" Here again, seek help from others with experience. Talk to individuals who are opposed to the decision, and talk to people who will be involved in carrying out the decision. Several individuals can often foresee future problems better than one person working alone.

Deal with one alternative at a time. Do not initially attempt to evaluate the possibility of each risk occurring in every alternative. Then, when you have completed your list of potential risks (problems) for the first alternative, evaluate each potential problem in terms of the probability of it happening, and its seriousness if it does happen. Again, use the numerical scale of 1 to 10 to assign "seriousness" and "probability" weights to each risk. Then multiply the two weights and add the numbers. The resultant score will show the amount of risk involved in that particular alternative. Repeat the process with each leading alternative.

In our example of Bill's team, two alternatives were left—applicants #1 and #2. Their last step, then, was to evaluate the risks for each, asking "If we hire that applicant, what could go wrong?" After talking with each other and the human resources department, they developed the following "risk list" for alternative #1:

Alternative 1:	Probability of it happening	Seriousness if it happened	
1. On occasion, heavy lifting is required: (about 110 lbs.) The applicant is not able to lift this amount.	10	1	$10 \times 1 = 10$
		Total risk for alternative #1 =	10

The team rated the probability that applicant #1 could not lift 110 pounds a "10" because it was a certainty that she couldn't lift that much weight. They rated the seriousness as only a "1" because it wouldn't happen very often, and she could always ask for help.

Then, the team wrote a second risk list for alternative #2:

Alternative 2:	Probability of it happening	Seriousness if it happened	
1. Because of low salary, he may stay with job only until he finds a job that pays more.	8	10	$8 \times 10 = 80$
2. There may be a possibility of significant lost time in the future due to illness.	4	8	$4 \times 8 = 32$
		Total risk for alternative #2 =	112

Although applicant #2 scored slightly higher than applicant #1 in terms of objectives, applicant #1 has a much lower estimated risk than applicant #2. Risk scores like "9 x 9 = 81" and "8 x 9 = 72" are probably a missed "must" alternative (i.e., they probable should have been "must" objectives from the start). Those "9 x 9" and other high-risk scores are rattlesnakes under the bed!

All things considered, applicant #1 appears to be the best candidate.

When you finish evaluating the risks of our various alternatives, do not subtract the risk score from the objective/alternative scores, because they are two entirely different factors. Simply compare the original objective/alternative scores with the risk scores to make a balanced decision.

Objectives, Alternatives, and Risks

If you have to make a major decision, try to use a grid analysis similar to the one just shown. You won't always have the time, so when time is short, use this approach:

1. **Objectives:** Ask, *"What factors should we consider?" "What resources are available?" "What restrictions exist?"*

2. **Alternatives:** Create and evaluate alternatives by asking, *"What other options might we consider?"*

3. **Risk:** Analyze risk by asking, *"What could go wrong?"*

Decision Making: Checklist

☐ **Step 1. Write an open decision statement.**

Start with *"Select the best way..."*

☐ **Step 2. List objectives.**

- Ask questions:
    - What factors should you consider?
    - What are your resources (money/time/people)?
    - What results do you want?
    - What restrictions are required?

- Determine *musts*.
- Weigh *wants* (1 – 10)

☐ **Step 3. Create alternatives.**

- Brainstorm a list of alternatives on another sheet (do not evaluate alternatives until list is completed).
- Select best 3 or 4 alternatives.
- Write date in "Must" objective/alternative boxes first.
- Eliminate any alternative that doesn't meet any "Must."
- Write in the rest of the data.

    - Verify information, if possible.
    - Try to avoid "yes" and "no." Use facts and figures whenever possible.
    - Use information. Don't use "good/better/best" classifications.

- Weigh alternatives on a scale of 1 – 10, assigning 10 to the best alternative for each "want" objective.
- Multiply objective weight by alternative weight, and record on grid.
- Add scores for each alternative.

☐ **Step 4. Analyze risk.**

- Select top two alternative scores for risk analysis.
- Evaluate probability and seriousness of risks for each selected alternative.
- Don't subtract risk scores from alternative scores.
- Don't double-load decision by rewriting an objective as a risk.

Decision Making: Worksheet

Step 1: **Write an open statement ("Select the best…").**

Step 2: **List all important objectives.**
- Identify and separate *want* and *must* objectives.
- Weight the *want* objectives, from 1 to 10 ("10" = highest weight).

Step 3: **Create and list the alternatives.**
- Brainstorm a list of alternatives on another sheet of paper.
- Select three or four alternatives for analysis.
- Write data in *must* objective boxes for each alternative first.
- Eliminate any alternative that doesn't meet every *must* objective.
- Then write in data for *want* objectives. Use facts, figures, and opinions (not "yes" and "no").
- Assign weights to each alternative for each *want* objective. (Assign a "10" to the best alternative reflecting each objective, and an appropriate lower score to the other alternatives.)
- Multiply each objective weight by each alternative weight, and record.
- Add column scores for each alternative, and compare totals.

Step 4: **Taking the top two alternatives, identify the critical risk objectives.**
- Assign "probability" and "seriousness" values (1 to 10 scale, 10 = highest risk).
- Multiply probability and seriousness ratings.
- Add risk totals for each alternative and compare.

Decision statement: _____

Objectives	Must or Want	Alternative	Alternative	Alternative

Alternative: _____

Risk: P   S
_____ ____ x ____ = ____
_____ ____ x ____ = ____
_____ ____ x ____ = ____
_____ ____ x ____ = ____

Alternative: _____

Risk: P   S
_____ ____ x ____ = ____
_____ ____ x ____ = ____
_____ ____ x ____ = ____
_____ ____ x ____ = ____

Quality Leadership Skills

14

The Importance of Planning

"Tell me, please, which way it is I ought to go from here?"
"Where is it you want to go?" said the cat.
"I don't care much where," said Alice.
"Then it doesn't matter which way you go!" said the cat.

– Lewis Carroll
Through the Looking Glass

After making a decision, plan before you implement. It's not complicated. Just follow these simple steps:

- Write a planning statement.

- List the action items necessary to implement your decision.

- Identify the most-important actions with the highest risk.

- For each critical action, list the things that could go wrong if you take the action (the problems).

- Prioritize the potential importance of these problems.

- Analyze each major potential problem in priority order.

- Add all major preventive and contingent actions to the original plan.

In this chapter, we will explain each of these planning steps.

Preventing Potential Problems

We make decisions in the present, but we plan for the future. Planning is something most people don't seem to get around to, because we are normally more concerned about today's problems and decisions than tomorrow's plans. Yet knowing where we are going helps us get there.

Of course, if you don't care what you do, then it really doesn't matter which way you go. Where we are going does matter to most of us, however.

Plans make destinations clear; they tell how to get there, and they allow us to measure the success of our efforts. Successful people plan everything they do—every day.

Do you think about the consequences of everything you do? Most of us seem to have a tough time imagining that our decisions (which of course are perfect) have negative consequences. But implementing a decision creates change, and most changes produce problems. It is not a question of "good" or "bad" decisions; change in and of itself creates a high probability for future problems.

Planning can reduce the worry. We all know someone who constantly worries—in fact, they worry so much that they lose sight of present happiness. Then there are perpetual optimists (like me) who rarely have problems big enough to worry about if they are in the future. I can just put my head in the sand, bury my body behind my desk, and let the problems take care of themselves. But I get in trouble when a problem doesn't go away and just gets bigger—then it is often too late to do anything about it. Fortunately, I was taught a problem-avoidance process a number of years ago; I use it religiously so I can go back to living my day-to-day life with much less hassle.

Future consequences may not be initially visible. Individually, you might think, "Of course I understand *all* the problems that might occur if I implement this decision." Time and time again, even though we believe without doubt that there are no problems with a decision, there are very real problems. By talking with others and sharing the decision and the resultant plan, you discover the power of feedback.

The planning process itself enables us to experience a daily sense of accomplishment, because every action we take toward achieving our goals feels good; we're moving forward and not procrastinating.

The most important things in life do not create a sense of urgency in us until we begin to see how they must be reached. When we bring our ultimate goals and objectives into the present by creating step-by-step action plans, we move forward.

Planning allows us to involve others—in this case, our employees and colleagues. Let your employees help determine the goals, especially if they are going to play a part in carrying out the plan. They will be more likely to be committed to the plan, which directly influences how successfully it is implemented.

Let's examine a process that will help us be more effective in planning and in avoiding problems.

The planning statement. When you have made a decision, you are ready to write a planning statement: a description of exactly what you want to accomplish. A planning statement should be quantifiable and have an end result and completion date. Let's look at each characteristic.

Quantifiable. The statement "To have productive cross-functional team meetings" does not communicate enough information. What does the word "productive" mean? How will I know when the team is productive? The planning statement must contain specific information about my goal so I will actually know when it is successful. To make the statement more quantifiable, specify behaviors or what the team will do when it is productive. Examples:

- *They will use the problem-solving process that we were taught.*
- *Team members will come to the meetings.*

End result. A planning statement that only identifies behaviors is not an effective way of specifying future direction. You must also include end results. The initial planning statement above should be expanded:

- *The team will use written problem-solving processes in four of the next six weekly meetings.*
- *Team members will have a meeting absenteeism rate of not more than 5%.*

Completion date. Specify a date by which the plan will be accomplished. The planning statement would now look something like this:

> *Create a productive team by January 5ᵗʰ by using a problem-solving process in four of the next six weekly meetings, and by reducing absenteeism to not more than 5%.*

There is nothing remarkable about a planning statement. It's a statement about a goal or objective that includes measurability, an end result, and a completion date.

Action items (action steps). After you have written a planning statement, develop a list of actions to achieve them. As you identify the action items in the plan, establish completion dates for each one. Do not assign a final priority number to the items at this point, as you might need to add additional action items later.

Here's what I mean: Elizabeth's planning goal was to become a manager in her organization within four years. The initial action steps in her plan looked something like this:

Planning goal: *"To become a manager in this organization within four years"*

Action steps:	**Completion dates:**
1. Meet with my boss and discuss promotional goal.	Sept. 15
2. Write 10 key development objectives for my present job.	Sept. 30
3. Analyze my managerial skills. Determine my strengths and areas of needed improvement.	Oct. 15
4. Take a minimum of two management workshops each year.	Dec. 1
5. Complete my B.S. degree at night school within three years. Sign up this semester.	Jan. 15
6. Identify management openings that might occur during the third and fourth years.	Mar. 1

This part of the planning process is simple. Most people can probably write a planning statement and then list the action steps in their plan. In fact, this is where most individuals stop their planning process. But wisely, Elizabeth realized that she also needed to look carefully at each action step to identify anything that might go wrong.

Critical action items and risks. From past experience, we know that some action items mean trouble. (Maybe you took that step before and it led to a disaster.) If an action is completely new to you, look out. "Murphy's Law" may get you. Major action items with lots of parts and pieces are especially vulnerable, particularly if you have no experience with it. Problems can also result when people have to communicate over distances by phone, letter, fax, or e-mail or when there are a number of people involved. If you must operate close to the limits of your space, time, or money, proceed with caution. If the plan requires that you order a new item that's exactly 3 feet wide and your door is 3 feet 2 inches, you'll have to do something about it. If someone tells you that the item you ordered will be delivered on Wednesday and you have to have it by Thursday, assume that it won't arrive until Friday. If one action item will only cost $9,990 and you have exactly $10,000, you know what's going to happen!

Ask yourself this question: When you take this action outlined in the plan, what could go wrong?"

If you anticipate potential problems before you carry out the plan, you can develop solutions that will greatly increase the chances of achieving the goal.

One of Elizabeth's critical action items was "Attend night classes and get the 24 credits I need to finish college." She viewed this action as problematic because it was new for her (she had never attended college at night). It was also a very important one. She once worked for a boss who said to her, "Your chances of being selected as a manager in this organization are a lot better if you have a college degree. In fact, your chances of making it without one are zero!"

List the action items:

Meet with my boss and discuss my goal to be promoted.

Write 10 key development objectives for my present job.

Analyze my managerial skills. Determine my strengths and areas of needed improvement.

Take a minimum of two management workshops each year.

Critical step: Complete my B.S. degree at night school within three years.

Identify management openings that might occur during the third and fourth years.

Possible problems. Having identified the critical action steps that might cause problems, select one and list the possible problems. In Elizabeth's case, she wrote down these:

Critical action step:

"Complete my B.S. degree at night school within three years."

List potential problems. (Ask yourself what could go wrong.)

I'll get bored and stop attending.
It takes longer than three years to obtain the 54 credits I need.
Night school will be very hard on my family.

Set priorities. The next planning step is to evaluate the probability and seriousness of each potential problem. That is, figure out what the probability is that the problem will occur, and then how seriously it will affect the success of the plan if it does occur. To rate probability and seriousness, use "H" for high, "M" for medium, and "L" for low.

In our example, Elizabeth felt that there was only a small chance that she would get bored and drop out (low probability of the event occurring), but if she did, it would seriously jeopardize her plan (high seriousness). Her boss would see her as a failure in something he considered very important (earning a college degree).

She also thought that there was only a low probability that it would take her longer than three years to obtain a degree. But if this did happen, she might still be eligible for promotion, given evidence that she was almost through with her education. When she considered her family, however, it was clear that not only was there a high probability that night school would be very hard on her family, but that it would be very serious indeed.

Her analysis now looked like this:

Potential problems:	Probability:	Seriousness:
a) I'll get bored and stop attending.	Low probability	High seriousness
b) It may take longer than three years to get my degree.	Low probability	Medium seriousness
c) Night school will be very hard on my family.	High probability	High seriousness

Problem analysis. Next, analyze the greatest potential problems by finding their likely causes. Then plan preventive and contingency actions. After you identify the likely causes, ask, "What can be done to reduce the probability that this event (or likely cause) will happen?" In other words, what preventive action can you include in your plans?

You then consider: "If the worst comes to pass and the problem does occur, what can I do now to reduce the seriousness of the consequences?" In other words, what contingency action should you include in your plans from the start?

For Elizabeth, the potential problem "Night school will be very hard on my family" had a high probability of happening, and if it happens, it would be high in seriousness. Thus she selected this problem for further analysis. She asked herself, her family, and others whose opinions she respected, "Why would night school be so difficult for my family?"

In real life, she received a long list of probable causes or reasons why night school might be difficult for her family. Those of you who have been through the night-school experience know that there are a number of likely causes leading to family hardship.

The information below answers these basic questions:

Column A: Analyze each major potential problem for the likely cause of the problem.

Column B: What can you do now to reduce the probability of the event (or likely cause) occurring?

Column C: What can you do now to reduce the seriousness of the event if in fact it happens?

Column D: What is going to trigger each major contingency action?

A. Likely Cause	B. Preventive Action	C. Contingency Action	D. Trigger
3 nights/week away from family	*See if college has courses I can take at home*	*Enroll Bill (spouse) in one or more courses with me*	*Me (Elizabeth)*
Lack of study time	*Buy course books now and start studying; take courses that are easier for me*	*Get family to help me study*	*Spouse complains and says, "You're never home!"*
Family not aware of hardships	*Involve family in pre-planning; have Bill talk to Joe (who is also attending night school)*	*(No action)*	*(If there is no contingency action, there is no trigger)*

Do the same thing for all of the other critical action steps. Conduct the same analysis: Identify the action steps with highest potential risk. List potential problems for each. Evaluate each potential problem on its probability of happening and its seriousness if it happens anyway. Lastly, analyze each major potential problem for likely causes, preventive actions, contingency actions, and triggers.

Preventive and contingent actions. The last important step in our planning process is to insert our major contingency and/or preventive actions back into our original plan. In our example, Elizabeth's plan will now look like this, with the new action steps placed in boldface type:

		Completion dates:
1.	**Have a family meeting and discuss plans.**	Sept. 1
2.	**Ask Bill to talk to Joe. Call Joe and ask him to talk to Bill.**	Sept. 2
3.	Meet with my boss and discuss promotional goal.	Sept. 15
4.	**Call college and see if it has online courses I can take at home.**	Sept. 20
5.	**Meet with my college adviser and determine elective course that my spouse would enjoy taking.**	Sept. 22
6.	**Buy course books now and start studying.**	Oct. 1
7.	Write 10 key development objectives for my present job.	Oct. 15
8.	Analyze my managerial skills. Determine my strengths and areas of needed improvement.	Nov. 1
9.	Take a minimum of two management workshops each year.	Nov. 15
10.	Complete my B.S. degree at night school within three years. Sign up this semester.	Jan. 15
11.	Determine management openings that might occur during the third and fourth years.	Mar. 1

As you can see, by adding these new action steps to her plan, Elizabeth has greatly increased the probability that she will successfully reach her goal. Obviously, in her real plan, she also analyzed other critical action steps and added additional action steps to her plan that are not shown in our example. Note, too, that some of her completion dates have changed to reflect her new activities.

Many of us spend a great deal of time dealing with a variety of problems, but we do very little planning. We can become so busy running from crisis to crisis that we don't take the time to plan for success. When we commit ourselves to careful planning before implementation, we can maintain our focus without getting so sidetracked. This will surely increase our level of achievement.

A Problem Avoidance worksheet follows.

Problem-Avoidance Worksheet

Step 1: Write a planning statement.

Step 2: List the action items necessary to achieve the goal.

Step 3: Identify the critical actions with highest potential risk.

Step 4: List potential problems for each critical action step. (Ask, "What could go wrong?")

Step 5: Prioritize the importance of these potential problems. Use High, Medium, or Low to rate probability of event occurring *and* rate the seriousness if it does.

Step 6: Analyze each major potential problem in priority order. Write down the likely cause, preventive action, and contingency action. Then assign a trigger for the contingency action.

Step 7: Add all major preventive and contingent actions to the original plan.

Step 1: Write a planning statement. Make the statement quantifiable, state the end result desired, and include a completion date.

_____

_____

_____

Step 2: List all the action steps.   **Step 3: Identify those critical action steps with the highest potential risk.**

Check if critical action step

1. _____   _____

2. _____   _____

3. _____   _____

4. _____   _____

5. _____   _____

6. _____   _____

etc. _____   _____

Step 4: List the potential problems for each critical action step.

Step 5: Set priorities for each potential problem.
Use H = High, M = Medium, and L = Low to rate probability and seriousness

	Probability	Seriousness
_____	_____	_____
_____	_____	_____
_____	_____	_____
_____	_____	_____
_____	_____	_____

Step 6: Analyze each major potential problem for likely causes, preventive action, contingency action, and trigger (if needed).

Problem: _____

Likely Cause	Preventive Action	Contingency Action	Trigger

Note: Do this for each major potential problem.

Step 7: Add all major preventive and contingent actions to the original plan. Write a new plan that incorporates important preventive and contingency actions (from Steps 6 and 7) as new steps in your original list of steps. Write all steps in chronological order, and number the steps. Finally, write a completion date for each step.

Sample

Step #	Step	Completion Date

15

Developing Objectives with Employees

The purpose of the work on making the future is not to decide what should be done tomorrow, but what should be done today to have a tomorrow.

– Peter Drucker
Managing for Results

Helping your employees write their goals and objectives provides them with a strategy for success. It allows the two of you to clearly and concisely specify their future activities and also provides a way of measuring their achievements. This kind of information is invaluable for managing their performance.

Preparation

Whether you are working with one individual or several, the process can seem a bit daunting until you get into it, so go slow. Begin by briefly meeting with the employee and:

- Discuss the purpose of the upcoming meeting.
- Explain how the process works.
    - Brainstorm a list of goals and identify those that are a priority.
    - Write priority goal statements that are measurable.
    - Develop a list of action steps to achieve each goal.
- Discuss the organization/department/section goals he or she needs to know about before completing his or her worksheets.
- Explain when and where the meeting will take place.

Explain the purpose of the upcoming meeting. You can require your employees to write goals, but it is important to obtain their acceptance and commitment to the process. In order to gain buy-in from your employees, you can review and then use the "reasons for planning" that were listed in the preceding chapter. For example, "Planning enables us to experience a daily sense of accomplishment" and "Good planning prevents procrastination" are especially appropriate reasons here.

Describe how the process works.

Brainstorm a list of goals. First, tell the employees to find a quiet place and brainstorm a list of the most important goals they see in their job. As they list their goals, ask them not to evaluate or judge them. Ask them to write down everything that occurs to them, even if it may seem "silly." If they have a burning secret desire to accomplish something different or special, ask them to write it down! Tell them to focus on all areas of their jobs—whatever goals are important to them.

Suggest that they not worry about writing measurable goal statements at this point. As long as they know what they mean by what they write, that's fine. At this point in the process, it is their list. They shouldn't have to show it to anybody.

Tell your employees that they can develop several different types of job goals:

- *Regular or routine* goals that simply specify the things the employee normally does in their job.

- *Problem-solving* goals to resolve a specific problem

- *Innovative* goals to facilitate new or creative ideas

- *Personal* goals

Most of your employees' growth on the job will be connected with efforts to achieve the last three kinds of goals.

Also tell them to put their energies into only two or three goals at any one time. Their chances of success are much better if they concentrate on a few important goals, rather than all of them at once. (Less-important goals can usually be addressed in the future.)

Measurable goals. The employee is now ready to write out his or her highest-priority goals using the "Goal Worksheet" found at the end of this chapter. A goal is simply a statement of exactly what the individual wants to accomplish. Such a statement should have three characteristics: It should be specific, measurable, and achievable.

Let's say that one of my goal statements is to "Learn more about motivating adjunct teachers." This does not communicate enough information. What does the word "motivating" mean? How will I know when I have learned more about motivation? By what date do I want to have obtained this knowledge? Since my goal statement doesn't give enough specific information about my goal, it will be hard to actually know when I am successful—or even whether or not I am successful. In a goal statement, you must specify behaviors and/or identify results.

Quantifiable goals. A good goal statement also should be measurable—*quantifiable.* "To learn more about conducting a performance appraisal session with my employees" sounds fine, but you really won't know when you have satisfactorily achieved this goal because you haven't specified the standard—or measure—of achievement. Here is a measurable goal: "To be able to conduct a performance appraisal session with my employees by January 1 of next year." The statement now contains a word that specifies behavior: "conduct" (rather than "learning"); and the statement now includes a specific time period so the individual will know when he or she has achieved it.

Achievable goals. A goal statement should also be *achievable.* There is little point in setting ourselves up for failure. A good goal statement will extend and improve performance.

Develop a list of action steps to achieve each goal. Tell the employees that after they have determined which goals they need to work toward first, they can then develop the steps they will take to achieve them, along with completion dates for each step. (But suggest that they not number to their steps at this point, as they may need to add more steps later.)

State any appropriate organizational goals. Next, in this initial meeting, we tell the employees about any specific organizational goals that should be included.

State when and where the meeting will take place. Finally, in this initial meeting with your employees, tell them when and where the principal meeting will take place. You should have located a meeting place that is private and where you can control interruptions. If it is impossible to hold your telephone calls for an hour meeting, then you need to go elsewhere. You can reserve the conference room, or find someone who is on vacation and use his or her office. You can even tell your boss what you will be doing and ask not to be interrupted. Whatever you do, treat this meeting as critically important: do not allow interruptions.

After this preliminary meeting with the employee, spend some time thinking of several key objectives that you would like to see the employee achieve during the upcoming year. Using the "Goal Worksheet" found at the end of this chapter, write out the goals as well as tentative plans and methods for how the employee will achieve them (the objectives). You can share these plans with the employee in the upcoming meeting, if needed.

The Meeting

Open the meeting. When an employee first walks into your office or conference room, explain that the purpose of this meeting is to help him or her better understand the organization's and department's goals and objectives, improve his or her goals and plans, and discuss any problems with the plans.

Next, help reduce any anxiety the employee may be feeling by setting out the meeting agenda. For example, you might say something like,

> *"Bill, I see my role in today's meeting as being a resource for you. I may have some information you need on our department's goals, some ideas or suggestions to help improve your plans, and even some ideas about anticipating potential problems. What I'd like to do is to discuss your goals and make sure that they are measurable statements, and then offer additional specific goals if appropriate. I'll also try to help you set some priorities so you know where you need to spend your time; review your strategies and plans and offer ideas if needed; and then set up specific follow-up dates. This is your meeting, Bill, and I am here to help you any way I can."*

Of course, you will use your own words to explain generally to your employee what is going to happen and your role in the meeting.

Discuss employee's tentative goals, and determine the measurability of each. Here, ask the employee to communicate the goals he or she wrote. Review only the goal statements at the top of the goal worksheets, since the specific plans and methods will be discussed later, after you set priorities. As the employee reads his or her first goal, you need to make sure that it is specific and measurable, and has target dates.

As the leader, you can help the employee in identifying his or her ideas for improving the goal statement by asking questions such as:

- "How will you know when you are successful?"
- "What will you be able to do (or avoid doing) when you have achieved your goal?"
- "What conditions will exist when you finish?"
- "What tangible results will be achieved?"
- "What are you going to do to make this happen?"

During the discussion of the employee's goals, it is not necessary to determine whether or not the goals are appropriate and feasible. You can deal naturally with the question of appropriateness when you set priorities, and you will discuss feasibility later when you review the employee's plans. Remember, what looks initially like an impossible goal may turn out to be possible after reviewing the employee's strategies and plans.

Offer additional goals if appropriate. After reviewing each of the employee's goals, you may have additional organizational, departmental, or sectional objectives that he or she hasn't addressed. So here is where you can offer additional topics that you feel are important. Since you took the time to write out several objectives before the meeting, you will be ready at this point to make any needed suggestions.

Determine goal priorities. Before employees start to spend time implementing their job-related goals, we should review their priorities. In conjunction with employees, decide which of the goals are "must do," "ought to do," and "nice to do." Since you will appraise their performance on what they do, it only makes sense for them to complete the high-priority goals that meet with our approval.

Ask the employee to arrange, in order of priority, the goals—both the employee's and yours— that were discussed. Then, two or three key goals should be selected for the immediate future. Goals that are not selected as first priorities can be deferred to quarterly follow-up meetings, and implemented as the initial objectives are achieved. You should deliberately restrict the number of objectives initially selected for two reasons. The employee's chances of success are better if his or her efforts are concentrated on only a few key objectives. Second, we can improve our chances of following up the employee's progress if we have a reasonable number of objectives to monitor.

Review employee's strategies and plans to achieve key goals, and offer ideas. As the employee discusses his or her plans and methods, you can do several things. First, if the employee has a good plan, be sure to say so. Second, ask what you can do to help the employee reach his or her goals, and offer your suggestions for how the plans could be further improved. Third, with each goal, ask the key question, "If you do this, what could go wrong?" to elicit any potential problems. Then, offer suggestions or ideas for preventive or contingency solutions, and include these ideas in the original plan. Finally, review the target dates for the goal and action steps, and adjust them to make them more realistic if indicated.

Set follow-up dates for review sessions, and conclude the meeting. Finally, tell your employee you will be available to discuss his or her plans whenever needed. To ensure that you will really follow up with the employee regarding progress, set specific dates in the employee's presence, and write them in your calendar. Normally, one follow-up meeting each quarter will be sufficient, with additional meetings scheduled as needed.

In concluding the meeting, ask the employee to provide you with a copy of the *Goal Worksheet* after the meeting. Then, you can spell out your positive expectation by saying, "I know you can do it!" Finally, express your appreciation for the time and effort that he or she spent preparing for this meeting.

A Leader's Checklist for goals and objectives follows.

Leader's Checklist for
Developing Objectives with Employees

☐ 1. **Prepare for the objective-setting meeting with the employee.**

- Tentatively complete the Goal Worksheet on key goals for this employee.
- Meet in advance to set the stage.

    – Discuss purpose of upcoming meeting.
    – Describe how the process works and give employee a copy of the Goal Worksheet.
    – Present any appropriate organizational, department, or section goals employee needs to know.
    – State when and where the meeting will take place.

- Plan minimum of one hour for meeting.

    – Make sure there is complete privacy.
    – Make sure there are no interruptions.

☐ 2. **Open the meeting.**

- Explain your role as a resource for:
    – Organizational goals
    – Department or section goals
    – Ideas and suggestions
    – Analysis of potential problems
- Outline the meeting agenda.

☐ 3. **Discuss the employee's tentative goals, and determine the measurability of each.**

- Ask the employee to share his or her goal statements. (Do not discuss specific action plans at this time.)
- Make sure that each goal is specific and measurable and has a target date.

☐ 4. **Offer additional goals (if appropriate).**

☐ 5. **Determine goal priorities.**

- Ask the employee to prioritize all of the goals.
- Discuss the employee's priorities. Reach a consensus, if possible.
- Limit the number of goals to two or three for the initial time period.

(continued)

☐ 6. **Review the employee's strategies and plans to achieve key goals, and offer ideas.**

- Provide specific positive feedback to the employee about any of his or her significant plans or strategies.
- Ask what you can do to help the employee achieve his or her goals.
- Offer ideas and suggestions to improve the employee's list of action steps.
- Analyze potential problems by asking, "What could go wrong?"
- Develop contingency or preventive actions for potential problems, and incorporate these into the plan.
- Examine the original target dates for each objective, and adjust if needed.

☐ 7. **Set follow-up dates for review sessions, and conclude the discussion.**

- Tell the employee that you will be available to discuss his or her progress whenever needed.
- Inform the employee that there will be follow-up meetings (e.g., quarterly).
- Write specific dates in your calendar (in the employee's presence) for the first follow-up meeting (in approximately 3 months).
- Ask the employee to provide you with a final copy of the list of goals (the Goal Worksheet, if one is used).
- Spell out your positive expectations.
- Express your appreciation for their efforts so far.

Goal Worksheet

Goals	Priorities	Plans/Methods to Achieve Goals
Goals should be **specific, measurable, attainable,** and **challenging.** They can be regular, problem-solving, innovative, or personal goals. Write your goals like this: "To…(verb)…(end result)…(subject)… (time)."	H = High M = Medium L = Low	Write specific and detailed plans and methods to achieve goals. a) Detail the steps of your plan for each goal. b) Ask, "What could go wrong?" and identify potential problems. c) Identify likely causes of potential problems. d) Develop key preventive and contingency solutions. e) Put solutions back in original plan as new (or modified) steps. f) Note new steps with an asterisk. g) Date and number all steps.
Goal:	**Priority**	**Plan:**

Goal Worksheet (concluded)

Goals	Priorities	Plans/Methods to Achieve Goals
Goal:		
Goal:		

16
Conducting Effective Performance Appraisals

To the extent that the level of performance, competitiveness, and innovation for individuals and groups continue to grow in importance, performance appraisal will remain one of the most critical management processes that organizations can undertake.

— Richard D. Jette and Edward G. Wertheim

Some years ago, I had a boss who was truly incompetent when it came to conducting performance appraisals. To compound the problem, he thought he was doing a good job. After every brief once-a-year session, I felt bad about him and about my organization. And most important, I felt bad about me!

But I knew that his short review of my strengths and weaknesses was ineffective. Since then, I have read everything I could about performance appraisals, attended many workshops on this subject, conducted appraisal sessions with numerous employees, talked to thousands of managers, supervisors, and employees, and taught hundreds of workshops on the topic.

And only now, many years after my first unfortunate experience, do I feel comfortable—most of the time—participating in a performance-appraisal session. I have learned a lot, and much of it the hard way.

This chapter is about performance appraisals: why they're important and what they should include. We'll also introduce an approach to conduct and manage them so that they are productive, balanced, and fair. It won't be a sit-back-and-listen-as-the-boss-tells-the-employee-his-strengths-and-weaknesses approach. It is participative. But there is a cost to you: It requires you to spend time preparing for the appraisal meeting. You will also find that your appraisal interviews will run longer. There will be open disagreement during your meeting, but an open discussion will allow you and your employee to reach a better understanding of his or her actual performance.

Performance Appraisals

There are a host of reasons why performance appraisals are win-win for everybody. They are great opportunities to obtain information useful in making decisions about salaries, promotions, or demotions and to tell employees what they have done right or wrong. These are important benefits, but there are even more important reasons for conducting performance appraisals.

For instance, you might want to work with an employee on professional development through coaching and counseling. Such appraisal discussions can create a mutual understanding of the employee's strengths and areas of desired improvement, which is the beginning for the creation of an action plan. They also help with career development, because you can learn where the employee wants to go and whether or not he or she can get there, so that you can help the employee achieve these goals. Appraisal discussions also provide opportunities to recognize and motivate an employee.

The leader has to sometimes play the role of a judge, which can lead the employee to quickly assume a corresponding role. A new employee can become passive and do very little talking, whereas an older employee might get defensive. The focus of this type of performance discussion is on the past: we are reflecting on what has already happened.

If the process is participative, however, the leader is more of a counselor. The employee's dignity is obviously being respected, and he or she will be more active and participative as a result. The focus is on where the employee is right now, and what can be done in the future to improve.

It is extremely difficult to play both roles in the same interview. If you play the role of judge and in effect tell the employee to "sit down, shut up, and listen while I tell you your strengths and weaknesses," then it will be very difficult to suddenly shift gears and say, "I'm here to help you in any way that I can."

I'm not saying that it's impossible to play both roles in the same interview. It's just very difficult. It is all in where we choose to put our emphasis. For real change to be made in the employee's performance following the interview, the emphasis has to be put on coaching, counseling, guiding, leading, training, and helping—not on judging. It is not so much what the employee has already done, but what he or she will do in the future that is important.

Factors Affecting the Quality of a Performance Review

There are four factors that affect the quality of a performance appraisal: the organizational environment in which the performance appraisal is conducted; the performance appraisal system that is used; the leader who conducts the performance appraisal; and the attitude of the employee.

The organizational environment. When you evaluate the quality of your performance appraisals, it is important to consider the support or lack of support on the part of executive management and the human resource department, the individuals conducting the appraisal, the number of employees whose performance must be appraised, the employee's job, whether or not there are job standards and legal considerations.

Executive management support. Do the executive managers demonstrate their commitment to performance appraisals by conducting quality interviews with their own department heads? Or do they talk about the need for good appraisals, yet fail to use them? Executive managers are responsible for leading their employees in the best way possible, using performance appraisals on a regular basis for performance improvement.

Human resources department. Has the human resource department designed a performance appraisal system (and forms) that help the process? If the organization expects leaders to simply hand an evaluation to the employee that reflects little or no input from them, it is essentially discouraging two-way communication during the performance appraisal discussions (which is essential for positive results). Try to conduct an informal appraisal shortly before the "official" appraisal session; this will not only make the appraisal interview fairer to the employee, but also will give you better information to use when you must fill out the appraisal form.

Delegation. Are the individuals who should be conducting performance appraisals allowed to conduct them? One department head I know had two first-line leaders and twenty-one employees reporting to him. He himself conducted all the performance appraisals with the employees to improve communication between the employees and management. He also met individually with his two leaders to discuss the performance of their employees before meeting with the employees. This was problematic, however: the department head attempted to do performance appraisals on too many people. He also bypassed the managers, who were in a much better position to know the details of their employees' performance. This led to poor appraisals and poor morale among the first-line leaders, who came off looking like they had little real authority.

The number of employees whose performance must be appraised. If you have only six employees, you have more time to conduct effective discussions about performance than you will have with twenty-six employees. Quality performance appraisals take time—time to prepare for them, and time to conduct them. The more employees you have reporting to you, the harder it is to find enough time to do in-depth preparation and work with the employee on performance.

The employee's job. The employee's job can influence the quality of the performance appraisal. Obviously, if the employee's job is monotonous and not very motivating, the performance appraisal will be more difficult. Contrast this type of situation with an employee who has an exciting or challenging job. Interested and challenged employees normally are easier to talk with about their performance.

Job standards. Appraisals are easier to conduct if both the employee and the manager understand the job, its standards of performance, and the established goals or objectives. Sometimes leaders run into problems during performance appraisal interviews because the employee does not know or understand his or her job expectations. Most of us have heard employees legitimately say, "I didn't know that I had to do that!" or ask such questions as "What is a good job?" "When am I not doing this job well enough?" and "When am I devoting too much time and energy to this task?" These questions suggest that the employee doesn't know what is expected of them in the job.

To avoid such problems, the manager should meet individually with his or her employees six to twelve months ahead of time to discuss their specific job responsibilities. They should each complete a job analysis worksheet similar to the one shown on the next page, independently of each other, and then meet and discuss how they both see the job. It is amazing how often managers and their employees do not agree on which tasks are most important, the standards for tasks, and the authority the employee has for each task. This kind of discussion helps ensure that the employee is on track. The next performance appraisal meeting with this employee will likely be fairer and more productive as a result.

This is a useful format for job analysis:

Job Analysis Worksheet

List the main tasks in your job.	How critical is each task? A = Highest B = Medium C = Lowest	What standards are used to measure your job performance in each task?	What problems exist that handicap your performance?	Authority Levels* 1, 2, or 3

* A "#1 authority level" means that the employee has total authority to do the task. He or she doesn't have to ask permission to do the task or even tell the leader that it was done. The employee simply does it because it's a routine part of his or her job.

A "#2 authority level" allows the employee to do the task without first asking for permission, but he or she is expected to let the leader know that it was done.

A "#3 authority level" indicates that the employee needs to obtain approval from his or her leader before doing that task.

Legal considerations. Changes in the laws require leaders to stay abreast of the latest requirements regarding privacy and Equal Employment Opportunity, policies on promotions or transfers based on past performance-appraisal data, etc. Astute leaders keep themselves informed so that what they do meets both the intent and the letter of the law.

The performance appraisal system. Another factor that must be considered is the appraisal system itself. How often are performance reviews scheduled? How is the appraisal form routed through the organization, and who has access to it? What information is requested?

These and other questions about the design of the performance appraisal system are important because although the organization's human resource department usually establishes the system, if it doesn't work for managers and employees, it should be reviewed and perhaps changed.

How often are performance reviews scheduled? At a minimum, reviews should be scheduled yearly for experienced employees, and every six months for newcomers. If your organization doesn't follow this schedule, try to schedule informal appraisal sessions.

How is the appraisal form routed through the organization? If your own boss must review and sign the form before you conduct a performance appraisal interview with an employee, the organization's system is inappropriate. A boss who must review the form before you are allowed to conduct an appraisal interview with your employee signifies lack of trust in your ability to complete the form properly with the employee. For effective interviews, the manager and the employee should complete the appraisal form together, and then send it through channels.

Who has access to the form? Restrict access to confidential information to only those who have a legitimate need for it, but you must also allow the employee to have full and ready access to blank forms and the completed forms. The employee needs blank copies of all appraisal forms to prepare properly for the discussion. In addition, he or she should be given a copy of his or her completed appraisal form to use as a reference during the year.

What information is requested? Some appraisal forms list general duties, personality traits, and work habits, and then rate the employee on each. Other forms are customized for the employee's specific job, with ratings assigned for each of his or her major job duties. (This is by far the better type of form.) The more subjective the form, the more difficult it is to use fairly and consistently. If the form asks managers to rate character and personality traits such as "attitude" instead of measurable behaviors, the appraisal cannot possibly be objective (or fair).

A good appraisal form can help you get a more-accurate performance appraisal, but some skilled leaders who use poor appraisal forms conduct excellent appraisals. So if you are required to use a form that measures personality traits, use it—but be sure part of your preparation for the review is to take a closer look at the employee's strengths and areas of needed improvement in light of his or her job performance. Then, in the discussion, you can talk about performance—not personality.

The key point is to use the system in the best way you can. Don't let the system use you!

The appraiser. The individuals who conduct performance appraisals greatly influence the quality of performance appraisal. Their attitude toward this part of their job, what they know about doing it, and how well they do it (skills) all make a big difference in the effectiveness of a performance appraisal.

Attitude. A manager's attitude will influence how much time is put into preparation, the priority he or she gives to performance appraisals over any crises that come up (and usually do), the amount of time set aside for discussions, and how important the employee feels the appraisal session is. If a manager considers performance appraisals to be a major part of his job, he is likely to devote significant time and thought to it.

Knowledge. Unfortunately, many leaders learn how to conduct performance appraisals from bosses who lack an understanding of how they should be done. There are very specific things that anyone can learn how to do to improve performance reviews. Later in this chapter, we will present some common-sense strategies.

Skill. We all nod intelligently as we discuss the key strategies for conducting an appraisal discussion, but because we are creatures of habit, we don't always use the steps effectively (though we may want to). You must have opportunities to develop your skills and apply the new things you have learned. That is why it is essential for you to select several key ideas presented in this chapter and use them for your next performance appraisal discussion.

The employee. The employee is the other person involved in the performance appraisal. The employee's attitude, preparation, and performance level all affect the outcome of the session.

The employee's attitude. The employee's attitude is vital to a successful appraisal session. If the employee is hostile or feels that the appraisal discussion is an exercise in paperwork, then the results will be poor. If you know that an employee has a negative attitude toward the appraisal process, it is up to you to find out why he or she feels that way and then to determine how you can help the employee see the positive benefits of a performance appraisal.

There are clear benefits for the employee. One-on-one sessions are great opportunities for you and the employee to talk about what the employee has done well in the past, and to discuss his or her future goals within the organization. Even poor performance can be discussed in a positive way (use phrasing like "in need of a little improvement," not "weaknesses").

The amount of time the employee spends preparing for the appraisal discussion is usually directly related to its success. If you want the employee to participate in a two-way discussion in the interview, then you must give the employee enough time to prepare adequately.

Help the employee in his or her preparation. In advance, make sure the individual has a blank copy of the appraisal form so that he or she knows what will be asked, and can think about strengths and areas needing improvement. Also explain that you expect them to do most of the talking.

The employee's performance level. Statistically, if you have ten employees, one will be a super-star, eight will range from "very good" to "meets minimum acceptable standards," and one will be a problem—your cross to bear. If an employee is outstanding in all categories, the appraisal will be fun to conduct. When this isn't the case, the interview is more difficult to handle.

Your ability to conduct a successful performance appraisal is far more dependent on what has been going on all year than on what you do or don't do during the appraisal. If you haven't been doing your job as a leader in guiding, coaching, counseling, directing, and training throughout the year, the most impressive interviewing skills in the world won't make your interviews successful. A performance appraisal session is not a substitute for ongoing leadership. It is the result of *good* leadership.

The Performance Appraisal Process

The country's best leaders have all had to evaluate the performance of their employees over the course of their careers. This section is about best practices. And much of it, when you read through the section, is common sense. Some general guidelines:

1. Talk about performance, not personality. It's about what he or she has or has not done, not about what he or she *is*.

2. Offer insight into the employee's problems, not indictment. Offer understanding and help, not blame.

3. Focus on development, not discipline. Focus on the future, not the past.

4. Discuss, not dominate. Talk *with* the employee, not *at* him or her.

There are nine steps that are considered critical in effective performance appraisal discussions.

1. Prepare for the discussion.
2. Welcome the employee and outline the purpose of the meeting.
3. Determine which topics the employee wants to discuss.
4. Discuss concerns not mentioned by the employee.
5. Develop written action plans for carrying out key solutions in a specific time period.
6. Give specific feedback on any positive performance that has not already been discussed.

7. Summarize the interview and discuss ratings.
8. Set follow-up dates.
9. Thank the employee for participating.

A number of years ago I was in Houston, Texas, leading a performance appraisal workshop. One participant sitting in the back hadn't said much. He didn't seem to want to be there, and I wondered if his boss had made him come. I had just presented the nine key steps for conducting performance appraisals when the participant spoke up. "Don't you think this is nothing more than a canned approach to a performance appraisal?" he asked aloud. Before I could say anything, someone in the group challenged the gentleman. "A football team spends a great deal of time practicing specific plays before a big game. Does that mean it's a 'canned approach'? Or a *planned* approach?" She made a powerful impact on this individual, because from that point on, he was an active workshop participant.

The following nine key steps and sub-steps will help you plan and conduct effective performance appraisal interviews. Think of them as a guide or a road map.

Prepare for the performance review. Approximately two to three weeks before the scheduled performance review, meet with the employee and confirm where and when the formal discussion will be held. Give the employee a copy of the performance appraisal form, and ask that it be completed before the appraisal meeting. Ask the employee to examine his or her ideas about the job and how well he or she is performing in each area and to be prepared to discuss any special problems or recommendations. They should also think about specific ways to improve job performance.

Filling out the form in advance will help the employee better prepare for the performance review. You should not ask to see the employee's completed form before or during the actual session; it's the employee's "worksheet" to help them plan for the meeting.

Fill out the performance appraisal form in pencil so you can see what kind of information you have not gathered. List the employee's key strengths and areas of needed improvement. For the areas where improvement is needed, identify potential causes of problems. Ask:

- Is he or she aware of what was expected?
- Is he or she aware of his or her performance?
- Are there uncontrollable factors?
- Does he or she lack ability or knowledge?
- Is there lack of motivation? If so, why?

Then develop possible solutions and tentative action plans (tentative because the information is not complete until you talk with the employee). You also want the employee, during the interview, to develop his or her ideas and solutions in order to establish ownership.

Set aside the time (normally an hour), but don't schedule it for the last hour of the day or the hour just before another critical appointment. In case you need more than an hour, schedule the session so that extra time is available if necessary. It is also your responsibility to make sure that there will be privacy and no interruptions. If you can't control interruptions at your office, go somewhere else.

Begin the discussion. When the employee arrives, relieve his or her tension with a warm greeting. Help the individual feel more at ease by sitting across the corner of your desk or by sitting in front of the desk with the employee. This will reduce the "I'm-the-Boss" problem and encourage the employee to communicate more openly.

The objective of this interview is to assist, guide, and help the employee to develop professionally. A judgmental attitude, as indicated earlier, can produce passive and/or defensive employee behavior that is not conducive to development. As you begin the discussion, stress your role as a counselor, not a judge. ("During this discussion, I'd like to offer any assistance I can give, and answer any questions you have. This is your meeting. I'm here to help in any way I can.")

Determine the topics the employee wants to discuss. Many managers still begin performance reviews by telling the employee what he or she did right and wrong. Asking the employee for the topics that he or she wants to discuss is a radical departure from this older method. There are four reasons why this is an excellent way to begin the interview:

1. The employee might raise a topic already on your list. It's much easier to deal with an area of needed improvement if the employee brings it up.

2. The employee might not be prepared to talk about a topic that you bring up, which will increase his or her tension.

3. You might discover areas of concern that you weren't aware of.

4. You want the employee to enter actively into a discussion, not just to listen to what you have to say.

Let's look at each of these three possible responses.

To open this part of the discussion, simply ask, "What topic would you most like to discuss today?" or "What's first on your list for today's discussion?" Note that both questions are neutral, in that they do not initially ask for a concern or a problem, but rather allow the employee to respond with whatever topic he or she wishes to bring up.

When you ask a question such as those above, the employee will usually do one of three things:

1. Mention an area of concern (i.e., something the employee feels he or she needs to improve)

2. Note an area of positive performance

3. Decide not to respond ("I don't know. What do you want to talk about?")

Let's look at each of these three possible responses.

First, if the employee brings up a performance problem or other area of concern, it is likely that the initial statement made by the employee will be general. Problems such as "I have trouble getting along with Jane" or "Those people over in information services won't communicate with me!" are difficult to address. Thus you may need to ask questions to help the employee be more specific. For example, "Could you give me an example?" or "Can you be a little more specific?" will provide you with more information to use to help the employee solve the problem.

When you feel the problem is defined in specific terms, the next step is to pose questions that help the employee explore the cause of the problem. Questions such as "What do you think is the cause of this situation?" or "What other causes do you see?" should be asked even if you think you already know the answers to the questions. You do this for three reasons:

1. The employee will be more open to your suggested solutions if he or she believes you understand the cause(s) of the problem.

2. Identifying the most probable cause(s) increases the chances that proposed solutions could work.

3. The employee may be closer to the problem and thus able to see causes that you can't see.

Last, when you are comfortable that the employee has identified the cause of a problem, you can ask further questions to obtain his or her solutions—even if you believe you know the solution. The purpose in asking for a solution, rather than offering yours, is that an employee who helps find the solution to a problem will more readily accept the changes the solution will require. In addition, there is always the likelihood that the employee will have a solution that is better than ours.

To elicit an employee's suggested solution, simply ask, "What ideas do you have for developing a solution to this situation?" or "What suggestions do you have for increasing your performance in this area?" or "What else can you do?" But be cautious here. The employee's response might be, "Well, I guess I'll just have to try harder!" The problem with this solution is that even though it communicates a willingness to change, it says nothing about how that change will occur. You will find it is very difficult to later follow up an "I'll-try-harder" solution. It is better to say, "Well, I appreciate your willingness to try harder. But how do you see yourself doing that?" or "What things can you do?" When you obtain specific solutions, you can better follow up and provide appropriate feedback. Surprisingly enough, an employee will bring up an area of concern (a performance problem) more often than a positive performance, or an "I don't know" response.

Now let's look at the second most frequent response to the leader's request for a topic of discussion: a positive performance statement. When you ask, "What topics would you like to discuss first today?" the employee may bring up something that he or she feels especially proud of. When this happens, immediately provide specific positive feedback (e.g., "I'm glad you mentioned that! I've noticed several instances where you've done extremely well. For example, ... describe events"). The reason for providing specific feedback is to increase its positive impact to the employee as well as to give believability to the compliment. If you can describe specific times and situations, the employee knows that you really have noticed his or her positive performance.

Finally, an employee may occasionally choose not to respond to "What topics would you like to talk about first?" This sometimes happens with a new employee who is still anxious, or an employee who had unpleasant experiences with past performance reviews. If you feel the cause of the reluctance is nervousness, then you can take the initiative and comment positively on a strength you have noticed. This will help reduce the tension the employee may be feeling and set the stage for a productive discussion. After you have discussed the employee's positive performance, however, you do need to follow up again with, "What other topics would *you* like to discuss?"

Discuss concerns not mentioned by the employee. After dealing with the topics the employee has brought up for discussion, it is now time for you to bring up any of your concerns that have not already been mentioned by the employee. This step uses a four-step model as follows:

Describe the employee's specific performance. Describe in specific terms the employee's actual performance (only describe behavior, not the personality):

"There were six errors made on the January report."

"The record shows that you have been fifteen minutes late five times during the past thirty days."

Describe the expected standard of performance. Then state exactly what the employee should be doing that he or she is not doing, or what the employee should not be doing that he or she is doing. Avoid nonspecific statements like:

"You've got to improve your production."

"You need to reduce the number of errors you're making."

Better:

"I expect a minimum of ten percent increase in your production."

"This job requires attendance at or before eight o'clock each morning."

"The performance standard for this job is zero defects."

Ask the employee to identify the causes for the deviation. It is important to probe for the cause of the problem, because it will make for a better solution that will be accepted and keep the discussion focused on the cause of the problem. This prevents premature focus on solutions. To help the employee analyze the cause of the problem, ask, "What do you think is the cause of this situation?" or "What other causes do you see?" (Note the less-judgmental term "situation," vs. "problem.")

Ask the employee for his or her suggested solutions. If the employee is going to play a role in making needed changes, it is better to gain acceptance by guiding him or her to identify the solution. Discuss each solution option and make suggestions based on your general knowledge or experience that might improve the quality of the solution. Then encourage the employee to select the solution(s) that will be employed.

Write action plans. Some solutions will not need action plans. The employee who is constantly tardy doesn't need a full-blown action plan to get to work on time. For more complex solutions, use a written goal statement with step-by-step plans.

If this is the first time a particular employee has written an action plan, put on your training hat and assist in writing a planning statement. However, be careful about who holds the pencil! If you write it, it's your plan, not the employee's. Letting the employee write a planning statement encourages ownership, which leads to acceptance and results.

Even though it needs to be the employee's plan, you can often make it better. Say, "I wonder if this might be something you could consider doing…?" "What can I do to help?" or "What would you like me to do?"

Give positive feedback. A performance review is an excellent opportunity to give employees positive feedback on their accomplishments. Plan to spend a significant amount of time on this step to balance needs with strengths.

Describe the employee's specific behavior and illustrate with examples. Give reasons why the employee's strength is important to you and to the organization. Spell out your expectations of continued high performance in the future. Express your appreciation for their efforts thus far, and for their commitment to improving their performance. Then work together to develop written action plans for further use of the employee's strengths (if appropriate).

Summarize the discussion and discuss ratings. Misunderstandings result when two people think they clearly understand what was said and agreed upon, when in fact they don't. Summarize the key points you made in the interview; then both you and the employee will have a solid feeling of accomplishment.

After you have summarized the highlights of the discussion, share with the employee your ratings. If you discuss ratings first, the employee won't understand the reasons for the ratings and might become defensive (which will make you want to defend the ratings). By summarizing the interview and discussing your ratings at the end of it, you will focus attention more on the job performance, rather than on the ratings.

Schedule follow-up discussions. Set follow-up dates with the employee and mark the date and time on your calendar in the employee's presence. This shows that his or her performance is important to you and clearly commits you to follow up.

Thank the employee for the time and energy he or she devoted to preparing for and taking part in the performance review. This is common courtesy, and will be greatly appreciated.

Use the Preparation Guide and Leader's Checklist as you plan and conduct your next performance appraisal discussion.

Appraisal Discussion Checklist

☐ **1. Prepare for the formal appraisal discussion.**

- Give the employee a copy of the performance appraisal form and discuss it with him or her 2 – 3 weeks before the meeting.
- Ask the employee to complete a copy of the form before the discussion.
- Reserve a place where you can control interruptions and have some privacy.
- Review incident files, and think about specific areas you need to discuss.
- Consider possible causes and solutions and create a tentative action plan.
- In pencil, jot down your initial thoughts about the employee's performance on the appraisal form.

☐ **2. Begin the meeting.**

- Put the employee at ease.
- Reduce physical barriers to communication.
- Stress that your role is as a counselor, not a "judge."

☐ **3. Determine topic(s) employee wants to discuss.**

If employee brings up an area of concern:

- Ask questions to help the employee be specific.
- Ask questions to explore causes.
- Ask the employee for solutions.

If the employee brings up a specific area of positive performance:

- Provide positive feedback.

If the employee does not bring up a topic for discussion:

- Comment positively on strengths you have noticed.
- Ask the employee again for his or her topic.

(continued)

☐ 4. **Discuss all your performance concerns not already discussed.**

- Describe the employee's specific performance.
- Describe the expected standard of performance.
- Ask the employee to identify causes of the performance shortfall.
- Ask the employee for his or her suggested solutions, and discuss.

☐ 5. **Develop written action plans for carrying out key solutions in a specific time period.**

- Let the employee select which key solution they want to employ.
- If necessary, assist the employee with writing a planning statement.
- Offer suggestions or ideas as the employee develops specific actions that he or she will take over the next six months.

☐ 6. **Give specific feedback on any positive performance that has not already been discussed.**

- Describe the employee's specific behavior, and provide examples.
- Tell him or her why the positive behaviors are important to you, to your organization, and to the employee.
- Spell out your future expectations.
- Express your appreciation for their efforts and positive performance.
- Develop action plans to build on the employee's strength(s), if appropriate.

☐ 7. **Summarize the discussion and discuss ratings.**

☐ 8. **Set follow-up dates.**

☐ 9. **Thank the employee for their participation and commitment to improve their performance.**

Preparation Guide:
Preparing to Conduct a Performance Appraisal Discussion

Use this step-by-step checklist as you prepare for the performance review. Feel free to look at the text for ideas on what you can say in each step.

☐ **1. Prepare for the discussion**

Have you met briefly with the employee one to two weeks in advance to prepare him or her for the formal review?

a) Did you give him or her a copy of any form that will be used in the discussion? ☐ Yes ☐ No

b) Did you discuss the forms with the employee? ☐ Yes ☐ No

c) Did you ask the employee to prepare for the discussion by filling out the forms before the meeting? (Don't ask to see the forms. They are to be used privately by the employee.) ☐ Yes ☐ No

Have you prepared for this performance review thoroughly?

a) Did you reserve an area where you can minimize interruptions? ☐ Yes ☐ No

b) Did you review incident files on this employee and think about specific areas to be discussed during this session? ☐ Yes ☐ No

2. Begin the meeting.

What will you do?

What will you say?

3. Identify areas of performance that the employee wants to discuss.

What are you going to say to encourage the employee to talk first?

When the employee brings up an area of concern:

a. What questions will you ask to determine the cause(s)?

b. What questions will you ask to generate ideas for solution(s)?

What questions will you ask to obtain a second or even third performance area for discussion?

(continued)

4. **Discuss your own concerns about the employee's performance that have not already been discussed. For each one:**

   a. Describe the employee's specific performance.

   b. Describe the expected standard of performance.

   c. What questions will you ask to determine the cause(s)?

   d. What questions will you ask to generate ideas for solutions?

5. **Develop written action plans for carrying out key solutions in a specific time period.**

   a. What questions will you ask the employee to help him or her generate ideas for solutions?

   b. What will you say to him or her regarding the action plan?

6. **Give specific feedback for any positive performance that has not already been discussed.**

   a. What specific example will you use to describe the positive performance?

   b. What reasons will you give this employee as to why the positive performance is important…

      to you?

      to the organization?

      to the employee?

   c. What can you say to let him or her know that you expect this positive performance to continue in the future?

   d. What will you say that is genuine in expressing your appreciation?

   e. How can this employee's strengths be even better utilized?

(continued)

Quality Leadership Skills

7. **Summarize the performance appraisal discussion and discuss ratings.**

   What will you say to lead into the actual summary?

8. **Schedule follow-up discussions.**

   What will you say?

9. **Thank the employee for his or her efforts and commitment to performance improvement.**

   What can you say that is genuine?

(concluded)

17
Managing Time

Our time is a very shadow that passeth away, and after its end, there is no return. For it is fast sealed that no man cometh again.

The Wisdom of Solomon
Apocrypha

Remember when you were young and those lazy summer days stretched on and on? Remember when the closer it got to summer vacation, the longer it took to arrive? Remember when the time from one holiday to the next seemed endless? Why do our days now seem hurried and shorter? What happened to time?

Certainly our perception of time is dependent on what we're doing. We all know how waiting for something we want to happen seems like forever, and how a disagreeable task seems to take so long. Our perception of time is also affected by the number of new events we're conscious of in a given period of time. For example, a drive from point *A* to point *B* on an unfamiliar road seems to take forever, but traveling that same distance on a familiar road seems shorter. Similarly, when we engage in familiar, habitual tasks, we often wonder at the end of the day where the time has gone. We're usually not aware of the way we have managed (or haven't managed) much of this routine time.

Most of us want to become more effective at what we do, but the desire to improve is not all that is necessary. We also need to become aware of how we have been managing our time so we can identify what to change.

We can improve the way we manage our time. Start by asking yourself some personal questions: What are the things that are truly important to me? How much of my time am I giving to these things? What takes up my time while contributing very little to my goals or to the quality of my life?

Time management also means accepting responsibility. It's easy to say that we have trouble managing our time because other people always interrupt us, or there is too much paper work, or there are too many emergency project requests. Many of these problems do occur, but they occur to everybody. And we know that some people facing these same problems are much more productive than others.

Effective leaders have learned to accept the things they can't change and to take responsibility for the things they can. They also recognize the difference. Exert some control over your life, make decisions, and accept part of the responsibility for what you do or don't do in the time you are given.

Awareness of Time

Okay. Let's say you have a positive attitude, want to be increasingly effective, and you are willing to accept responsibility for change. What's next? What are some things you can do for yourself and your employees to manage time more productively?

First, look closely at what you've been doing with your time, because what you *think* you did and what you've really done are often two different things. We all need to have some way of obtaining accurate data about our past actions to use in decisions for the future. The best method I can recommend is to use a "Time Log" to record accurately where you are spending your time. Record everything you do; write down when someone interrupts you, and when you interrupt yourself. Note telephone calls, incoming and outgoing; email contacts; visitors; trips to the water fountain; a coffee break. Write it all down. To obtain enough data for a complete analysis of your time, you should plan to record your activities for a minimum of three full days, both at work and at home.

A time log can be as simple as this:

Sample Time Log

Name: _____ Date: _____

Time	Activity	Time Consumed

When you have finished collecting information on how you actually spend your time, add up your time in categories. This will be a major help in determining whether or not the way you actually spend your time is really how you want to spend it. Use the chart on the following page to categorize and record each day's information from your Time Log sheets.

Weekly Time Analysis

Activities at Work	Day 1	Day 2	Day 3	Day 4	Day 5	Total Time	Percent of Day
Unscheduled visitors (pleasure)							
Unscheduled visitors (business)							
Scheduled visitors (pleasure)							
Scheduled visitors (business)							
Visitors subtotal							
Outgoing phone calls (pleasure)							
Outgoing phone calls (business)							
Incoming phone calls (pleasure)							
Incoming phone calls (business)							
E-mail Web (pleasure)							
E-mail Web (business)							
Communication subtotal							
Time with boss							
Meetings with an employee							
Group employee meetings							
Other meetings							
Waiting							
Breaks and lunches							
Reading							
Writing/typing							
Faxing							
Planning							
Physical work							
Other work							
Activities subtotal							
Total time for all activities							

(continued)

Personal Activities	Day 1	Day 2	Day 3	Day 4	Day 5	Total Time	Percent of Day
Meditation							
Spouse							
Children							
Friends							
Chores							
Eating							
Sleeping							
Civic							
Business							
Recreation							
Hobbies							
Telephone							
Television/video							
Computer, Web							
Computer, E-mail							
School							
Total time for all personal categories							
Total time for all work categories							
GRAND TOTAL							

After categorizing and recording your Time Log information, decide which areas you want to spend less or more time on. To do this, you'll need to ask some tough questions, including,

1. Did I use any time to plan for the future?

2. Have I recorded activity? Or "results"? (Activity = what I did. Results = what I accomplished)

3. What was the longest period of time spent on one thing without interruption?

4. Which interruptions took the most time?

5. What can be done to eliminate or control these interruptions?

   - Which telephone calls were unnecessary?
   - Which phone calls could have been shorter, yet equally (or more) effective?
   - Which visits were unnecessary?
   - Which visits could have been shorter, yet equally (or more) effective?

6. How much time did I spend in meetings?

7. Did I find myself jumping from task to task without completing the previous one?

8. Did "crisis work" push more important things aside?

9. As I recorded my time expenditures throughout the week, did I correct myself and change the numbers?

10. How much time did I take for quality employee development?

11. How much quality time did I spend with my family? What, if anything, do I want to change?

When you have answered these questions, you are in a much better position to decide what you should change to save time at work and at home. Of course, you might see that what you are doing is exactly what you want to do. If so, your final decision will be to do nothing. In either case, the information will help you make the right decision.

And when you do make changes, be aware of two points:

1. Increasing the amount of time spent on one activity will take time from another activity.
2. Changes can sometimes cause problems that, in turn, take even more time to fix.

What is urgent?

Charles Hummel once wrote an article entitled "The Tyranny of the Urgent." In it, he distinguished things that are truly important from those that seem "urgent." When important things and urgent things occur simultaneously, which ones usually win our attention?

Let me give you an example. Many years ago, I made a decision to leave the organization I worked for in St. Paul and move my family back to my home state of Virginia. I planned to be my own boss as an independent training consultant. After a couple of grim years, I finally achieved my bottom-line financial goal—we weren't starving!

At the time, my office was in our converted garage. Because we had many children, I had a business telephone line and a family line. One Friday evening, we were sitting down for supper when the business line rang. I asked the children to quiet down, and answered the phone. "International Training Consultants. Dick Leatherman speaking. How can I help you?" The caller was the program director of a local university's management center. He was extremely agitated—so much so that I could hardly understand him. Because I was also getting some noise in the kitchen, I put him on hold and went down to the garage to continue the call. "What's wrong?" I asked.

His story was a program director's nightmare. He was at the end of a weeklong seminar for about a hundred purchasing agents from up and down the eastern seaboard. The keynote speaker for Saturday morning, the dean of one of the country's leading law schools, had the flu. The program director called me right away. "Dick, will you be our keynote speaker tomorrow morning? We don't care what you do. Just come in and do something!" Let me tell you, that request made me feel good.

But let's put him on hold for a minute so I can tell you about several things I had already scheduled for the Saturday in question. First, because my office was at home, we had some pretty strict rules about the children bothering me when I was working. A week before the program director's call, I had been working in my office when seven-year-old Matthew careened in with a big emergency. Well, he wasn't broken or bleeding, and the interruption irritated me. As a result, I wasn't very nice to him. As he sulked out of my office, he said under his breath (but just loud enough for me to hear him), "Daddy doesn't have time for me anymore since he has his own business." And Matthew was right. I wasn't spending as much time with him as I once did. So I said, "Hold it, bud. You're right. I don't spend as much time with you as I used to. But I'll tell you what—let's you and me have a turtle day next Saturday morning. How about it?" "Oh, yes!" he exclaimed, and I got a big hug.

Do you know what a "turtle day" is? It's when you take a seven-year-old boy out to look for turtles. The fact that you probably won't find any is not the point—it's what you can talk about while you look. One-on-one private time between a father and his son is the point.

And there was another important thing I had scheduled for that Saturday. Laurie, my 16-year old, asked me the Wednesday before if I would teach her how to drive. I said, "Hey, honey, my tax dollars help pay for you to get professional driving instruction at your high school! Besides, you don't want to learn my bad driving habits." (I'm a lousy driver.)

"But Daddy," she replied, "I've never driven a car, and I get my 'behind-the-wheel' instructions next week. The other kids will be in the car, too, and I don't want to make a fool of myself in front of them!" "Oh, I see," I said. "I'll tell you what—let's spend some time next Saturday at the shopping center parking lot, and you can scare me to death!" "Fantastic!" she said. And I got a big hug for that, too.

The last thing I had scheduled for that Saturday was time with my youngest daughter, Leanne. Her "Uncle Frank" had made her a giant dollhouse. It was a marvel to see! It was carpeted, and it had real windows. It also had a low-voltage lighting system with a miniature chandelier hanging in the dining room.

Well, Leanne's house had an attic fire. Somehow the low-voltage wiring had shorted out, and the transformer had burned up. She had been reminding me to fix it for a couple of months. And the Tuesday before the Saturday in question, she asked, "Please, please, *please* (or were there four 'pleases'?) fix my dollhouse!" I said, "Tell you what I'm going to do. I'll put the transformer in your dollhouse this coming Saturday. At the same time, I'll teach you how to solder wires." I got another big hug.

Remember, we still have the program director on hold. What do you think I told him when he frantically said that Friday evening, "Dick, we don't care what you do. Just come in and do something!" Yes, I said "Okay." Then I walked up to the kitchen and said, "Guess what, gang? Your dad has a seminar at the Hyatt House tomorrow morning!" There was dead silence.

Then my oldest daughter said, "Daddy!" and walked out of the room.

Matthew said, "But . . . but . . . what about turtle day?"

And Leanne, with all the faith and trust of a young child, said, "That's okay, Daddy. I know you'll fix my dollhouse someday."

I did eventually fix the dollhouse, go turtle hunting with Matthew, and give Laurie some hints on driving. But not that day—when I let the "urgent" win out over those things that were truly important to me.

Two lessons can be learned from my experience. First, there is no end to it: the "tyranny of the urgent" is a battle we all will fight day after day. Do you imagine this was the last time I let a crisis get in the way of something that was really important? The thing we must try to do at home and on the job is to choose well when the urgent tries to displace the truly important.

Secondly, learn to say no so that you have time for the really important things in your life. If saying no is difficult for you, recognize that you can't say yes to everything; you have a right to say no. A simple "No, thank you" is often sufficient and appropriate for those situations where a personal relationship with the other person is not important to you. And sometimes you must say no more than once.

Here's an example: It's 6:30 p.m., and you're in the middle of supper. The phone rings.

You: "Hello."

Caller: "Is this Ms. Olson?"

"Yes."

"Wonderful! This is William Applebee from the Easy Glide Home Appliance Company. I am happy to inform you that you have won a matching set of stainless steel kitchen knives with genuine molded handles. One of our representatives will be in your area next week to deliver your prize. When would it be convenient for her to stop by?"

"Thank you, but I'm not interested."

"Ms. Olson, our computer selected you at random for this free set of superb knives that I know you will love having in your home. It won't take but a minute to have them delivered to you. So when would be the best time for you? Monday, or Tuesday?"

"Thank you, but I'm really not interested."

"I'm sorry, but I don't understand. Why aren't you interested in owning this free set of fantastic knives?"

"I'm not interested."

At this point, if the caller continues to be a pest, say goodbye and hang up. But if the relationship with the other person is important to you, first acknowledge the request, and then say no. Add a simple explanation. For example, suppose you are a great typist. You have a good friend who is taking evening classes at the local college. The conversation goes like this:

Friend: "Do you have a minute?"

You: "Sure, Jack. What's up?"

"I really hate to ask you, but I've got a special paper due Friday. I can't find anybody who can type it for me. Would you mind doing it?"

"It sounds like you're facing a tight deadline. I'd really like to help you, but I can't. I don't have time to do it."

"I know you are busy, and I really hate to ask. But you type so fast. It's only ten pages. Isn't there some way you could squeeze it in?"

"I'm really sorry, Jack, but I can't. I have other plans."

Note that you acknowledged his needs ("It sounds like you're facing a tight deadline"). You said no tactfully ("I'd really like to help you, but I can't"), and gave a reason ("I don't have time to do it"). Note, too, that when your friend persisted in his request, you said no again.

But how do we know when to say no? By realizing what is important to us. And how do we make sure that important things are not pushed aside by "urgent" things? By planning! Planning allows us to identify important goals and then put them into action. The resulting activities generated by this analysis then become a part of our daily planning.

Daily Planning

Daily planning is making a "to-do" list for each day. This list should include the priority items to be done immediately, as well as things that you can do today to help carry out long-range goals. It doesn't have to be anything fancy—just a small piece of paper you carry in your pocket or purse to jot down the things you have planned for that day or the next. It doesn't make any difference if you do it first thing in the morning or at the end of the day. Just so you do it daily.

But keeping a to-do list daily does take time. Even if you spend only 10 minutes a day making your list, that adds up to 3,650 minutes or 60 hours a year! So there is a cost for doing a daily to-do list. And thus there must be a compelling reason to do such daily planning.

In fact, there are many good reasons why effective people plan daily. First, when you visibly identify all the things you feel you need to do today, you can establish your priorities by seeing what's important and what's only urgent. Since everything on your list can't be a #1 priority, try using the categories of:

1 = Must do   2 = Should do   3 = Could do

Daily planning also helps the boss set priorities. For example, if your boss constantly interrupts you with new crisis requests, it's strategically helpful to hold up a daily to-do list and say, "Okay, boss, where does that fit on my list?"

Third, a to-do list acts as a memory aid. I, for one, have reached an age where if I don't write something down, there is only a very small chance that I'll remember what it was that I said I absolutely wouldn't forget.

I use a daily to-do list for yet another reason. It tells me what to do next after finishing a task. I am a very task-oriented person. While I'm working on a task, I'm usually not thinking of other things that need to be done. Then when I finish a job, because I can't think of what I wanted to do next, I may simply take a break. But if I have a to-do list in front of me, I can see exactly what I need to do next.

Others who keep daily to-do lists report that it simply feels good to scratch tasks off their list as they complete them. In other words, we have set up a way of giving ourselves immediate positive feedback as we complete each task.

Finally, I save my lists for a month or so and review them to see if I can discover any way that I can further improve my time management. If I haven't completed a task that I had planned to do that day, I immediately rewrite that task on the next day's list. And if I see that I rewrote a particular task more than once, I realize that I am probably procrastinating.

If you don't already use a daily to-do list, try it. It will be time well invested. Commit yourself to keeping a list for 20 working days. When you see that it pays off, you will continue to use such a list, because you've gotten into the to-do habit.

An example of a to-do list follows. Make as many copies as you need and then stack the sheets and staple them at the top to make your to-do pads. There are also some terrific computer programs that can help you keep track of the demands on your time.

Daily To-Do List			
Tasks to do:	Priority	Time	Date

Daily To-Do List			
Tasks to do:	Priority	Time	Date

In this chapter, we have presented several concrete strategies for managing your time well:

- Time logs
- Prioritizing important things over urgent ones
- Daily planning with to-do lists
- Creating a plan for the future

Use these techniques and you will complete key tasks on schedule and have more time for creative thinking, for your boss, for your employees, and for yourself. To become a better manager of your time, you need to spend your time on those things that are really important. In short, you need to take control of your life!

18

Conducting Meetings

Nero fiddled while Rome burned. Nero was in a meeting.

– Dick Dunsing

We are not born knowing how to conduct meetings. We learn, sometimes the hard way. We also learn by studying such things as meeting preparation, facilitation skills, and meeting follow-up. Let's take a brief look at the different types of meetings and the knowledge and skills required for each before we talk about the process.

There are four basic types of meetings: meetings that are primarily for providing information, providing instruction, solving problems, and obtaining information. Each of these types of meetings is a function of the flow of communication between the leader and the meeting participants. The individual conducting the meeting might be doing most of the talking in an informational meeting, while participants will be more involved in problem-solving meetings.

Each kind of meeting will call for specific skills, but some skills will be more important for one type of meeting than another. The ability to thoroughly prepare and organize meetings is useful for all four types, for example, but the skill of asking probing questions is usually not used when the leader "provides information."

Some of the skills and knowledge needed for each of these four meeting types are listed on the table on the next page. Note that this is not an all-inclusive list; you can probably think of other skills that belong here.

The Meeting

It's much easier to learn how to conduct a meeting if you break down this activity into steps and examine each one.

Preparation. People who prepare for their meetings conduct better meetings. It's as simple as that. It's up to you: If you want real results and you want your employees to feel good about your meetings, you must prepare. However, never leave preparation for important meetings to the last minute. Waiting too long to start the preparation process drastically reduces what you can accomplish. You might need a couple of overhead transparencies but don't have enough time left to get them made. You might discover at the last minute that your old PowerPoint presentation has out-of-date information, or learn that a key member can't come because he or she didn't have enough advance notice. Maybe you realize that you should have a written agenda to hand out, but you don't have enough time to have it typed, much less copied. These and many other problems can occur if you wait until it is too late. But if you take a few minutes to think

Providing Information	Instructional	Problem Solving	Obtaining Information
Prepares/organizes	• Prepares/organizes • Sets priorities	• Prepares/organizes • Sets priorities	Prepares/organizes
	Uses active-listening skills	Uses active-listening skills	Uses active-listening skills
Has expert knowledge	Is a subject-matter expert	Has some knowledge	Communicates expectations
	• Asks probing, open questions • Uses the Socratic method	• Asks probing, open questions • Identifies source of problem • Resolves conflict	Asks probing, open questions
	• Solicits feedback • Accepts/interprets feedback	Solicits feedback	Uses recording skills
	Uses nonverbal skills	Uses nonverbal skills	Uses nonverbal skills
Knows target audience	Has knowledge of instructional needs of audience	Uses basic problem-solving, decision-making, planning, and consensus processes	• Sorts important information out • Uses summarizing skills
Anticipates questions about content	Anticipates questions about content	Anticipates questions about processes	
Uses strong presentation skills	• Uses excellent teaching skills • Is interactive	Uses good facilitation skills	Uses excellent facilitation skills
Creates takeaway handouts	Creates takeaway handouts	Creates handouts on processes used	Has methods to compile information
Has excellent A/V skills	Has good A/V skills		

through the things that need to be done, you can usually determine how much time you need to prepare. (The Meeting Preparation Checklist included at the end of the chapter can help you prepare.)

Communicate. Let those who are to attend the meeting know, in writing, the who, what, when, where, and why of the meeting. If it is not a regularly scheduled meeting, it is especially important to confirm in writing the meeting time and place. Always make sure that the members receive the meeting objectives and agenda in advance; the more details the members have about the meeting ahead of time, the better prepared they will be.

The meeting objective. A meeting objective is simply a description of what leaders or participants want to accomplish as a result of the meeting. Some meetings really get crazy because the leader hasn't thought through in advance what is to be accomplished (and no one else knows, either!). One of your key tasks in preparing for a meeting is to think through why you need this particular meeting. What do you want the members to do in the meeting and do as a result of it? What do you want them to learn? To consider? To decide? To act on? What do you want to achieve in the meeting? What should happen when the meeting is over? Answering these questions will result in clear objectives. If you don't know the answers, save everybody a lot of time and think about not having the meeting at all.

The meeting agenda. An agenda is a list of topics that will be covered to achieve the meeting objectives and an outline of what you will do in the meeting—the activities that will take place to accomplish the desired results. If the objective of the meeting is to make a group decision, the announced agenda of topics/activities might look like this:

A meeting will be held on January 5 at 8:30 a.m. in conference room "B" to determine the best supplier for our electrical needs.

Objective:

The group will select, by consensus, the best supplier.

Agenda:

1. Discuss the need for a decision.
2. Determine the factors we should consider in making the decision.
3. Brainstorm a list of problem areas.
4. Make a final decision, using a consensus process.
5. Assign responsibilities to specific individuals to carry out the decision.

Prepare the content. To examine your own role in the meeting, consider what you need to do in the meeting and what you need to do to prepare for it. For example, if you are in charge of a meeting like the one described above, you would probably talk to your boss to find out what problems he or she has picked up on. You will also need to spend time thinking about the major problems as you see them. Then you would make a list of these problems in case others do not bring up some of them for discussion in the meeting.

You might want to prepare handouts, have reference material available, design a PowerPoint presentation, or even invite a subject matter expert to sit in on the meeting. The key thing to remember is that whatever needs to be done will take time (and the time to begin is usually way before the day of the meeting). Next, consider what you want the members to do in the meeting, and determine if anyone else needs to do something in preparation for it. Certain individuals may need to know in advance that they will be asked to offer their expertise or to bring their records and files for reference. Consider assigning specific meeting roles to key members, such as "Recorder," "Facilitator," or "Chair." Communicate with these members before the meeting, so that they will have time to prepare for their part in it.

Assign meeting roles. One of the best ways to manage and conduct successful meetings is to assign specific meeting roles to the members in advance. Assigned roles will not only get people more involved in the meetings, but will also create more-productive meetings. Involving participants by assigning roles is especially important in problem-solving and obtaining-information meetings. So let's look at our role in these meetings, and then at four other roles that can be assigned to employees.

Your role as the boss. The "boss" and the person running the meeting might be the same person, but they don't have to be. The boss doesn't have to lead every meeting—that responsibility can be delegated to a key employee. You might even choose not to be present at the meeting: Many organizations today elect to have their employees meet without the boss in order to solve production problems, improve quality, or help their non-exempt employees become more involved in and challenged by their work.

Don't worry about giving away your power by delegating responsibility and authority to subordinates to hold their own meetings; you will be surprised at how much time you will have saved for other more-important tasks! Your people will also become more excited about their jobs and come up with amazing ideas if you just turn them loose. Someone once said that a boss's job is to give employees what they need to do their jobs—supplies, tools, training, authority, and responsibility—and then to get out of the way. Of course, even if you don't attend meetings, you must still be in the communication loop. You will be asked to offer input, obtain resources for the team members, and make decisions.

The first time you try this, you will need to help them. Suggest that they assign meeting roles, use an easel or whiteboard, and utilize the best process for the task at hand. Tell them that you want to be informed of the meeting outcome and that you will help them in any way you can.

If your anxiety about allowing employees to hold meetings without you is too strong, try attending the meeting as a participant, and have one of your employees act as the chair. This will satisfy your need to keep some control (and also delegates increased responsibility). Your biggest problem might be keeping your mouth shut and letting your employees run the meeting!

The meeting chairperson. Someone needs to take the leadership role, whether it's you or someone you delegate the task to. So let's look at what a good chairperson does.

Effective chairs should establish and send out the meeting agenda, prepare needed handouts, arrive early, start on time and end on time, and use a flipchart or whiteboard to keep the meeting on track. Chairpersons also need to be able to handle problem participants.

Here are some common meeting problems and a few helpful solutions:

Problem: One participant monopolizes the discussion.

Possible cause:	Try this:
You (as the boss or the chairperson) talk too much.	Ask another supervisor, manager, or executive to attend your meetings to give you feedback.
This individual has expertise in the subjects being discussed.	Anticipate this and ask the individual to submit a position paper to all of the participants prior to the meeting.
The individual doesn't realize that he or she is doing it.	Ask the "monopolizer" for permission to conduct a frequency count of the number of times he or she speaks.
The person running the meeting doesn't exert control because he or she isn't the boss.	Tell the meeting chairperson that he or she has management's full support and needs to control a monopolizing speaker.

(continued)

| | Tell the participants that others are going to have a chance to conduct the meeting, and that they should treat the present chairperson the way they would want to be treated.

Provide participants with training on group roles and rules. |
|---|---|
| The person conducting the meeting doesn't know how to manage the situation tactfully. | Teach the individual how to:

- Interrupt tactfully and shift the discussion to others by using a question.

- Express his or her concern to the monopolizing employee privately, describe the negative results of monopolizing, and ask for cooperation. |

Problem: One of the participants is not participating.

Possible cause:	Try this:
The individual is shy.	Assign him or her the role of Recorder (see definition that follows).

Involve the individual in the discussion by asking him or her questions.

Give positive reinforcement for any contribution. |
| The individual is bored. | Assign him or her the role of Recorder, Facilitator, or Chair.

Get him or her more involved by assigning tasks for later completion. |
| The individual is angry. | In private discussion, determine the cause of his or her anger. Attempt to identify solutions to resolve the problem, and counsel if needed. |

Problem: One individual is continually tardy or absent.

Possible cause:	Try this:
The individual is habitually late or absent.	Stress the importance of being present and on time (tardiness and absence are not fair to the group).

Require performance by taking disciplinary action. |
| There is a work-environment problem. | Change the employee's environment so that he or she can attend the meetings and be on time. |
| The individual doesn't know what is expected of him or her. | Communicate expectations. |

These are the most common meeting problems. All leaders need to be familiar with and comfortable using a variety of meeting processes (problem solving, decision making, planning, etc.). Astute leaders are not bothered by conflict. They know that disagreements are expected, are healthy, and can be managed.

The recorder is responsible for recording who attended and who missed the meeting, the topics that were discussed, the key points that were made (not every word that was spoken) and who made them, and who agreed to do what (and when) as a result of the meeting. At the end of the meeting, the Recorder should also summarize the topics and task assignments, copy all easel paper and items that were written on the board (after the meeting), and follow up by promptly sending out minutes of the meeting to all participants. The Recorder should also keep files on all meetings.

The facilitator or chairperson plays the most crucial role in a meeting. Participants who take on the facilitator role need to be insightful, knowledgeable, tactful, and courageous. They must be insightful in order to keep their focus on the *processes* taking place in the meeting (not the topics or content of the discussion), and must therefore be knowledgeable about group process. They also need to be tactful when providing feedback in a non-judgmental way about participants' performance, and courageous so they can provide the boss with feedback when the boss is leading the meeting and make mistakes or talks too much.

Facilitators need to make an agreement with the boss and the participants as to what they will and will not do in the meeting. For example, should the facilitator interrupt discussion when it is off track, or wait until the meeting is over? Should he or she suggest an appropriate process for a topic that is going to be discussed? What will be the specific nature of the facilitator's involvement in the meeting? Questions such as these need to be answered prior to the meeting.

Most groups and leaders want this individual to be an active facilitator. If the group gets off course, the facilitator should let them know it, and when the group is uncertain about which process to use, the facilitator should make suggestions. However, most groups agree that the facilitator's feedback should be directed to the *group* (not to individuals), and that personal feedback to the boss should be given privately. Most groups seem to want their facilitators to focus on how the group is functioning, not on the content of the meeting. When the groups are small, however, the facilitator should probably have some input into the topic being discussed.

Because of their great influence, facilitators also need to refrain from sending nonverbal signals as they observe the meeting. Utterances (saying "Uh-oh!") or facial contortions (rolling the eyes upward, snorting, laughing, etc.) that indicate displeasure or any other kind of gesture or sound can affect the conduct of the meeting. The basic role of the facilitator is to observe, and to facilitate only when it is expected or necessary.

Here are a few good ways to guide or get participants to focus:

- "I have noticed that during the past hour only three of you have been involved in the discussion. Would it be possible to obtain input and involvement from everyone?"

- "It seems like we have gotten off the subject. How does the present discussion relate to our stated objective (or agenda)?"

- "Before we jump to conclusions and take action, how well have we identified the real cause of the problem?"

- "Rather than settling on that solution now, should we also consider other alternatives?"

- "Have we looked at the risks in our plan? In other words, if we adopt it, what could go wrong?"

The participants also have specific responsibilities in the meeting. For instance, they need to schedule their work so that they can attend all meetings and arrive on time. They need to cooperate with the other participants in the group: they should listen to one another; avoid interrupting others; and refrain from putting down another participant's ideas.

Participants also need to accept the responsibility of being involved. Although the problem of a bored participant needs to be addressed by the meeting chairman, it is that participant's responsibility not to become bored in the first place. On the other hand, too much involvement by one participant should also be avoided. Participants need to be very sensitive to "air time" and not monopolize the discussion.

Participants should also be honest with one another. They need to accept responsibility and say what they really think and feel. And if the boss is present, he or she must strongly encourage the members to "tell it like it is."

Finally, every group member should seek to become proficient in performing all four group roles—Leader or Chairperson, Facilitator, Recorder, and Participant.

Equipment, Materials, and Facility

Most of us are familiar with some of the subtopics in this section, but there are some helpful tips here. If you find just one helpful new idea that works, your investment of time has been valuable.

Note cards. If you are conducting a meeting where you are supplying information or instructing, don't read your presentation (or even parts of it), and don't write a script! Scripts are deadly dull reading. If you need notes because you are using PowerPoint and don't want to constantly look back at the screen or you are telling your story without audio-visual equipment, use small 3" x 5" index cards. Write your bullet statements on the note cards and use the statements as memory joggers to help you talk extemporaneously. However, if you plan to use PowerPoint to make your presentation, be sure you have backup notes in case of equipment failure. Note cards help you keep from having to constantly look back at the projection screen or sit in a corner of the room looking at your laptop computer screen. It is best to maintain eye contact with your participants and move around at the front of the room as you talk. (Just be sure you are prepared to give your presentation using only notes.)

Flipcharts. Try to use a variety of media to liven up a presentation. Flipcharts capture ideas in a meeting when the speaker is leading a discussion, but they can also be prepared in advance of a presentation and used as a supplement or even an alternative to a PowerPoint or overhead transparency presentation. If you are presenting information or teaching, you can write the key ideas on a flipchart in advance of the session so all the key ideas will be visible to the participants during the presentation while you present each of the steps in more detail.

When preparing flipcharts, use black, brown, or dark blue wide-tipped magic markers (avoid red—red is difficult for individuals who are partially colorblind). Be mindful that people seated at the back of the room need to be able to read the charts easily, however, so try out everything to see what is most legible from the back.

Try to use flipchart paper (easel paper) that has faint ruled lines already printed on the paper. This will help you to print professional-looking letters (the participants in the meeting will not be able to see the ruled lines). You can even pencil in your own notes in the margins that participants won't be able to see.

When presenting information to meeting participants for discussion, PowerPoint or the overhead projector is probably best. This is because the speaker normally has time to plan what information will be presented and has time to create transparencies or visual images to use in communicating these ideas.

Electronic/video projection systems. Electronic imaging systems such as PowerPoint look professional and eliminate the fuss of changing overhead transparencies. However, computer presentations have their limitations. Many of the older or portable systems have light images that are too dim to be easily seen with normal room lighting. When the lights are dimmed, you will have a more difficult time maintaining eye contact with the participants. In addition, such projection systems can trap you at the keyboard, which is usually located behind the podium (don't use a podium!) or on a desk or table. Try to use a remote-control device to advance your images, but be sure to prepare note cards with bullet points that match your presentations. Instead of note cards, PowerPoint has a feature that allows the user to print six small images on one sheet of an 8½ x 11 page. You access this feature in PowerPoint by clicking on FILE; then PRINT; in the PRINT WHAT, select SLIDES; then with HANDOUTS, select 6; and then OKAY.

Make sure that you can access the equipment. Arrange for a key to any locked cabinets. It is your responsibility to know how to set the system up and how to use it. (It is very embarrassing and distracting for the audience to have to wait for somebody to fix a system because it will not operate.) Be sure you know how to turn the system off and restore the room lighting to its customary level.

Creating images on your computer. Here are a couple of my own suggestions:

1. Use a "Times New Roman" type with a font size of 24 points (*never* less than 20 points) and larger point-size for headings (28-48 points), depending on the amount of information. This will result in clear, professional images that can be seen from the back of the room. Also, avoid using all capital letters in designing your images because they are more difficult to read. All capitals are okay for titles, but not for the body of the text.

2. Avoid the over-use of graphics. Any illustration that is used on a visual should serve a purpose. Also avoid using the popular, limited selection of graphic images that are included as part of the common word-processing programs that most of us use. The problem is that they are so overused they lack impact. We have all seen them (even used them ourselves), and we're probably pretty tired of them. There are dozens of high-quality graphic programs available at reasonable cost, and many can be downloaded free from the Web. You can always scan appropriate pictures or photographs and insert them in your document.

3. Be conservative in the use of some of the bells-and-whistles that can be found on modern graphics programs. Clapping sounds and images flying in from every direction should be minimized.

A/V Projection Research. The Wharton School of Business and the 3M Company conducted an interesting study that supports the use of projection systems. They asked 136 Master's degree candidates to conduct 36 meetings to introduce Crystal Beer, a new "product."

The case for Crystal Beer (a make-believe product) was cleverly written so that the reasons for and against accepting the product were statistically even. The variable in the study was the method of presentation—overhead transparencies vs. whiteboard (a whiteboard is like a blackboard, except that it has a white, glossy finish and can be written on with dry markers). The participants in the meetings were asked to listen to the presentations and then approve or reject the new product. The meetings and their outcomes are listed in the following table:

Number of Meetings	Presenters' Position	Presentation Method	Outcomes
12	Pro Crystal Beer	Overheads	67% "Go with the beer"
	Con Crystal Beer	Whiteboard	33% "No beer"
12	Pro Crystal Beer	Whiteboard	33% "Go with the beer"
	Con Crystal Beer	Overheads	67% "No beer"
12	Pro Crystal Beer	Whiteboard	50% "Go with the beer"
	Con Crystal Beer	Whiteboard	50% "No beer"

As the results indicate, the use of overhead transparencies had a positive impact on the subjects' decisions. Even more interesting was that the audience perceived the presenters who used transparencies as being more professional, persuasive, credible, interesting, and better prepared. For all these reasons, multimedia or overhead presentations are extremely effective.

Overhead transparencies. Transparencies are great for presenters and participants. They reduce preparation time because they act as a visible outline during a program. They make it easier to maintain eye contact with participants while presenting the program's information, and allow you to present more information in a given time period. It is also a very flexible method of presenting information: You can leave the lights on without dimming them, still get a bright image, and still see what the next slide (image) will be. Transparencies are also significantly less trouble than PowerPoint to prepare and use. Finally, a transparency can be used in conjunction with a PowerPoint presentation: the overall concepts, an outline of the presentation, and key points can be projected on a second screen while the PowerPoint presentation is made.

Using the reveal technique. You can control the group's access to the information by using the "reveal" technique. Simply place a sheet of 8½" x 11" paper on (or under) the transparency, and then turn the projector light on. Reveal each point by holding the transparency frame with one hand and pulling the paper out with the other hand, but do *not* do it line-by-line. Keep paragraphs intact.

However, too much revealing is annoying. Use this method only when you really need to limit the group's access to the information being presented.

Lighting. Turn the projector light off between transparencies, as the white glare on the screen (with no transparency on the projector) is distracting (too much on-and-off light is also distracting). Strike a balance. With a series of brief transparencies, leave the light on and remove the first one while you place a new visual on the projector.

Eye contact. In almost all cases, you can leave the room light on when using the overhead. Most overhead projectors are deliberately designed for this; it helps us maintain eye contact with the participants.

Avoid turning around and reading from the screen unless you want to strongly emphasize a specific point. Read the information directly from the transparency as you reveal it. This allows you to maintain better eye contact with your group.

The transparency. Use a pencil, pen, or small pointer to indicate specific items on a transparency. Do not use a finger, as it looks strange when enlarged ten times on the screen.

If you mount your transparency on a plastic or cardboard frame, you can write your notes on the white-frame margin. An ordinary fine-point permanent transparency pen will write on white plastic frames, and an ordinary ballpoint pen can be used on cardboard frames.

Read each word of a transparency as it is shown on the screen. Don't turn the overhead on and silently stand there while the audience reads—you won't have a clue when they have finished reading it.

The projector. I have used a variety of overhead projectors over the years, and prefer to use a projector that has a switchable spare bulb. The bulb will burn out—and usually at exactly the wrong time! Projector bulbs get extremely hot, and it is very difficult to replace a burned-out bulb in the middle of a program. Look for a brand that has a lever that allows you to quickly and painlessly replace the bulb simply by moving the lever from one position to the next.

Be sure you have an extra lamp bulb that fits your specific projector and that the extra bulb in the machine is not already burned out. Avoid moving or jarring the projector when the lamp is on, because the lamp's filament is soft and thus easily broken when the projector is on. Turn the projector off before moving it.

The projector should have a polarized, frosted-glass tabletop. This will keep the light spill from glaring in your eyes during an all-day program.

I do not recommend using a small portable overhead, because this type produces excessive light glare (there is no polarized glass). Portable projectors are almost guaranteed to give you a migraine headache by the end of a long presentation.

For best participant viewing, position the projector screen in the right-hand corner of the room, facing participants. Place the projector in the front center of the room at an angle so that the light is centered on the screen. If you are left-handed, simply reverse the above (i.e., position the screen in the left-hand corner of the front of the room). Unfortunately, architects don't have a clue as to how to design a room for audio/visual use, so they put the projector screens across the front of the room.

In summary, an overhead projection system offers these advantages over most other forms of imaging:

- Works with normal room light
- Is simple to operate
- Is reliable
- Eye contact with the audience can be maintained
- Is flexible
- Is readily available

An overhead projection system, when properly used, creates a professional presentation and is easy to use.

Making transparencies. Professional transparencies can be produced on your computer using software. If the transparencies are to be mounted on frames, be sure to create an image of the correct size so that the image can be seen within the margins of the frame. (In using the

Microsoft PowerPoint program to design overheads, go to the "File" menu and then down to "Page Set Up." Then change the default setting from 7.5" by 10" to 8.5" by 11"—the size of a standard sheet of paper.) After designing your images, print them directly from your computer to a color laser or ink-jet printer. In general, using a computer to print an image on transparency film loaded in an ink-jet or laser printer is easy to do and makes sharp transparencies. If, however, you don't already know how to use a computer desktop system to make images, learning to use one will require some investment of time.

In all cases, make sure that the transparency film you buy is the correct film for the printer you plan on using. There are many different types of film, and each is designed for a specific printer. Using the wrong film can be a disaster. I saw one presenter's words smear as he used his visuals, and they became unreadable. He was sick about it—he had about fourteen transparencies that nobody could read!

Here are some additional hints to make your transparencies more professional:

1. Use felt-tip permanent pens in a variety of colors and widths to highlight key statements or to box in an important paragraph. Make sure that the pens are of the permanent type designed specifically for use with transparencies. Washable or so-called temporary pens will smear badly and destroy the appearance of a finished transparency, and regular felt-tip pens made for writing on easel paper usually don't work at all (the ink beads up). On the other hand, if what is needed is a temporary notation on an existing transparency, don't use a permanent pen—use a transparency pen that is labeled "temporary" or "washable" so the ink can be rubbed off with a damp cloth or napkin.

2. Mount transparencies on frames. Handling is easier and they will give you space for "cheat notes." This will free you from your notes and allow you to make better, more-consistent eye contact with the audience. Frames also allow you to make horizontally lettered transparencies, since the frame will mask the light that would normally spill out the top and bottom. A transparency that is not in a frame will almost always build up static electricity.

Try not to put too much on one transparency, and do not write too small. Both are frustrating, especially to participants seated toward the back of the room.

When making transparencies, keep them simple. Using a maximum of six words across and six lines down will keep your transparencies from looking too busy. Transparencies are used to illustrate key points—not to present a lot of content.

Handouts. I am a firm believer in handouts. They allow participants to focus on the discussion, rather than on taking notes. If you use overhead transparencies or computer software to present information, they are a must to keep from presenting faster than participants can write or frustrating them because they will have to frantically try to copy down the information being presented. Handouts can also serve as memory aids back on the job.

People tend to judge a product's quality by the way it is "packaged," and this is also true for handouts. Participants in an important meeting will hear our points, but they see the media. They judge the quality of the transparencies or images, the flipcharts, and the handouts, and this influences their overall judgment about the meeting. The information that you present might be outstanding, but if you have poorly prepared handouts full of typos and misspellings, some participants will already be criticizing your work before you even have a chance to present all the information.

If you have twenty or more pages of handout material, it is usually best to collate and staple them or use some form of binding. Leave the back of each page blank (or lined), so participants have space for notes.

If you are preparing for an important, critical meeting, spend what you need to in order to get presentable handouts. Format them using one of the more common word-processing programs, and print them on a high-quality, 24-pound, bright-white laser paper. For handouts with fewer than one hundred pages, use a plastic or metal spiral binding so the pages lay flat. If there are more than one hundred pages, use three-ring binders—either silk-screened (more expensive, and normally used only when quantities are large) or binders with clear covers that will accept pre-printed inserts. Indexes, tabs, and numbered pages make for easy reference. You want your participants to say, "Wow! Are these ours to keep?"

When the participants later use their handouts for reference, they will appreciate you more if they are easy to read and understand. Clear writing usually consists of short sentences, written the way we speak. Most of us are much better writers than we imagine. Just dispose of self-consciousness and negative self-perceptions.

I was born dyslexic and always thought that I was a terrible writer. I can't spell. I mix up lower case *b's* and *d's*, and I even write my *2's* backwards on occasion. And I failed the sixth grade at Beverly Manor Elementary School in Staunton, Virginia. I naturally concluded that I couldn't write. Fortunately, I met a remarkable teacher—Bill Griffin, a professor of English at Virginia Commonwealth University. After looking at an article I had written, Bill said, "Dick, you are a wonderful writer! You've learned the secret of writing like you talk." Was that an exciting day for me! That was some twenty-five years ago, and since that time I have written thousands of published pages.

Don't misunderstand me. I still need the help of a proofreader, since my spelling, grammar, and syntax are awful. But I'm not afraid to write! I'm not afraid of being me as I write for you, and the end result seems to be adequate. If you feel that writing is hard or that you lack ability to write well, get some help with the mechanics of writing. But if you write like you speak—and you must be a fairly effective speaker, or you wouldn't be a leader—you will likely be a good writer.

This is not a book about writing, but on the following page is an example of two different writing styles. Consider the "audience" for your message when you choose the style.

Examples of "formal" style	Examples of "informal" style
It is the policy of AAA Power, Inc. that accident prevention be considered of primary importance in all phases of operation and administration.	Here at AAA Power, we believe that accident prevention is important!
It is therefore the desire and intent of the company to provide safe and healthy working conditions, and to establish and insist on the use of safe practices at all times.	It's the company's job to provide you with safe and healthy working conditions. It's your job to *always* work safely.
The prevention of accidents is an objective affecting all levels of the organization and its activities.	Preventing accidents is everyone's concern, from top executives to associates on the plant floor.
It is a basic requirement that each manager and team leader make the safety of associates an integral part of regular management functions.	Managers and team leaders are responsible for your safety.
It is equally the duty of each associate to accept and follow established safety regulations and procedures.	You are also responsible. Accepting and following safety regulations and procedures is part of your job.
This is the responsibility of each associate at AAA Power, Inc., regardless of position or area of responsibility.	Everyone here at AAA Power is responsible for safety. Everyone!

The formal writing in our example is at a grade level of 13 (a freshman in college should understand the message). The less-formal example has a grade level of 10.1 (a sophomore in high school).

Let's take a look at one more example: a handout to use in an instructional meeting to teach team leaders how to be more effective in conducting orientation sessions for new associates.

Do you remember what your first day on a "real" job was like? Do you remember the way you were treated? I do! I was told to report to my new boss at 9:00 a.m. sharp for my "orientation." When I got there, he was at his desk. "Have a seat and I'll be with you in a couple of minutes," he told me. He was busy, so I sat and waited. After about 30 minutes, I felt like maybe he had forgotten me. I certainly did not feel like I was very important. Finally, I saw him glance at the clock and look over at me. As he hurried by, he said, "Give me just a couple more minutes." I sat there another 15 minutes.

Not a very good way to start my new career! And we have all seen or experienced treatment worse than mine. Think about *your* first day. What was it like?

Turnover is expensive. New associates who are not treated appropriately on their first day often don't stay. Because labor is a significant cost of doing business, it is critically important to properly train new associates. And a new associate's training starts the moment he or she walks in the door.

This is what I mean by matching your style to the audience—in this case, team leaders and colleagues. Again, to make your writing interesting to the participants in the meeting who have to read it, write like you speak.

I have written over twenty pages of text about preparing for a meeting. This gives you some indication of how important I believe preparation is in conducting effective meetings. Now, let's look at how to begin or "open" a meeting.

The opening. It's time to begin the meeting—on time! Don't punish the early arrivals and reward latecomers by delaying. You'll develop a reputation for starting meetings late, and then participants will begin arriving late to all your meetings. Some people strongly feel that you are wasting their time by not starting on time. You'll also end up having trouble meeting the time schedule.

Write the agenda on the easel paper ahead of time and post it on the wall. If it is a problem-solving or obtaining-information meeting and you haven't already assigned the roles of Recorder and Facilitator, now is the time to do so. The Recorder and the Facilitator should know the processes that you will use. If you are delegating the Chairperson role, tell this individual well in advance so he or she has time to prepare. Begin the meeting by reviewing the meeting objectives and agenda, and move to the first order of business.

Using a process. For problem-solving meetings, select the most-appropriate process for the work the group is going to do from these four categories: problem identification; causal analysis; decision making; and planning.

- *Problem identification.* Some meeting processes are used to gather and arrange data in a systematic way in order to help identify problems. Note that these processes don't solve the problems—they provide information that tells what, where, and how serious they are. They help pinpoint and describe problems, and set priorities. They can also provide information for management to use in justifying funds needed to fix a particular problem. Such processes include situation analysis, Pareto charts, and histograms. Many have been explained in previous chapters. A few others are summarized here.

The *Pareto chart* is a bar chart that is used to show the frequency of occurrence for each of a particular set of problems.

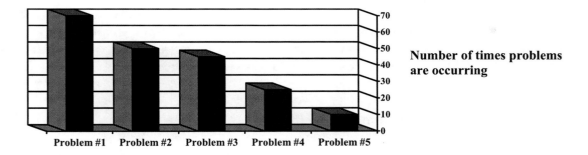

Number of times problems are occurring

The *histogram* is a bar chart that usually plots problem-frequency against some form of measurement (in contrast to the Pareto chart that plots frequency against identified categories). For instance:

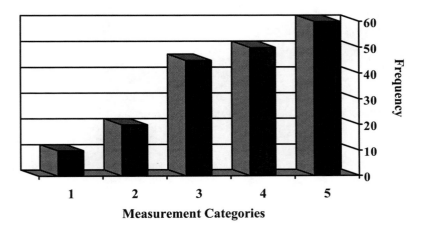

For example, suppose you conduct a survey to determine employee job satisfaction. One of the questions is, "How satisfied are you with your job?" Employees are asked to rate their satisfaction on a scale of 1 to 5, with 1 = "Not at all satisfied" and 5 = "Extremely satisfied." The histogram shows that sixty employees rated their job satisfaction a "5," fifty employees rated it a "4," somewhere around forty-five employees gave it a "3," twenty employees rated it a "2," and only about ten employees out of all the people surveyed rated it a "1."

Correlation analysis is used to examine the relationship between two things. For example:

> Does it really rain every time you go to the beach? Simply correlate the number of consecutive trips to the beach with rainy weather (probably not much correlation).

> Do children who are read to by their parents become avid adult readers? Correlate children who are read to with the number of books they read per year as an adult (likely a good correlation).

Does teller training make a difference? Correlate customer complaints or any other measure with bank tellers who have received training, as well as with those tellers who have not (probable a medium correlation).

Most groups doing problem identification need to be able to use basic statistics to analyze their data. They must understand the meanings of mean (an average), median (the middle number), mode (the most frequently appearing number), and standard distribution (the old "bell-shaped curve"), and must be able to calculate standard deviations, among other things.

- *Causal analysis* is used to identify the cause of a specific problem. A group can use this method to analyze data to determine where the problem occurred (versus where it did not occur), and when it happened (versus when it didn't). After answering these questions, a team can often identify the most likely cause of the problem.

- *Decision making.* Two major processes are used by teams to make decisions:

  Evaluation of alternatives: This tool is used to identify the best of several alternative solutions. Selecting the best computer or choosing the best way to do a task are examples of decisions that can be made through evaluation of the merits of each alternative.

  Force field analysis: This process helps you make a decision when there are only two alternatives (e.g., to buy a computer or not, or to change the way to do a task or not). Thus it is an especially good tool to use when there are two sides, pro and con, to an issue.

- *Planning.* A planning process is used by a team to do just that—plan. A goal statement is written, and then the team helps to develop appropriate steps in the plan. Next, a technique called "potential problem avoidance" is used to examine problems that might occur when the plan is implemented.

Involvement. Involving everyone is usually the best way to obtain acceptance. Encourage the team members to offer ideas or suggestions. As the boss, you should not offer to do everything yourself. Delegate assignments to others, such as key roles of Facilitator and Recorder, and even that of Chair.

Consensus management. Another way to obtain involvement and acceptance is to use a tool called *consensus management*, which is very different from the normal, oral "consensus" you may have used in the past. This is a technique often used in conjunction with other processes to help teams make better group decisions. It produces more agreement among team members than traditional voting does (which usually ends up with "winners" and "losers"). In consensus management, everyone wins, resulting in greater acceptance of the group's decision. Consensus management also generates more-creative ideas than does a traditional voting process.

Consensus management is employed at any point where a traditional vote would be taken. It is used to identify which problems a group wants to address or which topics to consider at a future meeting; to analyze a list of alternative solutions to a problem, select those the group wants to explore further, and choose the best solution; or to determine which steps to use in a plan.

Since consensus management is so critical to the functioning of an effective team, let's look in detail at how it works.

Arriving at Consensus

1. Write the question to be considered on easel paper.

2. Brainstorm a list of ideas relating to the question (topics, suggestions, alternatives, etc.). Don't stop to evaluate each idea—simply write exactly what each person says on the easel paper. Try to obtain everyone's suggestions without allowing any comments or discussion at this time.

3. When all the members have had an opportunity to present their ideas, ask if any of them can be combined or eliminated.

4. Then ask each person to explain *briefly* the reasons for his or her suggestion. (These presentations are limited to not more than two minutes per person.)

5. Next, ask each member to select and write down his or her first three choices, in order of preference, from the ideas listed.

6. The members then assign three points to their first choice, two points to their second, and only one point to their third.

7. Call on each member in turn to record on the easel paper his or her point-value rating.

8. Finally, add up the total score for each item and announce the group's selection.

If the list of items happens to be long (fifteen or more), it is preferable to have the members select their top four or five and then assign four or five points to their first choice (and so on). This decision process is usually superior to traditional voting methods because it better reflects the relative strength of the group's preferences for the particular ideas that have been generated.

Closing the meeting. One of the jobs of a meeting leader is to keep track of time. If a meeting is scheduled to end at ten o'clock, end the meeting at ten by announcing, "We are out of time" (unless there is a major reason not to do so). The members will have other appointments, places to go, and job tasks to finish. If someone still has something to discuss, suggest that it be covered at the next meeting (and ask the Recorder to make a note of it). The meeting leader can also invite those who are interested to stay for a short time after the meeting.

Make certain to leave enough time to

- Ask the facilitator for his or her comments on the group's process.
- Ask the recorder to summarize the meeting and review any tasks that need to be assigned.
- Ask for volunteers or assign people to complete these tasks.
- Announce the time and place of the next meeting.

Finally, privately thank the group members who served as facilitator, recorder, and meeting leader (if assigned) for their work in making the meeting a success.

Following up. Check to see that the people who were assigned tasks are completing them on schedule. Make sure that you complete any tasks that you agreed to do, also.

The ideas and strategies presented in this chapter won't solve every meeting problem, but they will help you resolve most of them, and will help you plan and organize meetings so that you will have significantly greater productivity and success.

Meeting Preparation
Checklist

Meeting date: _____ Location: _____

Time: Start at _____ End by: _____ Lunch: _____ to _____

Meeting objectives: Describe what you and/or participants want to accomplish as a result of the meeting.

_____

_____

_____

_____

Topics or Agenda:

_____

_____

_____

_____

_____

_____

_____

Who should attend?

_____   _____

_____   _____

_____   _____

_____   _____

(Check tasks required or completed)		**Notes** (Person to contact; person responsible, etc.)	**Date completed**
	Pre-Meeting Communication		
☐	Agenda	_____	_____
☐	Handouts	_____	_____
☐	Assignments	_____	_____
☐	Attendees confirmed	_____	_____
☐	_____	_____	_____
☐	_____	_____	_____

(continued)

(Check tasks required or completed)		Notes (Person to contact; person responsible, etc.)	Date completed
	Speakers or Guests		
☐	Approval received	_____	_____
☐	Contacted	_____	_____
☐	Advance copy of outline/speech	_____	_____
☐	Advance copy of handouts	_____	_____
☐	Lodging	_____	_____
☐	Invoice from speaker	_____	_____
☐	Speaker fees paid	_____	_____
☐	_____	_____	_____
	Meeting Leader		
☐	Outline of day's events	_____	_____
☐	Notes for commentary	_____	_____
☐	Handouts	_____	_____
☐	Prizes, awards, etc.	_____	_____
☐	Transparencies:	_____	_____
☐	Prepared	_____	_____
☐	Clear write-on film	_____	_____
☐	Marking pen	_____	_____
☐	Prepared flipcharts	_____	_____
☐	Videotape(s)	_____	_____
☐	Slides	_____	_____
☐	Disks for presentation software	_____	_____
☐	CDs	_____	_____
☐	Evaluations (if appropriate)	_____	_____
☐		_____	_____
	Lodging for Out-of-Town Attendees		
☐	Rooms confirmed	_____	_____
☐	Transportation	_____	_____
☐	Other	_____	_____
	Meeting Room		
☐	Room reserved	_____	_____
☐	Room key	_____	_____
☐	Appropriate size	_____	_____

(continued)

Meeting Room (continued)

- ☐ Loading entrance
- ☐ External noise checked
- ☐ Incoming phone calls held
- ☐ Restroom location
- ☐ Sufficient number of tables
- ☐ Sufficient number of chairs
- ☐ Room layout drawing for setup person

Equipment

- ☐ Overhead projector and spare bulb
- ☐ Slide projector
- ☐ Large screen
- ☐ Video player
- ☐ Video monitor
- ☐ Video recorder
- ☐ Presentation software equipment (e.g., projector)
- ☐ Computer
- ☐ Laser pointer
- ☐ PA system
- ☐ Microphone
- ☐ Wireless mike
- ☐ Volume control
- ☐ Flipcharts
- ☐ Extra paper
- ☐ Marking pens
- ☐ Masking tape
- ☐ Writing board
- ☐ Chalk
- ☐ Dry markers
- ☐ Erasers
- ☐ Electrical outlets
- ☐ Extension cords

(continued)

Equipment (continued)

☐ Room lighting

☐ Temperature controls

☐ Scratch paper

☐ Pencils/pens

☐ Name tags

☐ Direction signs

Refreshments

☐ Morning

☐ Afternoon

Meals

☐ Menu selection

☐ Written orders when to serve

☐ Cost

☐ Gratuities

☐ Billing

☐ _____

Travel for Meeting Leader (if meeting is out of town)

☐ Plane reservations

☐ Plane ticket

☐ Motel reservations

☐ Travel money

☐ Business cards

☐ Materials shipped

☐ Return-address labels

☐ Tape for repackaging

☐ Laptop or other devices

☐ Wireless phone

☐ _____

Notes:

_____

_____

_____

(concluded)

19
Interviewing and Selecting

Managers do not spend enough time making selection decisions, yet they often spend a great deal of time with problem employees, correcting mistakes or working out problems. If a small amount of that time had been spent in better selection, the problems might well have been avoided, and the managers could spend their time in the areas that would have a higher impact on the organization.

> – Bill Byham
> *Recruitment, Screening, and Selection:*
> *A Human Resources Management and Development Handbook*

Replacing employees when they don't succeed can be very costly to the organization in recruiting, interviewing, and employee training time and recurrent costs to repeat the process if the person who is hired doesn't work out.

Ineffective interviewing and selection also cost the company in less obvious ways. Employees are an investment. As with any investment, you need to realize a return. During an employee's career in an organization, the investment in terms of salary and benefits can easily exceed one million dollars. When you stop and realize that you are making million-dollar investments when you hire (often based on only an hour or so spent interviewing and selecting an employee), it's kind of scary.

Organizations operate within a larger community, and communities are quick to judge organizations with hiring turnovers. When the word gets around (and it doesn't take long) that the organization does a lousy job matching people and jobs, it becomes harder and harder to find good candidates—the good ones don't want to work for an organization with poor hiring practices.

Sometimes termination results in expensive litigation. Here again, nobody wins. In most states, a company can still terminate an employee who doesn't have a contract (written or implied) for almost any reason. But if the employee feels that hiring promises weren't honored and/or that he or she was unfairly terminated, the company loses whether or not it "wins" a resulting lawsuit. Have you ever had to sit for hours while an employee's attorney takes your deposition? I have, and it's no fun.

The morale in a section or department suffers when employees leave either voluntarily or involuntarily. Indeed, you're caught either way: If you don't terminate an employee who was poorly hired, morale will suffer. If you do terminate him or her, morale will suffer because of the termination. You lose no matter what you do. Therefore, it's tremendously important to put in the time and effort necessary to hire the right candidate in the first place. Prepare properly for the interview and you improve your chances of hiring the best person for the job.

The information in this chapter is presented sequentially, but some actions need to be taken simultaneously. Let's begin by examining all the things that need to be done in *preparation* for the interview. Then we will look at the *interview* itself, and finally the *selection* process.

Preparing for Interviews

Preparation is directly related to the outcome. When you are ready to fill a position, you must do several things before you meet with applicants:

1. Analyze the job to be filled.
2. Review the interview plan to make sure that it complies with the law.
3. Determine who will interview the applicants.
4. Establish an interview area.
5. Prescreen with telephone interviews.

Let's look at each of these in more detail.

Analyzing the job to be filled. Take a long, hard look at the job you want to fill by listing the major tasks of the job and then determining key knowledge, skills, and areas needed for each task. Also decide which tasks applicants must already be able to perform when they apply, and which tasks they can be trained to do after they are hired. Next, write out the questions you plan to use to determine the applicant's knowledge, skills, and interests for each task. And finally, have a strategy to discover whether or not the applicant is likely to be satisfied with the job conditions—salary, benefits, working hours, etc.

List the major tasks of the job. Here's how the task listing of an administrative assistant position might look:

- Files
- Types using Word
- Mails correspondence
- Handles supplies
- Answers phones
- Faxes messages
- Sends and receives e-mails
- Makes copies

Determine job knowledge, skills, and interests. Now you need to examine each task to determine what an applicant should know, be able to do, or be motivated to do. For example, for the job of administrative assistant, the applicant must 1) have basic reading skills, and 2) know the rules of filing (such as knowing where to file, say, "The 3M Company" folder, in order to do the filing). From this task detailing, you can later determine how well the applicant fits the job.

Decide whether or not the applicant should already have the required knowledge, skills, and interests. List the knowledge, skills, and interests required for a specific job, even though you are willing to (or even plan to) teach the employee some tasks. The administrative assistant's task of "making copies" is not one you need to ask an applicant about because you would likely plan to teach the employee how to do this part of his or her job. But by task detailing, you are able to determine prerequisites. An employee who will be required to spend most of the day typing must already know how to type; it's next-to-impossible to teach this skill on the job.

Identify prescreening questions. Now you need to determine 1) which job knowledge, skills, and interests an applicant absolutely must have in order to qualify for an interview, and 2) what questions you will ask the applicant on the telephone to obtain this information. The idea is to create "knockout" questions that will prevent you from wasting time in an interview. In a telephone prescreening interview, ask about the applicant's typing or keyboarding skills (if this is not already indicated on the application and it is important for the job) and terminate the conversation if the applicant can't type.

Ask open questions. In prescreening and for the formal interview, you must ask questions effectively. Write out your key questions in advance. Closed questions usually start with Do you...? Could you...? Will you...? Have you...? or Can you...?" and are normally answered with a yes or no. Open questions produce more information than closed questions, and that is our objective—information. The question "How do you feel about typing?" is likely to get more information than "Do you like to type?" Make them *open* rather than *closed* questions: start them with who, what, where, when, why, and how.

Avoid asking leading questions. Think of a movie or TV courtroom scene in which one of the attorneys jumps to his feet and shouts, "Objection! Objection, your Honor! The opposing counsel is *leading* the witness!" Whereupon the judge says, "Objection sustained. Counsel will please rephrase the question."

Pretend that there is a judge present who is listening to your questions. Every time you ask a question beginning with "Don't you... couldn't you... Shouldn't you... or Can't you..." this judge is going to jump all over you! Leading questions like these ask the applicant to agree with your preconceived opinions, and will usually bias his or her response. The question "Don't you think that it is very important to have good work habits?" quite clearly telegraphs the answer you seek, and can invalidate the information it produces. If you really want to know what applicants think or how they feel, use open questions. Don't lead the witness.

Decide how you will determine the applicant's knowledge/skills/interests. You can obtain information in a variety of ways. You can ask questions in the interview, require the applicant to perform certain tasks, have the applicant bring in samples of relevant work, and review the applicant's résumé and/or application form for specific information and questionable areas. Let's look at each of these techniques.

Technique #1. Ask questions. Interview questions normally should be composed at the same time you develop your telephone prescreening questions. Follow the same guidelines that were given for writing prescreening questions. You might want to ask the same question in the interview that you asked in the telephone prescreening call, but in a slightly different way.

Technique #2. Ask the applicant to demonstrate. One of the best ways to find out if applicants can do what they say they can do is to ask them to do it. It is remarkable how often interviewers ask job candidates about their skills, yet fail to ask them to demonstrate them. I suspect that the reason why many people in organizations today can't read (and no one knows it until a serious problem occurs) is because people lacking basic reading skills are adept at disguising this fact and are not always asked to read in selection interviews.

If I want to know if applicants can type, I ask them to type. If I need to know if they can use Ohm's law, I give them voltage and current and ask them to derive resistance. If I need to know how well they can answer the phone, I have them role play with me or answer an actual incoming phone call (with some preparation). If a particular job skill is important and I don't plan to teach it on the job, then I need to figure out a way for the applicant to demonstrate his or her degree of expertise for me.

Technique #3. Look at samples of past work. There are times when it is appropriate and extremely helpful to ask the applicant to bring samples of past work to the interview. If I am hiring someone to teach a one-day interviewing and selection workshop, I will ask for a video-tape of him or her conducting an actual workshop on this subject. If I want to hire graphic artists, I will certainly ask candidates to bring samples of their work. And if I am looking for a writer, then I will want to see some things that he or she had written. If computer programmers are needed, I will ask them to bring hard-copy samples of their work, and disks. If creative work that can be seen or heard is involved, ask the applicant to bring samples of that work to the interview.

Technique #4. Take a close look at the résumé and the application. Résumés are often written to present information in the best possible way. We seldom see on a résumé, "I really didn't like my boss, so I quit," or "After I work for an organization for a year or two, I need to move on to greener pastures," yet these are two of the main reasons why people actually quit. And when was the last time you read a résumé that said, "I am so desperate for work that I'll take any job. Even yours!"? The applicant will position his information in its best possible light on a résumé, so interpret what you see with this in mind.

An experienced eye can pick up on many things. Does the work history show much-too-frequent moves? What does this say about the applicant's intention of staying with your organization? Are there gaps in the employment history? What questions do we need to ask about those gaps? And is the applicant's work history actually a good fit for the job we are trying to fill?

Are there any sections in the application form left blank? If so, why were they not filled in? What questions do you need to ask to obtain the missing information? Has the applicant been unemployed? How long? Why did he or she leave one job before finding another?

The applicant's handwriting can also tell us something about neatness and carefulness. If an application is typed, do you also need to ask to see a sample of the applicant's handwriting?

Let's look at how all these things can be recorded on the interview planning worksheet, using the administrative assistant position as an example.

Interview Planning Worksheet

Key for Column 3:
R = Required when hired
T = Train after hired

Key for Column 4:
P = Determine information in prescreening
I = Determine information in interview
P/I = Both

1 Tasks	2 Job Knowledge, Skills, and Interests	3 R or T	4 P, I, or P/I	5 Prescreening Questions and Samples Required	6 Interview Questions, Demonstrations, and Samples Examined
Files	• Applies rules of filing • Has basic reading skills	R	P/I	*How well do you know the rules of typing?* *How well can you read?*	*Please put these files in order.* *(The above also tests for reading ability.)*
Types using Word	• Types min. of 45 wpm with only 1% error rate	R	P/I	*How fast do you normally type?* *Please bring three samples of papers or letters you have typed.*	*Please type this letter using Microsoft Word.* *May I see samples of papers you have typed?*
	• Likes using Windows	R	P	*How do you feel about using Windows?*	
	• Is proficient with Microsoft Word and Excel	R	P/I	*How well can you use Microsoft Word and Excel?*	*Type these numbers into a spreadsheet using Excel.*
Mails correspondence	• Can operate postage meter	T	I		*What's been your experience in using a postage meter?*
	• Adds and subtracts correctly	R	P/I	*What is your skill level in basic math?*	*Add and subtract these numbers.*
	• Demonstrates understanding of the U.S. postal rates	T	I		*What is the current postage required for a 1 oz. letter to Canada?*
Handles supplies	• Can fill out purchase order requests	T	I		*Please fill out this sample form.*
	• Can lift a min. of 25 lbs. (box)	R	P	*Can you lift a box that weighs a minimum of 25 lbs.?*	
Answers phones	• Has pleasing phone personality	R	P	Listen to how he or she sounds during the phone call.	
	• Knows telephone etiquette	R	P/I	Listen for key behaviors during the phone call.	Conduct a role play with a hypothetical customer.

(continued)

1 Tasks	2 Job Knowledge, Skills, and Interests	3 R or T	4 P, I, or P/I	5 Prescreening Questions and Samples Required	6 Interview Questions, Demonstrations, and Samples Examined
Faxes messages	• Knows how to dial a long-distance fax number	T	I		*What's been your experience with fax machines?*
	• Can position documents in machine and start/stop the operation	T	I		*Show me how you would send this document.*
	• Can load paper into the machine	T	I		*How would you insert more paper into the machine?*
Sends and receives e-mails	• Can use our network	T	I		
	• Can print e-mails	T	I		*Please print this e-mail.*
	• Can copy e-mails to computer	T	I		*Please copy this e-mail to the computer's hard drive.*
Makes copies	• Can turn machine on/off	T	I		*What's been your experience with copiers?*
	• Can troubleshoot machine	R	P/I		*What experience have you had troubleshooting copy machines?*
	• Can load toner	T	I		*How would you load toner in this machine?*

Determine other job requirements. Think of questions that will help you determine the applicant's expectations for other aspects of the job. For instance, if the salary was advertised, then the applicant has applied for the job knowing what the position pays. If salary has not been mentioned, you will need to decide how well the applicant's expectations match what the job pays.

One way to guess how satisfied the applicant is with the salary is to review any past salaries indicated on his or her résumé and ask appropriate questions during the prescreening telephone interview. If prior pay is not noted on the résumé or completed application, simply ask, "What was your salary in your last (or present) position?" or "What kind of salary range are you looking for?"

You might also need to ask questions about the applicant's desires and expectations concerning working conditions, work hours, vacations, holidays, benefits, and insurance. If the job requires that the employee normally work alone, then determine whether or not the applicant likes to do so. If the job hours are unusual, then ask questions to make sure that the hours will not pose a hardship.

A blank copy of the *Interview Planning Worksheet* we have been using as an illustration appears at the end of this chapter. Copy and use it to plan and conduct prescreening and selection interviews.

The interview plan, the law, and the organization's policies. It is impossible to fully understand the importance of correct interviewing and selection without looking at the legal considerations. But a word of caution: I believe that the legal information presented here is accurate, but it is nonetheless my understanding. I am not a lawyer, and the laws are constantly changing. Speak with an attorney about any process or practice you are using or considering, as well as any legal concerns you have concerning an applicant.

There are two key areas that you should evaluate to ensure compliance with the law: questions that should not be asked either on the application form or during the interview; and employee ratios with regard to minority status, gender, and age. Let's look at each of these in more detail.

Questions asked. The questions on application forms, as well as those asked in interviews, must be free of bias in terms of the race/ethnicity, religion, gender, age, handicap, and national origin of applicants. Most employers today are aware that asking informational questions of job applicants in these areas can be illegal, but do not assume that everyone is familiar with the law and legal guidelines.

Some questions are okay when asked *after* the candidate has been offered and has accepted employment. For instance, the human resource department will need to know the age of the new employee for retirement purposes, and family information will be needed for insurance purposes. On the other hand, questions about religion are not legally proper at any time.

Race/ethnicity. If the purpose and result of an organization's hiring procedure is to deliberately hire minorities, then most questions concerning race/ethnicity are legal. But if the intent *or effect* of the hiring procedure is to exclude minorities or that minorities are excluded; if the organization's present minority-to-non-minority ratios are suspect; or if a rejected applicant feels that he or she has been excluded due to race/ethnicity, avoid asking *What is your race? Where were you born? Where did your family originally come from? Are you a naturalized citizen? How did you learn to speak Spanish?* (or any foreign language); *What was your wife's maiden name?* and so on.

Asking applicants for a photograph, a birth certificate, or a baptismal record as proof of age *is also illegal* prior to hiring.

Religious preferences. Questions concerning an applicant's religion are always illegal. DO NOT EVER ASK questions such as What is your religious affiliation? What church do you go to? What religious holidays do you observe?

Marital and family status. Questions concerning marital or family status are generally illegal—unless, that is, you ask the same question of both sexes and have a job-related reason for asking. Some questions will get you and your organization into trouble. DO NOT ask questions like: How does your spouse feel about your need to travel in this job? (a potentially serious problem when asked of a female applicant); Are you married? Do you plan to get married? Have you ever been divorced? What are your plans about having children? What are you going to do about your children during working hours?

Height and weight. Unless height or weight information is clearly relevant to a job's requirements, questions about them are usually illegal. The issue here is why you or your organization would want to know. If particular height and weight qualifications are absolutely critical to a job and you can prove it, then the questions might be okay. Otherwise, it's none of your business. Don't ask such questions.

Age. Most interviewers today do not ask obvious age-inquiry questions, but I have heard people ask "disguised" questions to secure approximate age information, such as "How old is your oldest child?" and "What year did you graduate from high school?"

Minority representation. Are the applicants appropriately representative in terms of race or ethnicity and gender? If the effect of your hiring action is to either institute or perpetuate a policy of noncompliance with the law concerning race/ethnicity and gender, you might be in serious trouble. Take the initiative and talk it through with the human resource department or management to make sure that you are encouraging minority applications and interviews (and certainly not discouraging them).

If you are located in an area with a thirty-five percent minority population, for example, it is reasonable that you seek to interview at least this number of minority applicants.

Other cautions. **Do not** delve into areas that are not directly related to the job itself and the candidate's qualifications, or you will expose yourself and your company to liability claims.

DO NOT ASK questions like these:

- "Do you have any friends or family working for us?" (A hiring preference for friends or family members of your employees could restrict opportunities for minorities.) Of course, if your organization has a policy against hiring family members, then such questions are permissible.

- "Have you ever been arrested?" or "Have you ever spent the night in jail?" (Since some minorities have higher rates of arrest or incarceration than others do, these questions are discriminatory.)

- "Tell me about your credit rating." or "Do you own your own home?" or "What kind of car do you have?" (Unless such socioeconomic information is clearly important to the job, don't ask them. They tend to be discriminatory against certain minorities.) Likewise, DO NOT check on an individual's credit rating prior to hiring, unless the organization can absolutely document that doing so is a job necessity. This could be problematic; run it by your legal counsel first.

In general, the rule is that if the questions do not clearly relate to specific job requirements, they are probably illegal because they suggest a possible attempt to hire or not hire for reasons other than job qualifications. Asking them could result in charges of discrimination and costly legal action.

Determining who will interview the applicants. There are some very good reasons why you might wish to involve others in the interviewing and selection process (such as your fellow managers) to gain additional insight into an applicant's suitability for the job. Multiple interviewers, for example, can protect us from ourselves. I remember nearly hiring a candidate right on the spot after he informed me that he attended the same college I did. Fortunately, others who were also involved in the hiring decision helped me see my bias.

Involving others will indeed significantly increase your hiring costs, but if you are talking about million-dollar decisions, it's a good idea to invest additional up-front time and money to ensure that you make the best possible selections.

If the applicants are going to be interviewed by more than one person, provide all interviewers with copies of any planning notes or worksheets that list the knowledge, skills, and interests needed for each task and the questions to be asked. Decide in advance who will focus on what aspects of the job and which questions each interviewer will ask. Then set up a schedule and notify each interviewer by interoffice mail as to who will be interviewed and when and where this will take place. Applicants will begin to wonder about your organization if each of several interviewers asks, "What do you see are your weaknesses?"

One excellent strategy being used more and more today is to involve those who will have to work with the new hire in the interviewing and selection process. After all, if the employees are going to work with and probably help train the new person, they will feel much better about who is selected if they have had a hand in the decision. Most likely the current employees know the work better than anyone else. (They can even help develop the interview questions.) Finally, new employees appreciate knowing that their co-workers were involved in choosing them.

The location. Interviews are important, so schedule them in private locations where you can control interruptions. Use a conference room and put a sign on the door stating "Interviews in progress. Please do not interrupt." Or use the empty office of someone who is on vacation. Use your office if necessary, but do not allow any interruptions. Tell people who might normally interrupt you that you will be interviewing and do not want to be interrupted. Have all phone calls held until you are through.

Arrange the interview seating so that it is conducive to the sharing of information. Avoid an "I've got all the power" arrangement if you really want information from an applicant. Meet in a neutral area if possible, preferably a conference room. If you must use your office, don't sit behind the desk; sit across the corner of the desk or in front of it, using a guest chair. Whatever you do, set up the interview area so that it helps create a true conversation with the applicant. It is not supposed to resemble an interrogation.

Finally, place a small clock where you can see it while you are looking at the applicant, or put it where it can be seen as you look down at your notes. If you glance away from the applicant to check your watch or a clock, he or she will feel that you are pressed for time.

Prescreening telephone interview. After you have identified the job requirements, examined the résumé or application form, written prescreening questions, and decided what the individual should bring to the interview, you are ready to conduct brief telephone interviews. Prescreening allows you to separate applicants who are not suitable for the job from those whom you want to interview further.

If you determine that an applicant is a possible fit, let him or her know what must be brought to the interview (work samples, etc.). Also advise the applicant where, when, and with whom the interview will take place.

As you schedule prescreened applicants for interviewing, plan at least forty-five minutes for each interview, with a minimum of fifteen minutes between appointments. Interviews are exhausting to conduct. (Don't believe me? Conduct ten forty-five minute interviews and see how you feel at the end of the day!) A fifteen-minute interval between interviews will give you time to complete your notes and reorganize before the next candidate arrives. It will also give you extra time in case you go beyond your scheduled time with an applicant.

Forty-five minutes is a rough number; the time you allot will depend on the level of the job being filled, as well as on the experience of the applicant. If you are conducting an interview for a job that requires extensive experience, for example, you will need significantly more interviewing time to allow the candidate to present the needed information.

Conducting Interviews

A good interviewer has seven objectives in mind. They are to:

1. Determine what a candidate can do.
2. Determine what a candidate is willing to do.
3. Determine whether or not a particular job fits the candidate's values, interests, and preferences.
4. Present the job and organization realistically to the candidate.
5. Leave the candidate with a good impression of the organization and its people.
6. Reinforce or enhance the candidate's positive self-image.
7. Conduct the interview ethically and legally.

To accomplish these objectives, we will look at the actual interview process. Here are the five basic steps that lead to an effective exchange of information:

1. Start the interview.
2. Determine the candidate's suitability for the job.
3. Describe the job—honestly.
4. Ask for additional questions.
5. End the interview.

Let's examine each of these areas in detail.

Start the interview. A number of years ago, I wrote a book for employees titled, *Is Coffee Break the Best Part of Your Day?* I sent the manuscript to a few publishers, and received three contracts. Two of the three were from large publishers, who were not very friendly and were even a little bit arrogant (like they were doing me a favor by offering to publish my book). The third publisher was quite a bit smaller, but the representative was personable and flexible. In our discussion, he said, "I want this book. I want to be your publisher!" Guess whom I chose? Right! Not one of the big publishing houses, but the smaller one. HRD Press genuinely wanted my book. It is no accident that since that time, they have grown to be the largest publisher of human resource books.

It's the same way with job candidates. All too often, we see leaders acting like the old-line publishers I encountered: stern, distant, superior, and not very friendly. Remember: good candidates are likely to receive a number of job offers. If you want them to accept your offer, treat them the way you want to be treated—with interest, respect, and friendliness.

There is also a direct correlation between a candidate's willingness to share information openly and the consideration you show him or her. Treat all candidates the way you want to be treated. (Who knows—it might be your children out there job hunting some day—or even you!)

Avoid saying "I'm Mr. (or Ms.) So and So," because this sounds very formal and unfriendly. Instead, use your first name. If a candidate uses a title in speaking with me, I gently say, "Call me Dick." If the candidate continues to use the title, then that is his or her choice.

Establishing trust. The greater the level of trust between the job candidate and the interviewer, the greater the quality and quantity of information you are likely to receive—and you need information in order to make a good decision! Establish a trusting environment by preparing for the interview, scheduling interviews at a private location where you can control interruptions, not allowing yourself to be interrupted, having all phone calls held, and arranging the seating so that the candidate is comfortable.

But trust is also established by what we say. If you begin the interview by openly stating why it is important for both of you to be honest in the interview, the candidate is more likely to be honest—not just say what he or she thinks you want to hear. Tell candidates at the outset that you think it is important to let them know exactly what the job is: its good points, its bad points, and what it *isn't,* because if they are offered the job and accept it, they will expect it to be as you describe it in the interview. If it is not, then the new employee will have a serious problem, and consequently, you will have a serious problem, too.

On the other hand, if the employee provides you with "fantasy information" based on what he or she thinks you want to hear, you may have the makings of a disaster on your hands, starting with a new employee who is totally unsatisfactory for the job. And unsatisfactory employees make for unhappy employees—and unhappy bosses.

Here is an example of what an interviewer might say to a candidate:

Jack, before we start the actual interview, I need to say something very important. I think that you and I should try to be as honest as possible with each other. Not that I think you would be deliberately dishonest, but there is a natural tendency for applicants to try to appear as qualified as possible in the interview—as well as for the interviewer to make this organization sound great and the job even better. Sure, I'm proud to work here. I know you are proud of your accomplishments. But we're both going to get in trouble if we don't level with each other. You, by telling me what you're really all about; and me, by telling you what the job actually is, warts and all. If we don't do this, you may end up with a job you can't stand or aren't truly qualified for. And then I will end up dealing with all the problems this will cause.

If the interviewer and the candidate are both straight with one another, they both will win. If not, they both will lose.

Taking notes. If you do not take notes during your interviews, it will be impossible to remember what the candidates have said, even by the end of the day. Resist the temptation to use a tape recorder, and be sure you take notes. Tape recorders inhibit candidates, and not having notes to keep your facts and people straight makes it very difficult to remember what was said. Your handwritten notes are the way to go. Tell the individual that you will be interviewing a number of candidates, and that unless you take notes, it will be difficult to remember the important things that were said. Then ask the candidate if he or she minds.

But a caution here: If you try to write down everything that is said, you'll inhibit the conversation and slow down the free flow of information. Just make brief notes, and flesh them out immediately after the interview. You will then be able to maintain better eye contact and establish rapport with the candidate to enhance communication. Be aware of important visual cues that might otherwise go unnoticed.

If the candidate says something that might be viewed as negative, try not to write it down right away, because he or she might begin to feel uncomfortable and inhibited. Wait a moment or two before making such a note.

The interview format. In general, there are two ways to proceed with your questioning. The traditional method is to ask candidates prepared questions about their experience, knowledge, skills, and interests, and then to describe the job. The other approach is to show the candidates your list of job tasks and related knowledge/skills/interest requirements, and then to ask the individual to describe how their experience matches each task area. Both formats have advantages and disadvantages.

Ask—then tell. The traditional approach to interviewing holds that you should obtain information from the candidate before describing the job. This "ask—then tell" format, of course, allows you to learn about the candidate's background before he or she is fully aware of the requirements of the job. The theory is that keeping candidates in the dark about the specifics of the job will allow you to obtain more-honest information from them and keep them from slanting what they say toward the just-learned job requirements. It is obviously true that human nature will lead candidates who want a job to present themselves in the best possible light in relationship to that job (even when they really don't want the job, because it feels good to be made an offer.) Using the "ask—then tell" approach, you could say:

Sue, here's how we'll spend our time today. First, I'd like to ask you some questions about your experience and interests. Next, I'll tell you about the job, and you'll have a chance to ask questions. Finally, I'll let you know our decision within approximately a week. So, the first thing I'd like to ask you is....

The disadvantage of taking this approach is that it requires more work. Design a considerable number of relevant questions ahead of time, worry about their legality, and then ask them in such a way as to elicit the information we will need for selection. It's not an easy job.

Show—then ask. A different interview format preferred by some is to begin by showing candidates the list of job tasks and required knowledge, skills, and abilities, but not the prepared questions. Then you ask them to describe how their experiences and abilities relate to each task item, and sit back and listen. You will likely need to ask a few clarifying questions, but for the most part, the candidate will do the talking.

This approach has several advantages. First, it is a lot easier; you won't have to spend so much time and effort designing and asking prepared questions. Second, candidates are usually more comfortable because they are basically talking about themselves. And since they are more comfortable, you will probably get more information. Third, the information you obtain will likely be more useful. If candidates know what you want them to be able to do, they are better able to tell us their relevant experiences. This is the kind of information you need to make a selection decision.

To use this approach, say something like this:

Dan, first I'll give you some specific information about this job. Next, you will have time to tell me about yourself and how your experience fits the needs of the job. Then, I'll answer any other questions you have. Last, I'll let you know what happens about a week after the interview.

So, let's look at the job. Here's a list of the major tasks in this position, as well as the knowledge, skills, and interests we feel are required for it. What I'd like you to do is to take each task and its related knowledge, skill, and other requirements, and describe how your experience fits that part of the job. I have a copy of this list that I'll use as a reference as you talk. And I'll ask any questions I have as we go along. So, why don't you take the first task, and go from there.

The main disadvantage of this approach is that you are telling the candidate about the job first, which can result in biased information because they will probably shape their responses accordingly.

Quality Leadership Skills

Determine the candidate's suitability for the job. The next step is to ask your prepared questions to determine the candidate's knowledge, skills, and interests. We have discussed in detail how to design effective questions based on the task lists, but we also need to say a word about the way in which you should ask your questions.

Asking questions about sensitive topics. At certain points in the interview, you will need to explore "sensitive" topics, whatever they may be. Such questions will yield more useful information if they are carefully prefaced. ("In confidence, could you tell me more about...?" or "If you don't mind my asking, what can you tell me about...?") If what you are told is confidential, treat it as such.

Avoiding questions the candidate can't answer. If you are trying to determine factual information, avoid embarrassing candidates by asking questions they won't be able to answer but feel they should. For instance, if you ask, "Exactly how many days were you absent from your job last year?" the candidate will feel that you expect him or her to have that information at his or her fingertips, and might feel somewhat threatened by the question. It is much better to begin such factual questions with words like "Approximately," "Usually," "Normally," or "Generally." ("Approximately how many days were you absent from your job last year?")

Using repetition. Another strategy to encourage a candidate to talk is termed *repetition.* You simply repeat the last words of what the candidate has said, ending with the tone of a question in your voice. For example, suppose you are interviewing candidates for an office clerk's position. You just asked about the candidate's experience in taking incoming telephone calls. The candidate responds by saying, "Well, several years ago, when I was with the Intensive Care organization, I spent a lot of time on the phone." Then just repeat the candidate's key words in the form of a question: "So when you were with Intensive Care, you spent a lot of time on the phone?" The candidate will usually respond by giving you additional information. In this case, the candidate might add, "Yes, I was a telephone solicitor responsible for selling burial plots. It was a tough business. I really had to push for a sale!"

Probing questions. When you ask a prepared question, you might need to follow it up with another question in order to obtain more information. These *probing questions* include questions such as:

"Can you tell me more about that?"
"What else?"
"Why did that happen?"
"What happened next?"
"Then what?"

But when you ask probing questions, avoid using too many in a series, or you'll sound like a detective. Avoid making candidates feel like they are suspects in a murder investigation.

"Where were you on the night of the murder?"
"What time did you leave the party?"
"What happened next?"
"Then what?"

Remember, helping the candidate feel at ease is the best way to secure information. All the questions should be designed to produce confidence and relaxation by showing your positive interest.

Asking what-if questions. One excellent way to obtain information is to ask a hypothetical *What-if question.* ("Patricia, if you were given the responsibility for running this section, what would you do?" or "Suppose that you got this job, Ann. What strengths would you bring to it?") Such questions offer much insight about the candidate's approach to situations, as well as his ability to think on his feet. But keep in mind that what-if questions ask candidates to apply their own experience to a specific and hypothetical situation, and this can make some people nervous. So be supportive in asking what-if questions.

Listening. Asking good questions is only one of the skills you need to conduct interviews. You also need to listen. It is especially important to practice good listening skills during the interview. Avoid interrupting candidates while they are speaking. (There are exceptions, of course, even to this rule, such as having to interrupt a nonstop talker.) Normally, the more you listen, the more you'll learn. Maintain good eye contact, and remember that you can process the information you hear more quickly than the candidate can speak. Be careful that your attention doesn't wander as the candidate talks. Instead, use the extra listening time to consider and note questions you should ask when there is an opportunity.

Responding. A successful interview is one in which the candidate does most of the talking and the interviewer does most of the listening. But good listening is not just sitting there in frozen silence. There are many things that you can do and say to facilitate a natural flow of communication. For example, as you listen, you can use verbal prompts, such as, "I see," "That's interesting," "Good," "Uh-huh," or "I didn't know that," to encourage candidates to continue to talk. Often these comments elicit even more information than asking another question.

Silence is a powerful communication tool. It's okay not to talk—simply wait a moment to see if the candidate wants to say more about his or her thoughts (just as long as the silence doesn't become awkward for the candidate).

Attending. When actively listening to someone, posture matters. We *attend* a person when our body communicates that we are interested in being with them and hearing what they have to say. To attend, simply lean forward as they talk, and encourage them by nodding your head and using verbal prompts.

Clarify and summarize. Clarifying and summarizing are effective and useful listening tools. Clarification (sometimes termed "paraphrasing") is nothing more than repeating, in your own words, what you understood the candidate to have said.

Summarizing what has just been said is also a good way to ensure that what you heard was what was really stated. Summarizing will also improve your retention. After the summary, quickly return to listening; the candidate will often provide more information on what he or she was saying. Clarifying and summarizing cause us to listen better, and allow us to check our understanding.

Provide positive feedback. When candidates say something positive about themselves, it is important for you to respond in a positive manner by saying, for example, "That was quite an accomplishment," or "You must have been very proud of that," or even just "Very good!" and "That's great!" Listen carefully for things the candidate is especially proud of, whether it is the way that a job was done, recognition that was received, or accomplishments in school. Providing positive feedback helps increase your rapport with the candidate, and usually helps obtain more information.

Ask for a task demonstration. As mentioned earlier, if you want to know if a candidate can perform a task properly, the best way to find out is to ask him or her to do it.

Let me relate a humorous "parable" to illustrate. Suppose that I had a lifelong ambition to become a medical doctor, but my dream had not been realized. Then one day I was reading a *Popular Mechanics* magazine and came across a classified ad that said, "Make big money!!! Learn to be a physician at home on your own time through our approved correspondence training program!"

So I sign up, send in my check, and begin receiving my reading assignments. As it turned out, I am pretty good at learning the material, and made high grades on all my open-book exams. I found the section "Removing the Appendix" especially fascinating, and even earned an A+ on that particular lesson.

Now here's the question: How would you feel about hiring me to take out your appendix? Too often we only ask candidates, "Can you take out an appendix?" rather than asking them to demonstrate their ability as we observe. Arranging for them to demonstrate simple hands-on tasks is not difficult to do and is well worth the effort in what we will learn about the candidate.

Ask for samples of past work. Asking candidates to bring particular samples of their past work is also a concrete way to examine their ability to perform a task. (Be aware, of course, of the possibility of a candidate submitting someone else's work.)

If necessary, tactfully conclude the interview early. Even after careful prescreening of candidates, you may discover in the face-to-face interview that a candidate's qualifications are inadequate. When this occurs (and it will), don't waste your time or the candidate's time with further interviewing. If the candidate is not suitable for the position, tactfully conclude the interview. Provide a brief, general description of the job, answer any questions, and then stand as you explain that all candidates will be notified promptly by mail. Then walk toward the door and shake hands goodbye. If you do get questions from the candidate, answer them briefly and diplomatically.

For example, you might say:

Well, Betty, in closing, I really appreciate your taking the time to meet with me. As we stated in our ad, the job is for an office clerk. We are looking at a number of candidates and will notify each of you by mail of our decision. You should hear from us in about a week. Do you have any other questions? (Note: This is a closed question, requiring just a yes or a no.)

Describe the job. The point of an interview is to obtain information and to tell the applicant enough about the job so that if they receive a job offer, they will be able to make an informed decision about accepting the job. If you try to sell, persuade, or convince the candidate that this is the best job in the country in the best organization in the world, you might have trouble converting this person into a long-term worker, should they feel later on that they were hustled.

I believe that most leaders spend too much time in the "telling" mode. It's almost as if we say to job candidates: "Okay, I've asked you all these questions, and I've listened to everything you've said. Now it's *my* turn to talk!" And we talk… and talk. If you take the time to properly prepare, it is a simple matter to discuss the list of job tasks and details about related knowledge/skills/interests. Also review the good and not-so-good points of the job; as we've said, it's important that the candidate have a realistic view of the position.

This doesn't mean, of course, that you should be negative about the job—far from it! Begin by clearly presenting the positive features of the job, and then discuss any drawbacks. Here's an example of what you could say if you are interviewing people for a managerial job:

This job is exciting and challenging. The people are fun and easy to work with. Our customers are truly wonderful. The boss you would answer to is a leader who delegates both responsibility and authority.

Downside? The starting salary plus commission is low, though the job does have a high future-earning potential. (Then smiling.) *But for a job like this, maybe* you *should* pay us!

Answer questions. Give the candidate a full, final opportunity to ask questions. Try not to ask, "Do you have any questions?" This is a closed question (inviting only a yes or no) and actually makes it more difficult for the candidate to respond. Instead, say, "What questions do you have?" This assumes that the candidate does have questions, and encourages him or her to ask them.

End the interview. End your interview by 1) stating that your time is up, 2) summarizing the highlights of the interview, and 3) telling the candidate what comes next. Do not tell any candidate at this time that they are not qualified for the job. Do it later by mail, so the individual will not get defensive or bargain. Also remember that if the person you finally choose does not accept the position, you will need to re-evaluate the other candidates.

Here is a good way to close:

Sam, it looks like our time is just about up. I appreciate your openness in this interview. I feel that I've learned a lot about you and your work experience. You obviously like working with people, you enjoy doing paperwork, and you are efficient in managing your time. You don't care much for working evening shifts, and you feel that planning is not presently one of your strengths.

We are interviewing a number of candidates for this position, and should be finished in about two weeks. At that time, we will notify all candidates by mail.

Thanks for coming in.

Selection

Okay, you did an outstanding job of obtaining a number of qualified candidates for an opening in your organization. Now, you are faced with the task of determining which of the candidates is best for you and your organization. What follows are ideas in how this can be done to help make sure you select the right person for the job.

Schedule a selection meeting. Involving more people in the actual selection process generally produces a better decision, but strike a balance. If only one person is involved in the decision, it is likely to reflect bias, but if there are too many people in the selection meeting, it can become difficult to get anything done. If you use multiple interviewers, all of these people should be part of the decision process. You may wish to invite two or three of your peers to discuss the candidates and offer their opinions. Consider inviting those who will work with the new hire, whoever it is, to participate in the decision.

Making the decision. A structured decision-making procedure usually leads to a better choice. I often use the Kepner-Tregoe (KT) decision-making grid to select the best candidate for a job. It is an excellent method for sorting out data and arranging it so that it makes sense. It is also a good tool for making a final selection decision.

Simply do four things: Write a decision statement; develop and weight your objective; identify alternatives and write data; and evaluate the risks.

Here is what the grid would look like for the open position of administrative assistant:

Factors	Weight	Candidates		
		Sam	George	Edith
Knows filing	10	6 years experience	Never filed	Some filing experience
Has basic reading skills	(a must)	Yes	Yes	Yes
Can type 45 wpm	(a must)	Yes	Yes	Yes
Can operate postage meter	1	Never used one	Used daily in old job	Has seen one used
Can add and subtract accurately	(a must)	Yes	Yes	Yes
Can lift 25 lbs.	(a must)	Yes	Yes	Yes
Has pleasant phone personality	9	Acceptable in role play	Aggressive in role play	Very good personality on phone
Has good phone etiquette	7	Didn't know the "rules"	No mistakes	Super! One of the best we've seen
Can troubleshoot office equipment	2	Experienced troubleshooter	Lacks even the basics of troubleshooting	Did well after seeing the service manual
Meets salary requirements	5	Last job earned less	Last job earned more	Earned quite a bit less in old job
Can start work now	8	Yes	Yes	Needs to give 4-week notice
Has good work history	8	Excellent	Some gaps between jobs	Excellent

List all the "must" factors important for the job. Then assign priority numbers for the less-critical factors using a scale of 1 – 10 (1 is least important, 10 is most important). When you fill out the grid, be as specific as you can so you can fairly compare the candidates.

(Suggestion: Begin by choosing the most important factor on the list, and assign it 10 points. Next, pick the least important factor, and give it 1 point. Then assign relative weights to the other factors.)

After all the weights have been assigned, you will then multiply each alternative weight by its original factor weight, as shown below.

Factors	Weight	Candidates		
		Sam	**George**	**Edith**
Knows filing	10	x 10 = 100 6 years experience	x 1 = 10 Never filed	x 5 = 50 Some filing experience
Has basic reading skills	(a must)	Yes	Yes	Yes
Can type 45 wpm	(a must)	Yes	Yes	Yes
Can operate postage meter	1	x 1 = 1 Never used one	x 10 = 10 Used daily in old job	x 2 = 2 Has seen one used
Can add and subtract accurately	(a must)	Yes	Yes	Yes
Can lift 25 lbs.	(a must)	Yes	Yes	Yes
Has pleasant phone personality	9	x 6 = 54 Acceptable in role play	x 1 = 9 Aggressive in role play	x 10 = 90 Very good personality on phone
Has good phone etiquette	7	x 2 = 14 Didn't know the "rules"	x 7 = 49 No mistakes	x 10 = 70 Super! One of the best we've seen
Can troubleshoot office equipment	2	x 10 = 20 Experienced troubleshooter	x 1 = 2 Lacks even the basics of troubleshooting	x 8 = 16 Did well after seeing the service manual
Meets salary requirements	5	x 8 = 40 Last job earned less	x 1 = 5 Last job earned more	x 10 = 50 Earned quite a bit less in old job
Can start work now	8	x 10 = 80 Yes	x 10 = 80 Yes	x 7 = 56 Needs to give four weeks notice
Has good work history	8	x 10 = 80 Excellent	x 3 = 24 Some gaps between jobs	x 10 = 80 Excellent
Total Scores		**389**	**189**	**414**

Having multiplied each of our candidate's factor (job task) ratings by that factor's weight and totaled the scores, we can see that Edith and Sam appear to be fairly equal candidates and that George comes far behind. Our decision-making grid helped organize and evaluate a great amount of data on three very different individuals, and leads us to quite a clear (and measured) comparative ranking of them—a much-desired finding that is difficult to achieve without a systematic decision-making procedure.

But now we need to decide between Edith and Sam, so let's look at risk.

Evaluating risk. "If we hire candidate 'X,' what could go wrong?" Identify the risks for each candidate and evaluate each risk in terms of the *probability* of it happening and the *seriousness* if it does, again using a scale of 1 to 10. A "1" probability rating means the event is not likely to happen, a "10" probability rating indicates that the event appears certain to happen. A "1" seriousness rating means that if it does happen, it won't be very serious. A "10" seriousness rating means that if it does happen, it will be a disaster. When we have assigned our probability and seriousness ratings, we will multiply them to get a risk rating for each candidate. If there is more than one risk with a candidate, we will add the risk ratings for a composite score.

Since two of our office clerk candidates (Edith and Sam) are closely ranked and are far ahead of the third, we will do our risk evaluation only on these two. ("P" = the probability of the event occurring; "S" = the seriousness if it does occur.)

Candidate: Sam

Risk	P		S	P x S =
Poor attendance record due to several health problems. He may develop the same attendance problems here. (They are not health problems covered by Americans with Disability Act.)	3	x	7	21
Has been out of work for several months. He may be seeking this position only because he needs a job, rather than really wanting this one. We couldn't get a handle on this in the interview.	2	x	5	10
		Total composite risk:		31

Notice that we are analyzing the risks with each candidate separately. Different candidates will have different risks; if we find a risk that is common to more than one candidate, we have probably overlooked a factor (job requirement) in our initial task listing. For example, if past attendance is important, we should have added "Good attendance record," given it a factor weight of, say, "7", and evaluated all three of the administrative assistant candidates in terms of it.

Now let's look at the risks in hiring Edith. What could go wrong if we hire her for this position?

Candidate: Edith

Risk	P		S	P x S =
She made a number of errors in the typing test. She said it was because she had not had an opportunity to keep up her typing skills in her old job. There is some concern that she will not be able to improve these skills on the job.	1	x	10	10
		Total composite risk:		10

Note that we do not subtract a candidate's risk score from the factor score. We only compare our candidates' risk scores to help us make a balanced decision. Sam's risk score of 31 is well above Edith's score of 10.

Edith appears to be the strongest candidate, leading the second-ranked candidate, Sam, in job task qualifications (414 to 389) and lack of risk (10 to 31).

Notifying candidates of the decision. As soon as you have completed the decision-making process and selected the one individual you want to hire, you must notify all candidates of the hiring decision. It is inconsiderate and wrong to keep job candidates who are not selected in limbo for days and even weeks. They may well have other job offers pending that they don't want to accept until they hear from you, but apart from that, who wouldn't be quite anxious to hear whether or not they got the job? Not knowing the result of a job application can be even more stressful than learning that you have been turned down.

When you don't let them know your decision within a week at the most, they are placed in the dilemma of not knowing whether or not they should call you. If they call, you might think they are "pushy." And if they don't call, they have no idea as to when, if ever, they will find out how well they did.

If you plan to contact unsuccessful interview candidates by phone, try to write down what you plan to say. If letters are to be mailed, avoid sending form letters, such as this one:

> Dear Sir/Madam:
>
> We regret to inform you that you were not selected for the ___ sales ___ job. Thank you for your interest in our organization.
>
> Sincerely yours,
> *I. M. Lazie*

Also, try not to give unsuccessful candidates the impression that there was something "wrong" with them because they were not selected. Keep your focus on the positives, as in the following example:

> Dear Susan,
>
> Thank you for applying for the computer programming position here at INW. I know that the day you spent in interviewing would have been strenuous for anyone.
>
> Susan, you were asked to come in for an interview because of your excellent qualifications. Although you were not chosen for this position, you had many strengths. The person we selected, however, was slightly more qualified for this particular job.
>
> I am keeping your application on file in case we have additional needs in the future. Thanks for your interest in our organization.
>
> Sincerely yours,
>
> XXX

It is up to your management or personnel department to decide whether or not to give specific information to candidates regarding why they weren't selected. Provide feedback only if it is requested, because the decision might be appealed.

The specific job applied for should be referenced when you notify an applicant in writing, and you (or the interviewer, if it was not you) should sign it.

Maintaining records. The candidate whom you hire might not work out or might quit shortly after being hired. In spite of your best efforts, there will be people who aren't happy with the new job or that you aren't happy with. You might soon need to hire another person for a similar job. For these reasons and others, it is wise to keep all interviewing and selection information on file. This information was very expensive to obtain; keeping it might save the company a great deal of time and money if it reduces the need to interview additional candidates in the future.

In addition, if you are ever asked to justify the selection, you will have the data to establish that the decision was fair, objective, and impartial (as it should be). Keep on file any notes used to determine the job requirements and questions to be asked, and save any worksheets used to make the final selection (e.g., KT grid). These records on successful and unsuccessful candidates will be very important and useful to the organization if there is any appeal or subsequent litigation.

Various laws and regulations relating to discriminatory practices require organizations to keep their interviewing and selection records and notes for specified periods of time. These time periods vary, depending on the legislation and the type of job applicant, but two years is probably the minimum. Check with your organization's attorney to make sure you are complying with existing laws.

Summary

Preparing for job interviews, prescreening the applicants, conducting interviews, selecting the best candidate, and following up all require thought, time, and effort. There really are no shortcuts: The amount of time devoted to preparing for interviews directly affects the quality of those interviews, which in turn determines the quality of the information you have on which to base your selection. And the quality of information you have will determine the quality of the final choice. The legal requirements concerning discrimination must not be ignored or sidestepped.

The benefits to an organization because you made a good "million dollar decision" make all of your efforts worthwhile. When you take the time to prepare and conduct effective interviews and selection meetings, you can confidently expect to attract people who have the skills to do the job, a genuine interest in the job, and the information needed to accept or reject a job offer. The successful candidates are more likely to perform well on the job and stay with the organization. Those who don't get hired are more likely to feel that the process was thorough and fair, and thus might apply for other jobs in the organization. Should a hiring decision be challenged informally or legally, you will have evidence to support your decision.

In closing, I would like to offer two basic rules that will influence the quality of what you do throughout the entire interviewing and selection process:

Treat others as you want to be treated. There are few activities harder than looking for a job—especially if you don't currently have one. Have compassion. Treat job applicants with courtesy, respect, and consideration. What goes out comes back: The way we treat others is the way we in turn will be treated in life.

Take the time to prepare properly for interviews. The time you spend in preparation will save you time, help you be more comfortable interviewing (because you will know what to ask), and greatly increase your chances of hiring the best employee for the job.

Interview Planning: Worksheet

Position: _____

Page _____ of _____ pages

R = Required
T = Can train to do this task

P = Determine information in prescreening
I = Determine this information in interview
P/I = Do both

Job Tasks	Job Knowledge, Skills, and Interests	R, T	P, I, P/I	Write out all important prescreening questions to ask applicant. Note samples applicant should bring to the interview.	Write interview questions: specify what demonstrations are needed. Specify what samples will be examined.

Selection Instructions

1. Write a decision statement (e.g., "Select the best candidate for the job").

2. List all important factors (job task requirements). Identify Must (M) factors. Numerically weight the remaining factors from 1 to 10 (10 = most important).

3. List candidates and select 3–4 best candidates for analysis. Record candidate data for "Must" factors. Eliminate candidates who don't meet every Must requirement. Record specific data for remaining factors (facts, figures, opinions, impressions). Avoid non-specific notations such as "Yes," "No," "Poor," "Good," "Better," "Best," etc. Numerically rate each candidate on each non-must factor from 1–10; give 10 only to the best candidate. Multiply each factor weight by each candidate rating. Record the results and add column scores for each candidate.

4. Evaluate the risks for each top candidate by assigning *probability* and *seriousness* values (10 to 1 scale, 10 = highest probability, greatest seriousness). Then multiply probability and seriousness ratings, add resulting risk totals for each candidate, and compare. Make selections based on final comparison of job task scores and risk scores.

Decision statement (your objective):

Factors (Job tasks requirements)	Weights	Candidate 1 — Data and Rating (10 – 1)	Candidate 2 — Data and Rating (10 – 1)	Candidate 3 — Data and Rating (10 – 1)
Total Scores				

Note: P = Probability (10 – 1 scale); S = Seriousness (10 – 1 scale)

Risk for Candidate 1	P	S	
		x	
		x	
		x	
Total Risk:			

Risk for Candidate 2	P	S	
		x	
		x	
		x	
Total Risk:			

20

Developing Employees

To live means to experience—through doing, feeling, thinking. Experience takes place in time, so time is the ultimate scarce resource we have. Over the years, the content of experience will determine the quality of life. Therefore, one of the most essential decisions any of us can make is about how one's time is allocated or invested.

– Mihaly Csikszentmihalyi
Finding Flow

During the early 1900's, an entire generation of young people grew up reading a series of novels written by Horatio Alger. The books were titled *Strive and Succeed; Making His Way; Struggling Upward; Do and Dare;* and *Helping Himself.* The plots generally had to do with a young boy who had either a father (often a minister) who was kind and good, but not concerned with the practical side of life, or was an absent father. The family was always poor. And there was usually a rich villain who was going to foreclose on a heavy mortgage of perhaps $500, at a time when one could have purchased a house for $600.

But the ending always turned out "happily." "Happy" in the Horatio Alger stories meant that the boy earned the money to pay the mortgage because he was honest, hard-working, and kind, and loved God, his mother, and his country. The central theme was that if you are willing to work hard, success will come automatically because of the grand opportunities that exist in this country.

Today the Horatio Alger lessons no longer hold true because the facts of life in the business world have changed radically. We still view the individual as fundamentally responsible for his or her success or failure, but the maxim "Hard work will ensure success" has by now become more myth than truth. Look at the facts: Only a few decades ago, the chances of being promoted were one in five. Today the odds are more like one in thirty; employees are six times less likely to be promoted to leadership positions today than they would have been in the recent past.

Our expectations tend to be shaped by experience. A whole generation grew up with remarkable opportunities. Their children are now our employees, and they have similarly high expectations. They were told, "Work hard. Stay in school. Go to college. Get your degree. Do these things, and you will succeed!" As a result, they expect to have responsible jobs with opportunities for advancement. The truth, however, is that they are not going to have the same opportunities that our parents had. We need to manage these employees differently by using professional-development systems that can greatly help our employees overcome career obstacles and achieve success.

Development Systems

Good organizations know that their employees are their strength. The best organizations are helping their employees develop themselves so they can be more and more valuable to the organization.

Here is a picture of the way the parts of a modern professional-development effort fit together. As you can see, the central focus is on development and action plans.

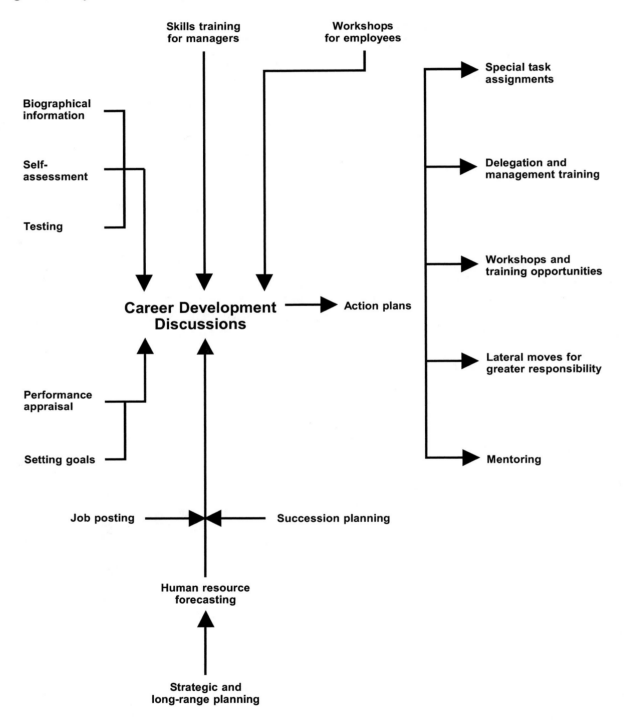

Organizational Strategies

Organizations are built on a foundation of strategic planning. Top management usually conducts this planning in order to define the organization's mission or vision. From the organization's definition of what it is about—its mission—a long-range plan is developed.

After the organization completes its long-range planning, it can then project its future human resource needs. When the forecasting is complete, the organization can then plan to determine who needs to be trained to do what in future jobs. Finally, the organization communicates its human resource needs to its employees by posting job vacancies.

If your organization does not do forecasting or workforce planning, you can still develop your employees. The first step is to help them figure out where they are going and what knowledge and skills will be required to get there. Then you'll need to determine what they need to do to acquire the needed knowledge and skills.

Useful Strategies for Determining Employee Needs

To explore an individual's developmental needs and desires, you need to analyze their past experience to determine their strengths, knowledge, skills, and values. This information will be very useful in helping them make sound decisions about where they are headed.

If you look at an individual worker's background and see that in nearly every past job the individual enjoyed making presentations, you might help this person focus on this interest and strength: public speaking and presentation skills.

Job history. One way to organize information about employees is to ask them to list each job they have held (a maximum of five), starting with their present position. A major job change within one organization should be counted as a new job.

Next, have employees break down each job into its major tasks, and enter the details on the form. They should then record their level of personal satisfaction for each task. Finally, for those tasks rated very high or very low in satisfaction, they note the reasons why they liked or disliked each one.

This list will provide clues and themes about the key things they want in their work life, as well as the things they wish to avoid. What follows is an example of one manager's past positions.

1. Job	2. Major Tasks	3. Satisfaction 5 = High, 1 = Low	4. Why did I like or dislike each task?
Department Manager	*Team leader*	3	
	Long-range planning	4	
	Handling budgets	1	*I hate dealing with budgets, because I am not very good at it.*
	Writing and creating new programs	3	
	Making presentations to executives	2	
	Acting as a resource for personal or technical questions	5	*I enjoy being the "expert" and helping people.*
	Speaking at local and national conventions	5	*The recognition I receive feels good to me. I also like feeling competent.*

5. What generalizations (themes) can you make about yourself from your job history analysis? What are the key things you want in a job, and what things do you wish to avoid?

1) I like the mentoring role.
2) Recognition for work well done is important for me.
3) I strongly dislike working with numbers.

Life history. The employee should also be given a form to record key positive events in their lives, either job-related or personal, that resulted mostly from their own efforts. For each event, they should list the skills or abilities they used and note specific reasons why each of the events was important to them. Ask them to examine each of their skills and abilities, and make a new list of the most-important ones. Finally, they should record the reasons why each positive event was personally important to them, and list the underlying values shown in the event. That is, what did the employee like or enjoy about each situation?

To illustrate how to use such a form, let's look at one of my own important life events. The teachers in my elementary school thought I was strange, because I could read at an astonishing speed yet could not spell.

It wasn't until I was in college that I learned I had a condition referred to as "dyslexia." Many years later, I was asked to give the commencement address to a special high school graduating class of twelve students, all of whom were dyslexic. It was an important honor for me. Here is the way I analyzed this positive event in the format described above.

1. Positive Event	2. List your skills/abilities that resulted in this event.		3. Why was this event important?
I gave the commencement address to a high-school class of students who are dyslexic.	*Speaking to groups*		*Recognition: I felt needed.*
	Writing skills (but not spelling)		
	Knowledge of how to conduct a needs assessment (I interviewed each of the 12 students prior to writing the speech).		*Deep satisfaction in helping others personally*

4. From #2 above, list your most important skills and abilities.	5. Identify your underlying values.	
Speaking to groups	*I like being in a situation where I can help others and am perceived as being exceptional.*	
	I enjoy the resulting recognition.	

It is difficult to understand the importance of this exercise until your employees have had an opportunity to go through it. Sample forms appear at the end of the chapter to use as-is or to customize.

Testing

There are a number of tests or questionnaires that can help you identify an employee's career interests and needs, such as John Holland's Self-Directed Search, the Myers-Briggs Type Indicator, the Enneagram personality type indicator, and the LLQ for leadership development. You can usually obtain tests such as these through your organization's human resource department.

There are two main kinds of tests to help people identify their work-related interests and needs: *perception* questionnaires, and *knowledge-based* questionnaires.

Perception questionnaires. Perception questionnaires are used to identify development needs. A questionnaire that begins by asking the employee "Which of the following topics do you feel are important for your future development?" is a *perception* questionnaire.

Perception questionnaires are easy and quick to complete. They can be filled out by the person being tested, the boss, a peer, or even a client or customer.

Unfortunately, perception questionnaires have very serious limitations. The employee might, for example, identify one or more topics from a list of topics that they say are "important," but they are not all truly the employee's needs. Topics such as "communication" and "time management" are almost guaranteed to be selected as critical, because they are what we call "umbrella" terms (they cover a number of different subtopics). They will usually mark "time management" as important, even if the other parts are not important to them at all.

Another problem is that what people think they need and what they really need can be quite different. An individual who is not competent in managing performance appraisal interviews might not even realize that he or she needs help in this area. Sometimes the entire organization as a whole doesn't know how to conduct performance appraisals effectively and has no idea of this shortcoming.

Knowledge-based questionnaires. Knowledge-based questionnaires, on the other hand, are used to determine actual knowledge in specific job-task areas. Here is a typical knowledge-based questionnaire item taken from the LLQ leadership tool:

The primary responsibility for employee development rests with…

A. The employee's immediate supervisor
B. The Human Resource department (for establishment of development programs and procedures, such as mentoring, training programs, development planning systems)
C. The employee
D. The chief executive of the organization, since his or her support is essential for the success of any development program

Unlike perception questionnaires, *knowledge-based tests,* when properly developed, provide very accurate information. Also, they reveal exactly what the individual knows, rather than what they think they know.

Performance Appraisal Systems

A performance appraisal, when it is properly done, can also help us identify our employees' needs and strengths. If you are honest and accurate in your feedback, if the appraisal system is designed to allow the employee to be a part of the discussion, and if the performance appraisal form includes information about their future, it will be an invaluable source of good development information.

In order for the performance appraisal interview to be meaningful for the employee and the organization, give employees an opportunity well in advance to discuss their job responsibilities with their leader (as much as one year prior to the interview, if possible). This pre-interview discussion is important because each employee needs to know precisely what they will be evaluated on. Here, there should be a full discussion of the job's tasks, the standards for each task, and the employee's authority level for the task. Be sure to do a careful analysis of any problems that might impede performance.

Leaders must give their employees honest and straightforward feedback, and must be willing to spend time discussing not only the employee's past and present performance, but their job future as well. And last, any performance appraisal system that is used should address such issues as developmental goals and objectives. Some organizations use a formal goal-setting process as part of a well-rounded performance management system. Employees (with leader help) write job-related goals and objectives, and then create plans to reach their objectives. This type of information, even though it is focused on an employee's present job tasks, can provide important data for development.

Employee Development Workshops

Most performance appraisal systems fall short of the desired standard. Many organizations are starting to encourage the employee to accept responsibility for his or her own development by setting up workshops so employees can assess their skills, experience, and interests, and design action plans that will help them achieve their goals.

Such workshops also assure individual employees that they are not alone in wanting to stretch themselves within the organization. A payoff for the organization is that employees often find that they have far better opportunities within their organization than outside of it.

Leader-Employee Discussions

One of the best ways you can help your employees with their professional or career development is to meet with them individually to:

- Determine whether or not their goals are realistic.
- Identify their strengths and determine whether or not these skills are necessary for future positions.
- Identify areas that need improvement.
- Become knowledgeable about career alternatives.
- Create action plans for continued development that factor in strengths and needs.

Now let's look at a few important areas for consideration in conducting a developmental meeting with your employees.

Preparing for the meeting. You should prepare for the meeting, but so should the employee. Meet briefly with each employee well in advance of the session and advise him or her of the date, time, location, and meeting objectives. Explain that you would like to discuss his or her goals and share ideas on the kinds of developmental activities that should be considered.

If appropriate, encourage the employee to consider all possible options. The focus should be on promotional opportunities, job enrichment, special projects or assignments, and lateral moves. You might say something like,

I'd like to meet with you in two weeks and spend some quality time reviewing the jobs you have held in the past, where you are today, what you might want to do in the future, and how you might get there. In short, one of the objectives of this meeting is to create a written plan that can help you reach your own realistic career objectives.

A word of caution: the purpose of this meeting is to help you explore your own goals, not to announce some sort of promotion. So, between now and when we meet I'd like to encourage you to think of a wide range of options, and consider things like how we can make your present job more challenging. Are there special jobs or tasks that you would like to take on? And what kinds of training do you feel you need to prepare you better for your future? It's important for you to consider a wide variety of possible goals, because it's a statistical fact that there are more and more highly qualified people available for fewer and fewer openings.

You might want to give the individual a realistic picture of what the future might look like. In most organizations, the chances of being promoted today are about six times less than they were three decades ago. It used to be that a promotion was the only measure of success on the job. But today, we all need to measure our success in other ways—like how happy we are doing what we have chosen to do. Or how productive we are. We can no longer use promotions as the major measure of whether or not an employee is successful. So it seems to me that the astute employee will explore a wide range of possible career options, rather than be limited simply to the idea of promotions.

Give the employee a copy of whatever forms you use to record job history and life history, and ask him or her to complete them in advance of the meeting. Here are some ideas on how to explain their purpose.

Now to prepare for this meeting, I'd like you to fill out these forms. They will help you identify the knowledge, skills, and abilities you have, and also enable you to determine the kinds of things you really enjoy doing, as well as the things you don't like doing. I think you'll find that they will give you an even better understanding of yourself—and also give us good information for our meeting. On the job history form, list five jobs or positions you've held in the past, starting with your present job and working backward. The life history form focuses more on significant events you have experienced, not only on the job, but in other areas of your life as well. See what you can do. And if you have any questions, come see me.

You will also need to find out if the employee already has a development action plan (few employees do). If so, ask him or her to bring it to the meeting. It is also advisable to urge the employee to come prepared to do most of the talking, since the responsibility for career planning is the employee's, not yours.

Please come prepared to do most of the talking in this meeting, since it will be a discussion of your career. My role will be to listen, ask questions, and offer suggestions to help you create a written development plan.

It is essential that you take the time to properly prepare the employee for such a meeting. If you expect the employee to do most of the talking, he or she needs time to reflect on the topics that will be discussed. It is a good idea to reserve a private area where interruptions can be controlled.

Beginning the discussion. You have arranged the meeting area so that the employee will feel as comfortable as possible. Here's a good way to begin your dialogue:

I'm pleased to have this opportunity to discuss with you your goals. In today's meeting, I see myself as a coach, a listener, and a resource for you as you explore your options. This is your meeting, and you're in charge.

As I see it, your objective is to explore your strengths, as well as areas where some improvement may be helpful, and to discover what you like to do and don't like to do. We also need to create a plan for implementation.

In addition to explaining your role and the meeting objectives, stress that there are no guarantees that what is planned will actually happen. However, by creating a well-conceived, written plan, the employee can increase the probability of reaching his or her goal.

Identifying and discussing knowledge, skills, and values. You will need information from the employee if you are to help with this person's professional development. A good way to start is to ask the employee to summarize the strengths he or she highlighted and determine the types of tasks that have been satisfying and those that were not. Then ask for a summary of knowledge, skills, and values highlighted by the life history analysis.

Help the employee do most of the talking by maintaining eye contact, listening carefully, and not interrupting. Rephrase the employee's comments throughout the meeting; this ensures that you understand what the employee said but also demonstrates to the employee that you are listening carefully. In addition, encourage the employee by giving verbal prompts as he or she is speaking: "That's interesting," "Please continue," and "Could you give me an example?"

Now provide feedback on what the employee has said. For example, you might wish to note any strengths you both agree on and list areas of needed improvement. Share your honest observations on strengths as well as weaknesses that the employee did not mention.

Don't challenge the employee's values. If the employee says, "Money is the most important thing to me!" do not say, "You mean that money is even more important than your family?" Determining what the employee values is the objective, so it is not appropriate here to challenge his or her values or make the individual feel that you are judging them.

Exploring developmental options and possibilities. Within reason, the more options the employee has, the better will be the final decision. Encourage the employee to look at many different possibilities, such as job enrichment of his or her present job, special projects, and/or lateral moves for more exposure or challenge. In rare cases, it may even be appropriate for you to help them explore opportunities outside the organization.

A good strategy is to help the employee brainstorm a list of possible developmental alternatives. The idea is to create a list of alternatives on paper without judging their viability. When the list is complete, he or she can drop those alternatives that seem impractical, combine the remaining ones where possible, and even add new ideas that come to mind. Help the employee select options that best meet the needs of both the employee and the organization.

Creating action plans. Once the employee has selected development options, it is time to create an action plan. Be careful who holds the pencil: if you write the action plan, it will be yours, not the employee's!

Why don't you start by writing out a general goal statement that includes one of your key options? This statement should clearly describe what you want to become or do and in what length of time you hope to accomplish this.

If the employee has more than one development option, he or she may need to write out a goal statement for each. And in some cases, there is one major alternative for which other alternatives become sub-steps or sub-goals in the final action plan.

After writing a goal statement, the employee should develop a list of actions that need to be taken to reach the goal. Again, the employee should explore, with your help, a number of different types of actions: mentoring opportunities, training programs, coaching, special task assignments, temporary lateral moves, and so on. Each of these actions or steps can then be dated and listed in sequential order. At this point, it may be necessary to revise the original goal date to meet the time requirements of the individual action (activities). For example, we could say to our employee,

Start by writing out a general goal statement. Then, after you finish the plan you will have a better feel for how long this will take to achieve, and you can write in a date by which you would like to accomplish your main goal.

Before finalizing the plan, look for potential problems in the list of activities or actions. It is important to do this with the employee, because if you both can identify potential problems now, you can anticipate likely causes and solutions.

We can develop solutions of two kinds: preventive solutions (which will reduce the probability of the problem ever occurring) and contingency solutions (which will reduce the severity of the problem if it does occur). These preventive and contingency actions can then be included as a part of the original plan. The time to consider problems and solutions is in the planning stage, where it will greatly increase the chances of successfully reaching the goal. When the plan is complete, it may be necessary to have follow-up meetings with the employee. Select key milestones and use these dates to plan meetings to review the employee's progress toward completing his or her goal.

Concluding the discussion. Encourage the employee to accept total responsibility for his or her development. In addition, check for any unasked or unanswered questions, and offer to answer any questions arising in the future. Thank the employee for his or her efforts in creating the career plan.

This is your plan, and its success is primarily dependent on you. I'll help in any way that I can, but for the most part, you're going to have to make it happen. I have confidence in you and know that you will give it your best effort.

Is there anything you have not asked, or that we have not considered?

I appreciate the work you did in filling out the forms and the time you've spent with me today. I feel very good about what we have accomplished together.

Following up. Sometimes we get so busy being a leader that we fail to take the time to follow up with the employee. Understandable—but a potential disaster. Employee development is no longer just "nice to do." It is critical. If all you do is help the employee develop an action plan and then ignore the employee's future efforts, the employee will have a legitimate reason to believe that you don't really care. Don't talk a good game and then fail to follow through with what needs to be done. Professional development is too important for the productivity and future of your employees, your organization, and you.

Samples of forms useful in employment development follow.

Sample Employee Preparation Guide
for Development Discussions

The forms in this guide will help identify your knowledge, skills, and abilities and the kinds of things you really enjoy doing, as well as those you don't.

Use the Job History form to list five jobs or positions you have held, starting with your present job and working backward. Use the Life History form to list significant events in your life.

Develop alternative career goals. Then, consider your talents and skills, as well as the things you like and don't like doing, and use this information to identify where you want to be in the future. Within reason, the more options you bring to the discussion, the better your decisions will be. Look at all the possibilities, including job enrichment in your present job, special projects, or lateral moves for more exposure or challenge.

A good strategy is to brainstorm a list of goals: Create a list on paper, without judging whether or not they can be achieved. When your list is complete, delete those goals that seem impractical, combine the remaining ones where possible, and add to the list any new ideas that come to mind.

Create a development plan. When you have identified the direction you would like to go (even a tentative one). Develop a step-by-step plan to reach your goal. Use a development planning worksheet, if one is available.

Analyze risk. A key question in planning is to ask, "If I do this, what can go wrong?" This is an important question you need to ask yourself—and others—as you prepare your plan. The idea is to try to develop preventive and contingency actions you can take if problems do occur. Preventive action includes those things you can do now to reduce the possibility that a problem will occur. Contingency action is what you will do to stabilize your plan if the problem occurs anyway.

You may wish to develop several possible career plans for your meeting with your leader: a primary plan and a second plan that can be used if your primary plan proves to be unrealistic for your organization. Your development plan is tentative at this point. To implement a plan, it must meet not only your needs, but the organization's needs as well. Therefore, after completing your forms, set up a time with your leader to review your plans and obtain his or her input.

Job History Form

Your name: _____   Date: _____

1. **Job:** List each job you have had (up to 5), starting with your present job (a lateral move within the organization counts as a job here).	2. **Major tasks:** List the major tasks in each of the jobs.	3. **Satisfaction level:** 5 = High 1 = Low	4. **What did you like or dislike about that specific task?** (Note reasons for only the highest (5) and lowest (1) satisfaction levels.)
Present job title:			
Previous job:			
Previous job:			

268   *Quality Leadership Skills*

Job History Form (concluded)

2. **Job:** List each job you have had (up to 5), starting with your present job (a lateral move within the organization counts as a job here).	3. **Major tasks:** List the major tasks in each of the jobs.	4. **Satisfaction level:** 5 = High 1 = Low	5. **What did you like or dislike about that specific task?** (Note reasons for only the highest (5) and lowest (1) satisfaction levels.)
Present job title:			
Previous job:			

Themes: From your analysis, list the key things you want in a job, and the things you want to avoid.

Life History Form

Your name: _____   Date: _____

1. **Positive event:** List a minimum of five positive events in your life.	2. **Skills and abilities:** List the skills and abilities you enjoy using that resulted in the event.	3. **Reasons:** Why was the event important to you? Be very honest and specific.
Positive event #1:		
Positive event #2:		
Positive event #3:		

270

Quality Leadership Skills

Life History Form (concluded)

1. **Positive event:** List a minimum of five positive events in your life.	2. **Skills and abilities:** List the skills and abilities you enjoy using that resulted in the event.	3. **Reasons:** Why was the event important to you? Be very honest and specific.
Positive event #4:		
Positive event #5:		

4. List your most important skills and abilities from the list in column 2.	5. Analyze the reasons in column 5 why the event was personally important to you, and see if you can determine your underlying values.

Goal Planning: Worksheet

1. Write your goal statement: _____
   _____
   _____

2. List the steps in your plan to achieve this goal in sequential order. Do not number or date the steps yet.

   Completion date

   Step 1: _____ _____

   _____ _____

   Step 2: _____ _____

   _____ _____

   Step 3: _____ _____

   _____ _____

   Step 4: _____ _____

   _____ _____

   Step 5: _____ _____

   _____ _____

   Step 6: _____ _____

   _____ _____

   Step 7: _____ _____

   _____ _____

3. "What can go wrong?" Identify potential problems with your plan.

   _____
   _____
   _____
   _____

4. If possible, develop solutions (preventive and/or contingency actions) for any identified potential problems, and incorporate these solutions into your plan as new steps.

   _____
   _____
   _____
   _____

5. Finally, number the steps in your plan, determine a completion date for each step, and then review the plan with your leader.

21
Managing Organizational Transitions

After a major change there is often a decline in productivity, quality, and innovation—precisely those things the action was designed to improve! Experts agree that the key to better results is helping employees see that the new situation is not the end of the world, and that with some readjustments—however painful—the organization can become healthier and stronger than ever before. Doing this requires that we first understand what employees are experiencing after change and why.

– Anthony J. Mulkern
Transition and Recovery from Organizational Change

Change causes problems. Not only do we have to deal with external problems resulting from change, but we also need to deal with our emotions. Fear, anxiety, and worry are all common reactions to change.

Most of us have at least some apprehension about the unknown. We're not certain what's coming or whether or not we will be able to handle it, and we're not sure we want to give up where we are. Will we be as comfortable with the future as we are with the present?

Human beings react differently to change. Some people feel overwhelmed even by the thought of making a change, while others seem to thrive on it. Whatever our own personal tolerance, this chapter is for those who must cope with change. We'll explore ways to increase our tolerance for change and how to manage it to our employees' benefit.

An individual's ability to manage change is directly linked to the feeling of being in control and to the personal benefits to making the change. The challenge we face is to discover the ways that a change will benefit us and our employees. If there are no apparent benefits and we have to go through the change anyway, we will need to find strategies to control its negative consequences.

Let's look at the major causes of change and examine some strategies used to manage change.

Kinds of Change

There are two major categories of change: external and internal. External changes are those that originate outside our organization. They cause us the most distress because they tend to make us feel that we have no control over what is happening. For example, if the economy turns downward and the organization starts to lay off workers, it might be difficult to maintain the morale of our employees. That would undoubtedly cause significant emotional distress.

Internal changes are those that result from an organization's own initiatives. If your organization decides to relocate its operations, you can be assured that you and your employees will have to deal with major internal changes.

External changes. Major kinds of external change include new technology, governmental regulations, variable economy, job mobility, constant increases in wage levels, union activity, and personal relationships.

These external changes cause major problems, but they can also create positive opportunities to do things differently, or better. Let's examine each of these kinds of external change.

Technological advances can create havoc within any organization. It is rare for new technology to cause industry-wide disruption, but it can cause great distress in an organization. Even if the employees don't lose their jobs, they may feel anxiety over the possibility of having to be retrained or transferred to another job.

New technology, however, can also result in jobs that are even more secure. Suppose your organization decides to reorganize its reporting procedures, and therefore installs a new system to speed the flow of information. Employees must be provided with hundreds of hours of training so they will know how to use the new equipment. Their new skills will make them even more valuable to the organization.

New governmental regulations can also have a great impact on organizations. The Americans with Disability Act, privacy acts, tax regulations, automotive emission and gas consumption regulations, wastewater disposal guidelines, environmental regulations, and safety regulations are all examples of laws and regulations that create major concerns within organizations.

But even changes in governmental regulations can produce opportunities. For example, look at what has happened to the automobile industry: Continued change in the government's regulations concerning automotive gasoline resulted in the development of high-efficiency engines that are among the best in the world. The net effect of this has been that the U.S. was forced to become more competitive in world markets, thus saving many U.S. jobs.

Economic fluctuations can create inflation, stagnation, and depression. Third World debt, balance of payments, national debt, wars, and competition from a world market are all economic realities of our time. Since we have little chance of preventing these problems, we can reduce our anxiety when they occur by taking action ahead of time to protect ourselves.

Note that I said when, and not if. Large-scale economic changes have taken place, are taking place, and will continue to take place. You know that you will be affected by some or even all of these global economic problems, and that they will have a profound effect on your organization. It is to our benefit to do those things now that will help us cope with such problems when they occur. In our personal lives, for example, we can save more, get rid of high-interest credit cards, and reduce our expenses. On the job, we can make ourselves and our employees ever more valuable to our organization by increasing the quality and quantity of their output. The people who survive swings in the economy are those who are the least dispensable to their organization. And it's much easier to make such changes now than after trouble comes.

Job mobility has both positive and negative consequences. It's great to attract high-quality applicants from other organizations, but it's not so great to lose our people to other organizations. Therefore, we can't just work on attracting good people; we have to figure out ways to keep them. For the most part, employees don't leave organizations for financial reasons. There are some people, of course, who are always hungry for more money or simply new challenges, but even when employees earn fair wages, some will leave because another job offers an opportunity for more responsibility, greater challenge, or better leadership. Today's employees are often more committed to their professions than to their organizations; the leaders of these highly mobile employees may need to implement training programs to help create challenging environments that attract and energize good people so they don't want to leave.

Constant increases in wage levels can induce some employees who can afford it to take frequent unofficial three-day weekends. This might call for internal changes such as instituting tighter time-off policies, keeping careful records of attendance, and immediately dealing with abuses when they occur.

Union activity is another major external factor that can radically affect the way we manage. Unionization is often a response to poor management—management that *talks* about leadership, but doesn't *do* it. In other words, if an organization and its leaders treat their people fairly, a union is less likely to win a union vote.

If the organization already has a union, there will be stress each time a contract is up for renewal because employees will not know all about the contract issues or how they are to be interpreted. The organization should tell its leaders the key issues so they are prepared to handle any changes that may be required.

Personal relationships are sources of external change. Marital problems, separation, divorce, alcohol- or drug-dependent family members, children leaving home, death—all these are examples of external changes that cause untold stress and more change in our lives. The best strategy to deal with such realities is to encourage your employees to get professional help and group support. It is far better if employees seek help than to try to tough it out by themselves; trained resource people outside the situation often make a critical difference. Be sure you and your employees know about the services available through the company's Employee Assistance Plan. If you do not have one, set one up. In the long run, it might be one of the most important and cost-effective programs a leader establishes.

Internal change. External forces can cause internal organizational changes—sometimes sweeping ones. But internal initiatives also cause major changes within an organization. These actions fall into three categories: personnel changes, job changes, and organizational changes. Let's look at each of these in turn.

Personnel changes can have a strong impact on an employee's ability to cope. Suppose you receive a promotion and your employees get a new boss, or one of their co-workers leaves the organization, or you hire a new employee to work in your group. These changes take some adjustment.

When there is a new boss, people become understandably apprehensive. What will the new boss be like? What will be his or her expectations of them? This problem is even more difficult if the employees had an extremely good relationship with their old boss. We have all been through this kind of change with close co-workers or supervisors. Some of us have strong reactions to incompetence, while others have trouble with personality differences or the new person's leadership or communication style.

There are things we can do to help our employees constructively cope with personnel changes. For example, new bosses have histories—they come from somewhere! The odds are that the new boss was promoted from within the organization; if so, it is often easy to obtain some background information on the new leader for your employees so they will be less apprehensive.

If the new boss comes from your section and is now the leader of what were his or her co-workers, it is especially important that you spend time with the new leader and the employees to help them all manage this transition. If the leader is new to leadership responsibilities, you might need to help him or her understand the difference between the new job and the old one. Try also to be sensitive to the feelings of those employees who wanted the job. My point here is that it is normal for the new leader and the employees to have strong feelings about this change. Your job is to listen—and to help them manage their feelings and responses so the transition is as smooth as possible.

Losing a valued co-worker can also be distressing. Close relationships that develop within a group are normally altered when one individual leaves. When an employee loses a friend through resignation, termination, or transfer, try to encourage them to plan specific outside activities and develop common interests that have nothing to do with work. This will help them maintain a continuing relationship, though they will no longer work together. If an employee must give up the relationship, it is important to let them grieve this loss. I once had a wonderful boss, an ex-football player who was a mountain of a man with a heart of gold. I liked him a lot. Our boss-subordinate roles had not allowed for a friendship away from work, and when I resigned my position and took another job, we could not maintain our relationship. I permitted myself to fully experience the sadness and deep sense of loss that this change caused. Openly acknowledging my feelings at work helped, though I miss him still.

Another type of change occurs when hiring a new employee. Most new employees are anxious about their new jobs and feel great discomfort about the strangers they will be working with. Your job as manager is to help them overcome their anxiety in order to adjust to the change. This person is probably nervous about the new job, so don't say, "This job is simple. You'll catch on in no time." Rather than relieving tension, this can make it worse. If you say that the job is easy, some people might think that you won't think they are smart if they have trouble. Better to say something like, "I know that most new jobs appear difficult, but I am confident that you can manage it."

You can also help new employees overcome some of their anxiety by finding out what their outside interests are, and then introducing them to others who have common interests.

Job changes ranging from the addition of a new job task to a new job due to promotion or transfer are not always easy to adjust to. The more different a new job is from the old one, the greater the employee's anxiety will be.

A key strategy here is to take the time to describe the employee's job tasks on paper and then go over each task with the employee and devise an on-the-job training plan. This will take some of the mystery out of the unfamiliar assignment and reduce the employee's anxiety. It will help him or her to see that what may at first appear to be an overwhelming job is really a series of particular tasks that he or she can handle successfully.

Organizational changes such as efforts to be more competitive in the marketplace, introduce a new product or service, increase profits, reduce operational expenses, or pay bigger dividends to stockholders often cause employees deep concern. They become worried about their future with the company when there's even a hint of a merger, acquisition, downsizing, rightsizing, or spin-off. In the past, workers who were laid off due to changing economic conditions were recalled, but today's layoffs are usually permanent because jobs have been eliminated. In the past, these changes usually affected a specific industry. Today, they affect all industries. Yesterday, these changes were caused by economic downturn. Today, new equipment, new technology, new processes, and new policies and procedures cause them. These major changes affect all our employees—and us.

A major problem occurs because high-level decisions are usually made in secret (often for good reasons). Major decisions are argued, fought over, discussed, and finally accepted at the executive level, and then presented to the organization's employees. Executives who have had months to come to grips with their momentous decisions and iron out all the details expect the announced changes to be reasonably well received by the rank-and-file employees. ("We know there will be some minor disruptions, but nothing that middle management can't handle.") Much to their surprise, the very things they wanted to have happen—things like lower production cost, better quality, greater effectiveness, and increased earnings—don't! Good people, the very ones they want to keep, are the first to put their résumés on the street. Turnover is up. Morale is down. Production falls. Quality is out the window. Creativity disappears. Loyalty to the organization vanishes. And executives wring their hands and wonder what happened.

Competent leaders know that employees are going to experience strong emotions: anger, guilt that they still have a job and their friends don't, anxiety, fear, and betrayal. They also know how to help their employees adjust to these internal and external changes: communicate, communicate, and communicate; give employees time to adjust to what they think are cataclysmic changes; and listen, listen, listen.

This means spending most of their time communicating with their employees one-on-one and in group meetings about the change. And when they do, they need to tell the truth! They need to explain what has happened, why it really happened, what other changes are planned, and what changes will not happen.

Sometimes managers don't even know the details. This is unfortunate. They must be assertive about their right to know what is going on and press their boss, the human resource department, and even their boss's boss. Most employee concerns about organizational change are due to a failure to keep them informed and in the loop. If you don't want morale to sink, rumors to fly, and productivity to drop, make every effort to get the facts from those people who, in fact, know the facts—and then communicate this to your employees as soon as possible.

Managing Change

The way a leader approaches organizational change and helps employees deal with it is extremely important. Here are a few tips:

1. Give the employees an opportunity to express their feelings about the change. Do not react to anger or other strong emotion by becoming defensive. Just listen and let them talk.

2. Change frequently comes with significant personal benefit. Your job is to identify those benefits and to discuss them with your employees in order to create within them a genuine understanding of what's in it for them, so they accept the change.

3. Determine which aspects of the situation you can control, and take positive action on these things. Some negative effects of a change can be turned to your advantage if you creatively take charge in the areas you still control.

4. Seek the assistance of others. Simply talking to someone who is a good listener is sometimes enough to reduce anxiety to a manageable level and free our energy.

Above all, don't let any of your employees quit in a huff. Ask the individual to think through all the reasons for staying with the organization. If he or she still wants to leave, encourage them not to resign until they've found another job, because it will be much easier for them to obtain another job while they have this one. The plain fact is that prospective employers think the employee is more valuable if someone else thinks so as well.

Many of you might be thinking that it's better to let an upset employee go ahead and quit, especially if the employee was only an average performer. But the best policy is always to treat employees the way you want to be treated. Besides, it may be easier (and cheaper) to turn the employee around than to hire and train a replacement. And if the employee leaves anyway, don't you want him or her to say good things about the organization and about you?

Using "Force Field Analysis" to Manage Change

Many years ago, I used to write books in longhand. Then computers arrived. Talk about a major change! I bought the simplest word-processing program I could find, and sat down to use it. A computer expert obviously wrote the instructions, using words I had never heard of to explain things I couldn't picture. I became so frustrated that I almost gave up. The fact that the word processing program had a built-in word speller to help me overcome my spelling problem was the only reason I stuck with it. I finally learned how to use it.

Force field analysis is a great way to understand the positives and negatives about an issue (in this case, the decision years ago to use a computer to write). You begin by listing on one side of a vertical line all the reasons or *forces* that support the change. Then you list all the opposing forces or reasons against changing on the other side of the line. The final step is to draw opposing arrows to represent the competing forces, with longer arrows indicating stronger forces.

Force Field Analysis
Changing from Longhand to a Word Processor

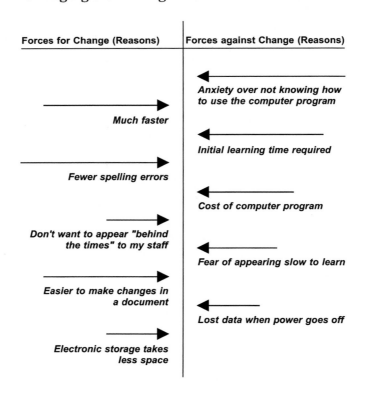

Forces for Change (Reasons) | Forces against Change (Reasons)

Anxiety over not knowing how to use the computer program

Much faster

Initial learning time required

Fewer spelling errors

Cost of computer program

Don't want to appear "behind the times" to my staff

Fear of appearing slow to learn

Easier to make changes in a document

Lost data when power goes off

Electronic storage takes less space

Force field analysis helped me decide to make this change by graphically showing me the factors that were influencing my feelings about the change. I could see at a glance all the positive reasons for accepting this change, as well as the ones against it. I could then begin to minimize the effects of the opposing forces through specific actions.

Now that I've learned how to use a word processor, I'll never go back to writing in longhand. But notice that I had an overwhelming reason (my need for a spell-checker) to continue my efforts to master this new process.

A force-field chart can help you and your employees deal openly with feelings about change, and increase employee acceptance of the need for change. Your job is to help employees discover the reasons for change and its possible benefits. If you show employees all the factors in favor of change, then they can more easily accept the possibility that the organization (or others) had what it believed were good reasons for the change, no matter how idiotic it might have initially seemed.

To analyze a specific change, start by sketching a force-field chart as just shown. Then, work with employees to list all the benefits and disadvantages. If the benefits side looks sparse at first, you may need to uncover additional reasons why the change was introduced; ask your boss or peers whose opinions you respect, and talk to others outside the organization to get their views.

Remember that the objective is to identify other positive reasons for the change—not to affirm any present discomfort with it. Help them find out the reasons for change so that they see the need for it from a knowledgeable position. Help them look for ways to control the opposing forces (negative effects) coming from the change to enable them to cope with the change constructively, creatively, and to their advantage.

A sample worksheet for managing change follows.

Worksheet for Managing Change

1. Write a brief description of the change that concerns you or your employees.

   _____

   _____

2. Using the force field analysis chart below (use easel paper if you are working with a group), list the reasons or forces that support the change on the left side, and list the opposing forces on the right. Place an arrow over each force, with the length indicating the strength of the force (reason).

Forces for Change	Forces against Change

3. What information do you need to complete the chart further?

   _____

   _____

4. Who has the needed information?

   _____

   _____

5. What are the major benefits of this change for you or your employees?

   _____

   _____

6. What specific actions can you take toward the opposing forces (negative results) that will minimize or even reverse their effects, putting you or your employees in better control?

   _____

   _____

7. What additional actions will you or your employees need to take to make this a beneficial change?

   _____

   _____

Quality Leadership Skills

22
Leading Your Employees

One reason corporate and governmental bureaucracies stagnate is the assumption by line executives that, given their rank and authority, they can lead without being leaders. They cannot. They can be given subordinates, but they cannot be given a following. A following must be earned. Surprisingly, many of them do not even know they are not leading. They mistake the exercise of authority for leadership, and as long as they persist in that mistake, they will never learn the art of turning subordinates into followers.

– John W. Gardner
Leaders and Followers

Times are changing! In a world of global markets, scarce resources, and tougher competition, the winds of change are being felt everywhere. Employees are changing, too. They are better educated and more highly specialized, and they have gained greater mobility. They also cost more—more to find, more to train, more to replace.

And how about you? Are *you* moving with today's changes? Do you understand what's happening in your organization? Do you know your employees and their real needs? Do you know how to lead your employees through the often-bewildering tasks they face? And do you really understand that every change is an opportunity to do something better—a chance to grow in your leadership skills?

A number of key principles have been woven throughout this book. I would like to end by listing some of the most important ones as simply and clearly as possible.

If you want to be a truly effective, helpful leader, you can. In a nutshell, here's how:

1. Prepare before every important interaction with your employees.

2. Do the job *with* your employees, not by yourself.

3. Lead your employees—don't order them around.

4. Keep everyone informed.

5. Talk *with* employees, not *at* them.

6. Trust your employees with responsibility. They *want* to be challenged.

7. Set high standards. Employees tend to fulfill their leader's expectations.

8. Involve your employees. It will raise their morale, stimulate their creativity, and increase their commitment.

9. Focus on what was done well, as well as what was done wrong.

10. Provide feedback that is specific and positive to balance feedback that is corrective.

11. Follow up to ensure that what is planned happens, and to make performance matter. Provide needed and timely guidance.

If you follow these principles, you will become a good leader. Your organization will thank you, and so will your employees.

References

Byham, William. (1994). Recruitment, Screening, and Selection. In Tracey, William R. (ed.), *Human Resources Management and Development Handbook*, 2nd edition. New York: American Management Association.

Ciulla, J. (1998). *Ethics, The Heart of Leadership.* Westport, Connecticut: Quorum Books.

Cameron, Kim S., Robert E. Quinn. (1999). *Diagnosing and Changing Organizational Culture.* Reading, Massachusetts: Addison-Wesley.

Csikszentmihalyi, M. (1997). *Finding Flow.* New York: Basic Books.

Dunsing, R. (1977). *You and I Have Simply Got To Stop Meeting This Way.* New York: American Management Association.

Gardner, John W. (1990). The Cry for Leadership. In T. Wren (ed.), *The Leader's Companion.* New York: The Free Press.

Hummel, Charles E. (1967). *Tyranny of the Urgent.* Downers Grove, Illinois: Inter-Varsity Christian Fellowship.

Kotter, J. P. (1995). Leading change: Why transformation efforts fail. *Harvard Business Review,* 73(4), 59.

Kepner, Charles and Benjamin Tregoe. (1981). *The New Rational Manager.* Princeton: Kepner-Tregoe.

Kinlaw, Dennis C. (1989). *Coaching for Commitment.* San Diego, California: University Associates.

Maslow, Abraham H. (1954). *Motivation and Personality.* New York: Harper & Brothers.

Mohrman, Resnick, and West-Lawler. (1989). *Designing Performance Appraisal Systems.* San Francisco: Jossey-Bass.

Mulkern, Anthony J. (1992). *Transition and Recovery from Organizational Change.* Houston, Texas: International Training Consultants.

Schein, Edgar H. (2004). *Organizational Culture and Leadership,* 3rd ed. San Francisco: Jossey-Bass.

Steinmetz, Lawrence L. (1985). *Managing the Marginal and Unsatisfactory Performer*. Reading, Massachusetts: Addison-Wesley.

Thom, Bruce E. (1996, November) More navigation through the heart of darkness: 14 guides to becoming a successful leader. *Public Management*.

Tushman, Michael and Philip Anderson. (1997). *Managing Strategic Innovation and Change*. New York: Oxford University Press.

Whitmore, John. (2002). *Coaching for Performance*. London: Nicholas Brealey.

About the Author

Dick Leatherman served as a manager of education and training for the 3M Company, and then spent twenty-five years as the CEO of International Training Consultants, Inc., growing the company from a one-person organization to a major producer of training packages, videos, and assessment instruments. After retiring from ITC, he taught full time at the University of Richmond, where he was an associate professor and the academic program director of human resource management for the School of Continuing Studies.

Dick is widely recognized for his pioneering work in the areas of trainer training, employee development, and needs assessment. His published instrument, the Leatherman Leadership Questionnaire (LLQ), measures leadership knowledge. He is the author of several professional books, including *The Training Trilogy* and *Is Coffee Break the Best Part of Your Day?*

He has been a presenter at major conventions of the American Physiological Association, American Society of Training and Development, and The American Association of Higher Education. In 2000, he received the University of Richmond's Distinguished Teacher Award.

He attended the University of Minnesota and earned his M.A. in Adult Education and Ph.D. in Urban Services, Human Resource Development from Virginia Commonwealth University.